NO BUDDY LEFT BEHIND

Bringing U.S. Troops' Dogs and Cats Safely Home from the Combat Zone

TERRI CRISP WITH CYNTHIA HURN

LYONS PRESS
Guilford, Connecticut

An imprint of Globe Pequot Press

Lyons Press is an imprint of Globe Pequot Press.

Permission granted for use of the FedEx logo on the plane in the photo on p. 208. © 2011 FedEx. All rights reserved.

Text design by Sheryl P. Kober

Library of Congress Cataloging-in-Publication Data

Crisp, Terri.
  No buddy left behind : bringing U.S. troops' dogs and cats safely home from the combat zone / Terri Crisp with Cynthia Hurn.
    p. cm.
  ISBN 978-0-7627-7386-2
  1. Animal rescue—Middle East. 2. Animal rescue—Middle East. I. Hurn, Cynthia. II. Title.
  HV4763.C76 2011
  636.08'320956—dc23

                                                              2011024558

Printed in the United States of America
10 9 8 7 6 5 4 3 2 1

This book is dedicated to all the animals that have suffered and died in Iraq. They are my reason not to give up.

CONTENTS

ACKNOWLEDGMENTS

Terri Crisp

If I were a dog, I would have long ago worn out my tail—wagging it to say "thank you." In the three years that I have been the manager for SPCA International's Operation Baghdad Pups program, a human "pack" of animal-loving individuals has entered my life and given me countless reasons to be grateful for these remarkable comrades.

Since this journey began in the fall of 2007, I have become well acquainted with a select group of stalwart individuals serving in the U.S. military. While bravely fighting for our country, these men and women balanced out the cruelties of war they faced daily by finding it in their heart to protect a stray dog or cat—many on the verge of certain death. Our troops may be trained to be tough and to battle for the freedoms all Americans hold dear, but I have seen their compassionate side, too, the side that won't allow them to turn their back on a suffering animal.

I have cried and laughed with these individuals while working together to give some deserving four-legged—and in a few cases three-legged—wartime buddies better lives. Not many people get the privilege to save the lives of animals and at the same time to give some kind-hearted, uniformed individuals the peace of mind that comes from knowing that their companion animal will never suffer again. What has grown out of these lifesaving efforts is a kinship with these stellar individuals—ignited by our shared love for animals.

I will forever be grateful to SGT Eddie Watson for falling in love with an Iraqi stray dog. If these two souls, caught up in the Iraq war, had not found one another, my life would have undoubtedly been quite different. I imagine I'd still be helping animals because I cannot fathom my life not immersed in what I love doing the most. However, I suspect I would have continued my work much closer to home—not in the middle of a war zone.

Thankfully, I responded to Eddie's desperate plea to save Charlie, and SPCA International let me go. This development led me to Iraq and to all the other animals after Charlie, rescued by Operation Baghdad Pups. These animals suddenly showed up at a moment when their gentle and reassuring presence was so desperately needed by the men and women called to fight a war.

Operation Baghdad Pups would not have saved one Iraqi animal if we'd asked the military for permission before launching the program. When contemplating the growing number of requests to save dogs and cats befriended by U.S. troops, it quickly became clear what had to be done—break the rules. After eighty-seven successful missions to Iraq, it is quite clear we made the right decision. I want to thank all the men and women who made the decision in the first place to risk so much in order to care for animals struggling to survive. These animals were destined for a short and miserable life in Iraq had their caregivers not broken the rules and given their wartime buddies the chance to live the kind of life they should have been dealt in the first place.

I have worked in the animal welfare movement since 1983, rescuing more animals than I could ever begin to count. While doing this I have encountered all kinds of people—from those who find it easy to be cruel to an animal to those who on a daily basis make enormous sacrifices to make sure animals are safe and well cared for. The people I have worked with who are connected with Operation Baghdad Pups are some of the most unselfish individuals who don't think twice about putting animals first. If the world were filled with people like them, animal suffering would end. They are indeed an inspiration.

As of May 2011, 280 dogs and 58 cats that had been born in the Middle East now call America home. They escaped a life of deprivation because of a team of tireless volunteers. Barb Hartman and Bev Westerman were the first two Operation Baghdad Pups volunteers. Their unselfish natures and complete devotion to all animals are remarkable. Since the program began we have laughed together hysterically and cried until we had no more tears. Throughout this journey we have never lost sight of how fortunate we are to be a part of an endeavor abundant in goose-bump moments. Barb and Bev are true friends to all creatures and my friends, too—the kind of friends who are few and far between. I will forever be grateful to them for being who they are and for always being there for the animals and me.

The other members of the Operation Baghdad Pups team who have transported animals halfway across the world have time and time again proved their commitment to animals, enduring some tough times but never complaining. The long hours sitting in airports and on planes flying animals from the Middle East to the United States are quickly forgotten when we witness those animals being reunited with the individual who means the world to them—who saved their life.

Flying into a war zone is indeed risky, but, thankfully, we have avoided the dangers. The precautions we continue to take have kept us safe. Still, the fact that the Operation Baghdad Pups team members are willing to take this risk proves they are a special breed of people. No amount of applause could show my appreciation for my traveling partners. These individuals have escorted animals to their new homes: Danielle Berger, Cassandra Dawes, Jerry Elfrank, Rebecca Fenner, Cindy Hurn, Sharon Maag, Matt McDonough, Janet Mercer, Linda Pullen, Charlene Ruttle, Billy Schweizer, Donald Smith, Mickey Sonstegard, Dave Souligne, Christine Sullivan, Michael Walsh, Bev Westerman, and Bev Wolfgram. I say to them, "Job well done!"

Four other team members deserve an even higher level of thanks for their exceptional support. They are my husband, Ken, and our daughters, Jennifer, Amy, and Megan. The choices I have made in my career have meant I have been absent from their lives more than I would have liked. To help make up for this, I have been able to take them with me to the Middle East to bring animals to the States for our troops. Seeing a part of the world many people never get to see, I believe, has helped them to see that they are a part of a global family, too. They have all gained a greater appreciation for what we have as Americans while being able to share their talents, kindness, and laughter with some incredible people they have met along the way. I am so incredibly proud of my family members, and I always feel their love no matter where I am in the world.

I would like to thank the SPCA International staff members who have been working right alongside me since Operation Baghdad Pups began. JD Winston, SPCA International's executive director, trusted me from the get-go and gave me the freedom to develop the program as I saw fit. We have shared some hair-pulling moments, but we always got through them as a team and as friends. It has been a learning experience in more ways than one, and I am grateful to have stepped outside the box, with JD always there to fall back on.

Stephanie Scott, SPCA International's director of communications, was the voice of Operation Baghdad Pups when we needed to gain the support of the public so more animals could be saved. Her persistence in getting the media to pay attention definitely kept the program moving forward. We've had some comical moments as we've tried to get animals to cooperate with producers in unfamiliar TV studios, some just hours after stepping foot on American soil for the first time. There have been the struggles, too, but each bump in the road has only strengthened Operation Baghdad Pups and our friendship.

Jennifer McKim was the first person to accompany me to Baghdad. Maybe, being my daughter, she did not have a choice, but I know she did it because she believed in the program. Working for SPCA International, she had the added insight as to why this program was so necessary. Her years of helping animals definitely added to the strong foundation Operation Baghdad Pups rose from. It has not always been easy having me as a mom, but Jennifer rarely complains. When she does, I know it is only because she loves me, and I feel the same way. A mother could never ask for a better daughter. She continues to make me extremely proud, and the accomplishments she has made on her own have greatly benefited animals, too.

The SPCA International board of directors has been in my corner from the beginning. The board has listened to the success stories and has cried with me when another animal was lost. The board members are as proud of Operation Baghdad Pups as I am, and their support has many times given me the strength to keep going.

In Iraq and Kuwait are people who have become treasured friends. Most of them originate from other countries, but their need to make a living has brought them to a part of the world that has welcomed me and given me some of the richest experiences of my life. I have shared some unbelievable experiences with this multicultural blend of people, all of them ensuring in their own way that Operation Baghdad Pups was able to save more animals. I say "thank you" to them in over a dozen languages.

Included in my new circle of friends are the security team members. They have been my heroes time and time again. What they were willing to do in order to get animals from point A to point B in Iraq proved their tenacity. On one of many missions, I got word that one of the vehicles in their convoy had rolled over an improvised explosive device (IED). I thought my worst fear had finally been realized. What a relief it was to learn that no one was hurt, including the Operation Baghdad Pups cat that was riding in the heavily damaged vehicle. This brush with disaster was a wakeup call about just how dangerous it is to travel around Iraq.

Some people might think it crazy to put human lives in jeopardy to save dogs and cats, but the security men reassured me repeatedly that they understood why they had to do what they were doing. They were doing it for the troops and the animals that had made a difference for them in a harsh and dangerous place.

While writing this book I spent five months at the Reed villa in Erbil, Kurdistan, located in northern Iraq. Reed is the security company that Operation Baghdad Pups has been using since October 2008. Their generosity allowed me to be in the country where the Operation Baghdad Pups animals were from, inspired me, and gave me my own understanding of what animals in Iraq endure every day. I could not have asked for a better place to be uninterrupted so I could focus on writing. The distractions were definitely few and far between. When the mid afternoon temperature hit 120, 130, and even 140 degrees in August 2010, I felt the same mind-frying heat that our troops and their wartime buddies had suffered through. I must confess I did not get a lot of work done on those afternoons. It's hard to work on a computer while getting drenched by garden sprinklers.

While I wrote, my good friend, Ameer Khoshaba, the dog handler and trainer for Reed Security, was there to support me. His cooking nourished me. His refreshing laughter and his spirit-lifting smile were welcome encouragement. The cups of tea he set on my desk provided much needed comfort. Our walks helped to clear my mind and to remove the infamous writer's block. Ameer kept me on track when I wanted to do anything but write, and he is a big reason my book got completed.

Watching my book become a reality has led Ameer to believe he, too, has a story to tell. Being Assyrian and Christian and living in Kurdistan have put Ameer and his family members in life-threatening situations since he was a child. In spite of all they have suffered, this family whose members I hold dear has endured, and it is indeed an inspiration. It's a story that needs to be told, and Ameer will one day be the author he wants to be.

Deciding to write my third book came at a time when once again I was juggling a lot in my life, Operation Baghdad Pups being the biggest attention grabber. Thankfully, Andrea Hurst, my agent, found me. She knew that this story needed to be told, and she offered her expertise to ensure that it was published. Her lifelong love of animals also gave her a clear-cut reason to persuade me that I had time to share the stories piled up in my head. She was right.

Andrea suggested that a professional writer should join me on the book-writing project. Her recommendation brought a very special person into my life— Cindy Hurn. It turns out that we were practically neighbors and had shared a longtime love of writing and rescuing animals. We met at a coffee shop in November 2010 to explore how she might help me with my book. What I thought would be a two-hour meeting, stretched to six—and we could have stayed longer if other demands had not stopped us.

It was clear to Cindy and me after that first meeting that she and I had work to do together. I knew that Cindy, a talented writer with a keen sense about animals and people, would add another dimension to what I had already written. I could not be more thrilled to have gained a writing partner and a friend.

Facing an almost impossible deadline to complete this book, Cindy and I surprised everyone and got it done. Initially, completing this book required days of being holed up together in Cindy's house, sitting side by side on the couch as we worked. During January and February I was back in Iraq, so the final chapters were completed across the ocean. Throughout the process Cindy kept us on schedule, and for that reason you now have our book—truly an effort of love—to hold in your hands.

Maybe I was a dog or a cat in another life. That would explain why I feel so happy and content when I am around animals. I have felt this way my entire life. My love for animals comes as naturally to me as breathing. Their unconditional love has continuously enriched my life, giving me friendships more valuable than any material possession. The 311 animals that came into my life, between February 2008 and March 2011, through Operation Baghdad Pups, are some of the best buddies I have ever known.

This book is for them—the four-legged heroes from Iraq that I have been blessed to know and help. As many people worked to save them, they were unknowingly mitigating the scars of war that U.S. service men and women suffer. What started as an effort to save one dog has turned into so much more. May the hard work of everyone associated with Operation Baghdad Pups continue to result in no buddy left behind.

The face of each of the Iraqi dogs and cats will forever be etched in my mind and heart. Each time I am reminded of one, I smile. It is a comfort to know that they are now smiling, too.

—*Terri Crisp*

. . .

Cynthia Hurn

My first and sincerest "thanks" goes to Terri Crisp for this incredible six-month story-telling mission, during which our joint writing effort spread between California and Iraq and crossed thousands of cyberspace miles.

It didn't take long for me to discover that Terri really is "all about the animals." While staying with her in Iraq, I watched her in action as she constantly focused on planning the next rescue and on making the world a safer place for her four-footed friends. Whenever someone says, "it's impossible," Terri quietly leaves the room, gathers the people who she knows can help, and, before you know it, the impossible has been accomplished while those she left behind are still shaking their heads and murmuring, "it can't be done." She is a remarkable person in many ways, a good story-teller who is fun to write with, and when Terri sets her mind on helping an animal in need, she truly becomes a miracle worker.

I also want to acknowledge some of the people whose bravery is often unnoticed and unappreciated. These are the folks who stay behind when their loved ones go into a war zone. While collecting hours of taped interviews, I could not listen—or later—write without a box of tissues beside me. Their pride in those who serve our country was clearly evident in their voices, and their quiet courage inspired me. I hope they will feel honored in the telling of their tales. My sincerest thanks goes to Rhonda Beardsley, Danielle Berger, Pam Bousquet, Lorna Brooks, "Jean Mathers," Jolene Matlock, Janet Miller, and Adela Vodenicarevic.

To the U.S. soldiers and civilian contractors who delved into their memories for the sake of this book, I want to express my deepest gratitude and appreciation for how willingly you did so. Most of you have risked your lives under incredibly difficult circumstances. The depth of emotions you visited when recalling painful moments was humbling, and it served to make your funny stories and the laughter we shared that much sweeter. Even though this book doesn't go into detail about the tragic events of people you lost and injuries you came home with, I hope the sacrifices you have made and the courage you have displayed come through these pages loud and clear. Your candor opened my eyes to a world that few people have the nerve to walk into, let alone stay in until the job is done.

I thank the following soldiers and civilian workers for sharing their stories with me: Andrew Bankey, Bruce Bousquet, "Kevin Connors," Erin Kirk, Thomas Liu, Jenni Mann, Matt McDonough, Bryan Spears, "Jessie Walker," Eddie Watson, and the Captain who rescued Mama Leesa.

The volunteers whom I interviewed never failed to prove that human beings are capable of great kindness, enthusiasm, and generosity. I thank them for saving animals, for supporting U.S. troops, and for helping with the production of this book in any way they could. Each person gave freely of his or her time, transporting me from the airport in D.C. to the veterinary hospital and staging kennels, sharing photographs, videos, and memories, and confirming many story details. I'd especially like to thank Dena DeSantis, Barb Hartman, Dave Lusk, Linda Pullen, and Bev Westerman. As their personal accounts unfolded, I was often astounded and always heartened by their selfless actions. Our world truly is a better place for their living examples of love in action. One of the soldiers in this book said it so well: "You guys are the real heroes."

I thank Terri's daughters, Jennifer, Amy, and Megan, for answering so many of my questions. They were instrumental in helping me to better understand their mom and in revealing more of her character as the book developed. Terri never failed to tell me how proud of her daughters she is and rightly so. They've all sacrificed in many ways and have worked hard for the sake of our four-footed friends.

I also salute JD Winston and Stephanie Scott. Although their characters remain mostly in the background of these stories, not one of the Operation Baghdad Pups rescues would have happened without their constant dedication, commitment to, and passion for animals. I thank them for their support, for giving me interview time, and for doing everything they could to ensure that this project was completed by the publisher's final deadline.

The most influential person in the production of this book is hidden behind the pages, yet she deserves to be recognized with boldfaced capital letters and exclamation points. Andrea Hurst, literary agent and manager extraordinaire, is the person who originally approached Terri and convinced her to work in tandem with another writer, ensuring that the story was completed within an incredibly short deadline.

Throughout the writing process Andrea was there for us any time we needed her, day or night. Andrea's professionalism went above and beyond expectation and included her playing the roles of literary manager, editor, coach, cheerleader, mentor, advisor, and go-between. Her humanity comes from a heart that is full of compassion, courage, and great wisdom.

With many years of experience in the literary field, Andrea has earned the respect and friendship of many writers, editors, and publishers. She knew that without time to distance ourselves from the story, Terri and I would need feedback from qualified readers. Andrea rounded up a team of the best reader-critics a writer could hope to work with.

Freely giving their time, these fine authors and editors read the first and second drafts of many chapters. They commented on anything that needed attention, made excellent suggestions for material to include, and encouraged us by their keen interest in the stories. I cannot thank them enough for their hours of intense concentration and great feedback: Katie Flanagan, Brandon LaFave, Audrey Mackaman, Sarah Martinez, and Vickie Motter. What a great team indeed.

Holly Rubino of Lyons Press deserves mention for her wonderful work as editor. She is the person who read the completed manuscript and gave us the benefit of her professional know-how. While Holly held the much-feared red pen in her hand, she wielded that pen with respect and skill. She took a good story that rippled over stones and split course at times, and she made it flow strong like a river that knows exactly where it's going. Holly also worked with Lyons Press designers to come up with a cover that we were proud of. Listening to feedback from Terri, Andrea, and me, she worked hard to make sure that the cover honestly represents the bravery and selflessness depicted in this book. Thank you, Holly.

Turning a manuscript into a published book requires a series of steps that involve more editors and support people than most readers would ever imagine. Writers often dread the scenario of too many cooks spoiling the stew and they pray it won't happen to their precious tome. Terri and I feel so lucky that our manuscript went through the capable hands of Lyons Press editors and designers and onto the desk of Meredith Dias, project editor at Globe Pequot Press. Their combined professional handling of our labor of love and their personal attention to detail has resulted in the book you now hold in your hands or see on your screen. If Terri and I were the parents of this baby, then they were the doctors and nurses who delivered it, and made sure everything went as planned. To all of them we give an enthusiastic "thumbs up."

For supporting me through six months of a writing schedule that started at dawn and often stretched long into the night seven days a week, I have to thank my sweetheart and my rock, Rich Eldredge. The number of times he came home from work to find empty cupboards and uncooked dinners and never complained but instead kept me laughing is worth mentioning here. Rich washed the dishes, did the shopping and laundry, cooked suppers, and took me out for many a meal after long days of running his own demanding business so that I could finish another chapter. My sweetheart could not have been a better partner and friend.

Last of all, thanks go to Jody and Mike Jones of Homeward Bound Golden Retriever Rescue and Sanctuary in Elverta, California. Their dedication to rescuing over eight hundred golden retrievers a year brought me my foster "old golden" and best buddy, Cherokee. While I was in Iraq helping Terri bring home more soldiers' animals and observing the final stages of Operation Baghdad Pups rescues, Jody and Mike took care of Cherokee at their home.

Throughout the long hours and days of the last six months, Cherokee sacrificed a lot of playtime, she leaned against me when sad-story tears ran down my cheeks, and she made me go out for three walks a day, refreshing my brain with much-needed oxygen. With Cherokee constantly by my side, writing about the stray dogs of Iraq always seemed that much closer to home. Somewhere in the pages of this book, I'm sure her gentle spirit has left its paw print.

—*Cynthia Hurn*

Chapter 1

HOW IT ALL BEGAN

SGT Eddie Watson and his inseparable buddy, Charlie *Eddie Watson*

When night was setting in, and the last unit of the 82nd Squadron hadn't returned from patrol duty, it was hard not to imagine the worst. SGT Eddie Watson was stationed at the guard desk, knowing that his men were patrolling in one of the most unstable neighborhoods on the outskirts of Baghdad. Until the previous week his platoon had been lucky. SGT Watson wondered if that luck had worked against the men, perhaps encouraging them to feel almost invincible. On April 28, 2007, reality hit hard when their first soldier made the ultimate sacrifice and lost his life to an enemy bullet. Since then, life at the outpost had been pretty grim.

SGT Watson's platoon occupied one portion of an Iraqi police station and shared responsibility for security operations with the police and the Iraqi Army. U.S. military operations took up most of the second floor. When the soldiers reached the top of the stairs, the first thing they saw was the guard desk.

As soon as the familiar sound of boots and voices rose up the stairs, Watson let out a big sigh of relief. Smith came in first, holding a scrap of material that had been wrapped around something about the size of a big baked potato. He laid it on the desk and stood there grinning at Eddie.

"Got a present for you, Watson," Smith said. The Sergeant looked down just as the cloth moved.

"You got a rat in there or something?"

"Naw, it's a puppy. He was hiding in a shelled-out building. When we entered to check it out, he took one look at us and started to follow. We tried to lose him, but he wasn't about to let us go. Stubborn little mutt—a real soldier."

"What's he look like?"

"Damn cute. You'll see."

The guys circled around as Watson began to unfold the material. A flea jumped onto his arm. "Shit, that's all we need—a bunch of those critters in here."

"We couldn't just leave him," Smith said. "Iraqis were all over the place, and they would have kicked his butt if they'd seen him. Besides, he's got guts, this dog. And he's just a little fella."

The Sergeant pulled the puppy out of the tattered folds. A black head, back, and tail, plus a white ruff, chest, and belly made Watson wonder if the dog was a border collie. Black freckles were splattered up and down his legs and snout, and his ears flopped over at the halfway point. His eyes held an inquisitive intelligence, but they didn't disguise his pathetic state. Bone-skinny and covered with fleas, ticks, and filth, the puppy felt hot to the touch and shivered uncontrollably.

"He's cute all right, but I don't think he's going to last long," Eddie said. He didn't want to encourage friendship with all those fleas that were crawling over the small animal, yet he couldn't help but pick the puppy up and cuddle him. "Poor mutt, you're a mess, aren't you?"

Smith reached out and scratched behind the pup's comical ears, then ruffled the fur on his head.

"We've got to get those fleas off you, buddy," he said.

"Take him out back and give him a bath," Eddie said with a sigh of defeat.

After two baths, the dirt and ticks were scrubbed away, but the fleas held their ground. One of the guys filled a bucket with JP8 diesel fuel.

"Here, dip him in this. Those fleas will be dead suckers in no time."

"Hey, you can't use that! You want to kill him?" Already SGT Watson felt himself getting attached to the dog.

"We've got to do something," said the soldier with the bucket. "It's not like there's a pet store around here. It won't hurt him if we do it real quick. We'll just dunk him."

So they did. And it worked.

SGT Watson feared that the pup's biggest problem was that they were breaking all the rules by having him there. Included in the U.S. Military General Order 1A is a prohibition against befriending animals or keeping pets. If an unsympathetic officer found out the men had this dog, he could shoot it or make the men dump the puppy somewhere far from the outpost. One way or another, this little guy had a death warrant hanging over his head.

"What are we going to call him?" Eddie asked.

"Let's name him after our company."

"Yeah, that's good." Eddie reached across the desk and stroked the puppy's wet chin. "Hey, little guy, your name is 'Charlie,' and as of today, you've joined the Army."

"He's still shivering," said Smith. " Do you think we gave him too many baths?"

Watson grabbed a clean blanket. "Here, let me have him. He can stay with me while I'm on guard duty. I'll keep him warm."

Wrapping the pup like a baby, Eddie held Charlie in his arms and did his best to keep him warm. The pup studied Watson's face as if he were trying to memorize every pore, until a few minutes later, when he stopped shivering and fell sound asleep.

The next morning soldiers were running around like wet nurses, getting Charlie water, taking him out to pee, wiping up his accidents. The barracks took on a new life with everybody wanting to play with Charlie.

"What are we going to feed him?"

"Give me an MRE," Eddie said, referring to the military's self-heating meals-ready-to-eat. He opened the package, dumped it into a bowl and offered the food to the pup, but Charlie turned his nose away at the first sniff. The guys squatted around him, looking worried.

"Try another one. Maybe he doesn't like that beef stew."

Five packets later a soldier's buffet was spread in bowls across the floor. Charlie sniffed at each one, then backed up and turned his head to look at the soldiers as if saying, "You think I'm gonna eat that? Hell, no!" The men began to laugh.

"Looks like he's one of us already. He's about as fond of bag nasties as we are."

"He's gotta eat something. Maybe we can get one of the Iraqis to buy some meat scraps at the market."

The squad members had made friends with a few of the men with whom they shared the building, so it was easy to convince one of them to start bringing in bones and meat scraps for Charlie. That solved the food problem, but they still had to engage in "Operation Hide the Pup" so Charlie wouldn't be discovered by the senior officers.

Not many days passed before Charlie began to fill out. He was getting cuter than ever and a lot more active. Four of the men took turns doing pee and poop duty, and for Charlie's exercise they took him into the guard tower or up onto the roof, where he could charge around without getting into too much trouble. It wasn't long before Charlie knew which of the soldiers gave him the most attention, and he'd go looking for his favorites. When SGT Watson wasn't on patrol, Charlie always sought him out. Maybe that's why Eddie started thinking about Charlie all the time, looking out for him, as if they belonged to each other.

The second floor of the building was wide open and sectioned off for communications and other tasks. At the far end, a couple of smaller rooms were used by senior officers and Commanders, and a big room off to the side was crammed with enough bunks to accommodate about thirty men. In these close quarters the wrong person was bound to see Charlie at some point.

"Damn, hide him quick!" Smith whispered.

Before Eddie had a chance to grab the puppy, the Battalion's Command Sergeant Major (CSM) entered the barracks. Charlie ran up to him and stood there, wagging his tail.

"What's this dog doing in here?" the officer demanded.

"Sorry, sir," Eddie replied. "The puppy followed the squad home, sir, and he was starving."

"I don't care. Rules are rules. Get rid of him."

Before Eddie could obey the order, Charlie tilted his head from one side to the other and looked straight into the Command Sergeant Major's eyes as if to say, "You're a friend, right?"

"I don't want to see this dog or any other animal inside the barracks again," the CSM barked.

Charlie responded with a noise halfway between a growl and a woof as if adding emphasis to the Sergeant Major's order.

The high-ranking officer looked down at Charlie, surprised at the sound. Eddie could swear that the officer's stern face nearly cracked a grin. Watson couldn't help but smile. Just then the CSM squatted and scratched Charlie under the chin.

"He *is* a cute little guy. I guess he'd have a tough time on his own. If he was to find a corner in the courtyard to lay out his roll, I probably wouldn't notice him there." With that, the CSM stood and marched out, barking orders at someone else.

Sighs of relief flooded the room as if half of the platoon had been holding a single breath.

"I can't believe what I just heard."

"Me either," Eddie said, scooping up Charlie. "Sorry, buddy, but from now on, you're sleeping outside."

The police station that SGT Watson's squadron occupied was smaller than most military outposts. Fifteen-foot-tall concrete barriers, topped with rolls of concertina wire, surrounded the property. A guard tower and manned gate at the entrance had essentially created a castle keep. From that day forward Charlie became an outdoor dog and lived in the comparative safety of the walled outpost courtyard.

SGT Watson was surprised at how much he missed having Charlie in the barracks, and he hoped Charlie felt the same about him. When Eddie came back from patrol a few days later, Charlie hauled ass straight past the other guys, leaped into Eddie's arms, and licked him all over. That's when the soldier knew: Charlie had decided that Watson belonged to him.

The outpost was manned by three platoons on a rotating schedule of three weeks. Each time their week-long rotation came about, SGT Watson hoped that the replacement soldiers would look out for Charlie until he got back. He worried about his puppy the whole time he was gone.

Every time members of Watson's platoon returned to the outpost from their week away, they found Charlie waiting for them in his usual spot at the gate. It seemed as if he always knew when they were coming back. He'd snatch an empty water bottle and invite the soldiers to play, his elbows on the ground and butt in the air, wagging his tail as if it were wagging him.

When Charlie was about four months old, Watson's platoon came back from its three-week rotation. One of the men who belonged to a unit that had remained at the outpost came over and joined Eddie as he played with the dog.

"Did you hear what happened to Charlie while you were gone?" the soldier asked.

"No. What?" Watson stopped playing as a look of concern flashed across his face.

"We let him follow us on foot patrol last week, and he acted like a seasoned trooper. As we were walking down a street behind the market, a pack of dogs came after us, looking like they meant business, and Charlie stood up to them. He didn't even stop to think they might rip him apart. He's one tough little mutt. At the end of the day, when we started walking back to the outpost, a soldier stopped and offered us a ride, so we climbed into the Humvee, but Charlie refused to get in. That's when the Sergeant sitting next to the driver told us to leave him behind."

Something in Eddie's gut gripped. He fought the urge to release the anger that was rising inside him. Why didn't one of them get out and walk with Charlie? Before he could say anything, the other soldier continued with his story.

"Two days later, guess who came marching down the street?" he laughed. "You should have seen him. Charlie's tail was down, and he kept looking over his shoulder, but as soon as he heard us shouting his name, he ran through that gate with his tail raised like Old Glory on the Fourth of July. Man, it was one hell of a reunion."

Eddie was madder than hell that the guys had left Charlie behind but felt relieved that he'd found his way back to the outpost. When American soldiers got to Iraq, they soon learned that many Iraqi people have different attitudes about dogs and cats, despite the Koran's bidding not to abuse animals. To them these dogs were a threat, riddled with disease and living in packs that roamed the streets, and they often chased after people who got too close. With no veterinary services to provide a sterilization program, the number of strays had multiplied quickly, creating a serious problem for city residents. A dog's rank in Iraq, therefore, was lower than that of vermin, and many people treated them as such.

American soldiers often intervened to stop groups of children from throwing stones at stray animals, and they saw Iraqi soldiers kicking dogs, torturing them, or shooting them. From the shocking scenes he'd witnessed, Eddie knew that if Charlie was left to survive on his own in the streets of Baghdad, he'd be dead in no time.

It was soon after hearing about Charlie being left behind on patrol that Eddie got his hands on the book *From Baghdad with Love*, which was written by a Marine who had befriended a dog in Iraq.

Against impossible odds, LtCol Jay Kopelman had managed to bring his buddy Lava home. Eddie began thinking that maybe he could save Charlie. He started asking everyone at the outpost for ideas, and he started a blog called "Operation Bring Charlie Home."

Some people asked SGT Watson why he was determined to bring Charlie to the States when so many American dogs were homeless.

"You have to understand that being in Iraq is nothing like being in America," Eddie would explain. "In Iraq you can't relax. You've always got eyes in the back of your head watching for that surprise attack. The enemy here looks exactly like the friendlies. The Iraqi who works beside you in the day may be the enemy at night. And when you come back from patrol, the adrenaline that pumps through your body while you're under fire stays with you, so back at the barracks, you can forget about sleep. At the slightest crack or thump, you're up and armed, ready for an ambush. You tell your body to calm down, but it doesn't listen. When I get like that and can't sleep, I just go outside and hold Charlie. There's something about holding him that settles me down, and relaxes me enough that I can finally grab a few hours."

Watson wasn't the only one who took comfort in this little dog. During the summer the Baghdad thermometer hovers at around 120 degrees. When soldiers are toting full battle raffle, which means carrying nearly sixty pounds of gear and wearing a helmet, flak jacket, long pants, and boots, the heat is brutal. Despite their exhaustion, when they returned from those butt-busting patrols, the first thing the men in Eddie's platoon did was start yelling for Charlie. Their faithful friend was always there, wagging his tail and jumping up to greet them.

The soldiers would drop their weapons and gear, then get down in the dirt and play tag with the puppy. Charlie would dodge the soldiers, keeping one eyebrow arched in a catch-me-if-you-can expression. Before long the battle-weary men were laughing. Charlie provided the kind of innocent distraction that reminded the soldiers of what they had left back home. When they played with the puppy for a little while, they were just a bunch of guys fooling around with their dog.

Companionship and entertainment weren't the only benefits of having a puppy. When Watson got notified of his first tour to Iraq, he'd half-expected to be killed, and had accepted that he probably wouldn't be coming home. He hadn't thought about a future in America. He hadn't thought about anything beyond what he had to accomplish on any given day. But after Charlie came into his life, something inside Eddie changed. Now that he started thinking about trying to get his dog to the States, he visualized himself going home with Charlie—for the first time since he'd come to Iraq, he saw a future with himself in it.

As soon as Eddie set up Charlie's website, people began to respond to SGT Watson's plea for help. Several offered to send money toward the cost of Charlie's transport. Others sent dog food, treats, toys, and even an airline carrier. But when it came to providing the transport out of Iraq, nobody had any feasible answers. SGT Watson sent an e-mail to every animal welfare organization he could think of, asking each one to forward his plea to others who might be able to help

Charlie in the outpost courtyard *Eddie Watson*

Charlie. No matter where Eddie's plea landed, no one could help him. He wasn't having any luck. Logistically it's not easy to get a dog out of a war zone. Some say it's downright impossible.

Charlie needed more than luck, Eddie realized. He needed a miracle.

Chapter 2

GETTING THE CALL

Charlie on patrol in Baghdad *Eddie Watson*

The afternoon staff meeting in late October 2007 had reached the point where I began to doodle in the margins of that month's agenda, and I couldn't stop thinking about the unfinished pile of work on my desk.

"Before we finish," said Nancy, one of SPCA International's web team members, "I have one more item to bring up."

A small groan escaped. *Was that me?*

"This e-mail came through our website last week." Nancy passed a copy to each of us as she spoke. "I haven't been able to get it out of my mind. The original was written several weeks ago by a soldier stationed in Iraq, and since then it has been forwarded from one organization to another."

At the mention of Iraq, I stopped doodling.

The e-mail had been written by a SGT Eddie Watson and was addressed to "Whoever Can Help Charlie."

"This is really sad," said Stephanie, the Director of Communications. She echoed what I was feeling as I read the following message:

> Our unit rescued Charlie from the streets of Baghdad, and since then he has become a mascot and loyal friend. But it is against military rules to befriend animals or use military vehicles for animal transport. In March of 2008, we will redeploy. I'd like to find a way to bring Charlie home to America, but the biggest stumbling block is finding transport. At around six months of age, he's still just a puppy. He deserves a chance. Please, can you help us get Charlie home?

The room filled with silence as each person read SGT Watson's history of how the soldiers found Charlie and what the dog meant to the men in his platoon. Scanning the long list of forwarded addresses, I realized that we at SPCA International might be Charlie's last hope.

"How can the military expect soldiers to leave their beloved friend behind? Don't soldiers give enough to this country?" Matt, another member of the web team asked. "I mean, how much space could a dog take up?"

Having some prior knowledge about the military policy on animals, I explained that General Order 1A had been issued by U.S. Military Central Command in 2000 to clearly state prohibited activities and conduct for U.S. military troops and contractors in war zones, particularly in countries like Iraq and Afghanistan where cultural and religious differences needed to be respected. Any conduct or activity that threatened the good order and discipline of troops came under the umbrella of General Order 1A, including befriending, feeding, or transporting stray animals. Any person who broke the rule risked punishment under criminal statutes.

"I can understand that the military has to maintain standards," said JD Winston, our new executive director, "but it sure seems harsh to expect these guys to ignore a starving puppy that follows them and has no chance of survival without some help. I know I would find that extremely difficult to deal with."

"Welcome to the dilemma faced by the guys at the top level of military," I said. "They know it's a problem, and most of them feel sympathetic to the soldiers who get caught in this situation. A lot of them agree that having a loyal four-footed friend in a war zone is a great morale-booster and comfort for the men. But their main concern is not about saving animals. They have to focus on getting in, getting the job done, and getting the soldiers back home—alive."

No longer anxious to return to my desk, I stood up to replenish my coffee and looked around the room. I hadn't seen us this collectively captivated in a long time.

"I can understand how a dog would make a big difference to the soldiers," Stephanie said. "Can you imagine the horrific scenes these guys have to face every day?"

Nancy looked around the table as we all shook our heads in sad agreement. "This isn't only about saving a dog," she said. "It's about supporting our troops."

My eyes wandered to the windows, and I stared at the smoggy haze hanging over southern California. This wasn't the first time I had heard about soldiers bonding with a dog while fighting a war far from home.

JD spoke up. "Let's give it a shot and see what we might be able to do." Then he turned toward me and continued, "Terri, you've had lots of experience with disaster rescues. My guess is that saving Charlie will present the same kinds of coordination issues you've dealt with before. It makes sense for you to look into this. Besides," JD smiled, "you have been saying you wanted to take on a new challenge. How about taking on this one?"

A quick succession of practical questions flooded my brain. How would Charlie adjust to living in the States? What if the changes were just too much for him, and he didn't fit in? We certainly couldn't send him back.

Everyone at the table waited for my answer.

"Last year," I said, "a woman I know helped her brother to get a dog that he had befriended out of Afghanistan and into the United States. It took months of hard work, but thanks to volunteers from across the globe, they did it."

No one said it, but I'm sure we all thought it: If a dog from one country at war could be saved, why not another?

"So, does that mean you think you can do it?" Stephanie's question drew all eyes to me again.

Talk about pressure. Taking a second to consider, I responded with an unequivocal "Yes!"

"That's great," said JD, closing his notebook. "See what you can find out and report back to me. Hopefully, we'll be able to help SGT Watson and Charlie."

Returning to my desk, I pushed aside my other work. I couldn't wait to start the preliminary research on my newest challenge, but where should I begin? Already I felt stuck.

"Come on, Terri," I said to myself. "You've taken on the seemingly impossible before in disaster situations. Don't freeze up. Remember what you've learned."

I hoped no one overheard my private pep talk.

"Push aside negative thoughts. Focus on the goal, keep walking forward, and trust that the right things will happen."

Panic moment over, my brain slipped into gear and identified transport as the first priority. I began a computer search using Expedia.com. I typed in "Baghdad, Iraq" for the flight departure city and randomly picked "Washington, D.C." for the arrival city.

"Destination Currently Unavailable," Expedia reported. I had to admit that I wasn't surprised. No one in their right mind would be traveling between Iraq and the United States unless Uncle Sam was their travel agent.

Using less familiar avenues for booking air travel, I came no closer to finding flights in or out of Iraq. If we couldn't get a flight out of Iraq, maybe we'd have to drive Charlie to a neighboring country and fly from there; but which one? I couldn't remember the countries that bordered Iraq, so I Googled a map of the Middle East. Iran was out of the question. Kuwait might work. After all, American troops did come to the rescue when Saddam Hussein tried to take over that country. Jordan, Saudi Arabia, Turkey, and Syria provided other possibilities. Good. Now I had some options to explore and no longer felt stuck.

Seeking sources of land travel, I discovered that no trains in Iraq cross the border, and the few Google images of public buses showed what looked like death traps on wheels. Major car rental companies weren't available either. Turning to websites that specialize in transporting animals all over the world, I learned that none of them does business in Iraq. This was turning out to be a travel agent's worst nightmare.

In twenty-five years, responding to seventy-one major disasters, I had met challenging logistical situations that drew upon all my resourcefulness. But none had been like this. It was time to start thinking way outside the box, but by the day's end, even years of experience hadn't been much use in solving the problem.

That night, as I lay in bed with Eddie's dilemma swirling around in my brain, I realized that his plea had taken my routine day and turned it into one that presented a familiar kind of excitement, one that I thrive on during disasters. It felt good, once again, to be faced with seemingly insurmountable obstacles. Yet, just before I fell asleep, I thought, "I have to e-mail Eddie tomorrow, but what on Earth am I going to tell him?"

The next morning I calculated the time difference between California and Iraq and determined that it was 5:30 p.m. in Baghdad. I wondered when Eddie would check his e-mails and hoped he might be preoccupied with hunting down insurgents. The longer it took for the two of us to connect, the more time I would have to find at least one tidbit of good news. The frustration I felt after only one day of searching made what Eddie had been grappling with for the last few months uncomfortably clear. I repeated the mantra, "You'll find a way. You can do it."

The morning produced no more answers, despite brainstorming with my co-workers Matt and Jennifer, both members of the web team.

"I've got it," I laughed. "I'll call the Commander-in-Chief and ask him to intervene. You know, to put Charlie on *Air Force One.* If he refuses, I'll call Mrs. Bush. Surely she'd let me borrow their plane for a few days if it's helping one of our soldiers."

"Either that, or do a PETA-style stunt to attract awareness," offered Jennifer.

"You mean, strip down to my birthday suit and chain myself to the White House fence?"

Laughter helped to ease the tension, but by the time Matt finished his second cup of herbal tea, we hadn't come up with any workable solutions.

"Don't give up, Terri," Matt said as he walked back to his cubicle. "You'll figure it out."

Before doing anything else, I had to e-mail Eddie. It wasn't fair to leave him hanging. He'd done enough of that already. Having read articles about servicemen and women returning from Iraq with emotional scars, I didn't want to contribute to Eddie's burdens by dumping my frustration on him. This had to be a message of hope. I also needed to ask him some key questions before I could go much further in my search.

Taking care of how I worded my reply, I wrote that we at SPCA International were moved by Eddie's request. After hearing his story, we all agreed we wanted to help him save Charlie. I assured Eddie that he deserved all the assistance he could get, considering how hard he had been trying to keep his four-legged friend alive. I also explained that I would be his SPCA International contact, but I was a novice at finding transport out of war zones, so it might take me a while to unravel the puzzle.

"What I lack in experience," I wrote, "I make up for with determination" and ended the e-mail with "Keep yourself and Charlie safe!" The only thing I could do now was to wait for Eddie's reply.

I returned to my backlog of work and throughout the day kept checking my inbox. When I left work at 6:00 p.m., I still hadn't heard from Eddie. Late that night I sat in front of an idle computer not knowing what the next step was. It seemed I had reached the end of the road, unable to build a bridge between Iraq and the United States that a dog could cross. Nevertheless, I wasn't willing to give up just yet. Exhausted, I turned the computer off and went to bed.

The next morning at breakfast I noted the newspaper's October date. It had been barely forty-eight hours since my quest began, one that had completely derailed my pre-Eddie life. As I scanned the pages, stories concerning Iraq assumed much more importance; articles and photos that I would have quickly glanced over or ignored before, I now studied with consuming interest. This man and dog caught up in the conflict gave me a connection to Iraq I never expected to have.

When I got to work, I called or e-mailed all my contacts who had extensive experience in emergency management, logistics, and international travel or who had served in the military. They came up with some of the same ideas I had already explored, but when all was discussed, they, too, had no answers. Each conversation ended with the suggestion that I should give up.

At noon my co-workers went off to lunch while I ordered in a sandwich instead. Just as I swallowed the last bite, a familiar ping indicated that an e-mail had arrived.

It's him! Eddie has replied!

I faced the screen with mixed emotions, somewhere between excitement and apprehension. My finger hovered over the "Enter" key. "Please make this be okay," I prayed.

"This is such amazing news!" Eddie's first words burst onto the screen. "I'm at home on leave, in Phoenix. This is by far the greatest news I've had to date. Oh, man, this is awesome. I'm so totally stoked right now. Thank you for offering your help!"

I couldn't help but smile at Eddie's heart-stirring response. It proved that he'd been grasping for any bit of hope he could hang onto. In his shoes I, too, would be holding out for a miracle. There was no way I could disappoint Eddie now. The pressure on me kicked into high gear, but, knowing I work best when faced with a good challenge, I believed I'd find a way.

I replied to Eddie immediately, hoping to catch him before he left the computer. His leave from Iraq could not have come at a better time. The sooner my growing list of questions was answered, the quicker I could get the ball rolling. With renewed energy, I sent Eddie my phone number and asked him to call me ASAP.

He called eight minutes later.

No longer just words on a screen, Eddie's voice came through with a jolt of reality. Buried in logistical details, I had almost forgotten that I was dealing with a person who was risking his life every day for me and my country. As Eddie's story unfolded, I grew more impressed with his persistence and the earnest mission he'd undertaken to save his buddy.

From that point on, each decision we made would result in the life or death of Charlie. Suddenly I felt proud to be working for SPCA International. People in our organization didn't say, "Sorry, it's impossible." We might not succeed in getting Charlie home, but we sure as hell wouldn't go down without a good fight.

"Tell me everything you can about your efforts to date," I said. "Maybe there's a lead I can work on."

"There's one lady whose name I promised not to give out. She got a lot of military mascots out of Iraq, but so far, she's lost almost as many dogs as she saved due to her lack of resources. If she helped Charlie, the handoff would have to be done on short notice, and I can't just grab a truck and drive him myself. Military rules on vehicle use are really strict. She relies on local nationals for transport, so the person driving is probably afraid of dogs. If anything went wrong, they'd be just as likely to take the money and abandon Charlie."

"Would it be possible for me to speak with this woman? She might know something that will help us. I promise that her identity will remain confidential."

"I can give you her phone number, but please don't share it with anyone. I sure don't want somebody getting hurt or killed trying to save Charlie."

That sounded ominous. Animal rescue work is often risky, but in a country reeling from years at war, serious danger was a reality. Were we at SPCA International really prepared for this?

I called the number that Eddie gave me and left a message describing myself as someone who wanted to help SGT Watson get his dog to Arizona. I assured her that any information we shared would be kept confidential, and I left my number.

Later, after I finished wrapping up my work for the day, I walked down the hall and knocked on JD's office door.

"You got a minute? I wanted to give you an update on the soldier and his dog."

"Great! I was wondering how that was going. Make any progress?"

"Not really, but I did talk to Eddie this afternoon."

"Really?" JD picked up his water bottle, took a long sip, and put it down slowly. His mouth did that tight-lipped thing that I had learned was his way of collecting himself when he was concerned about something.

"Don't worry. I didn't call long distance to Baghdad," I said, laughing. "Eddie is home on leave in Phoenix for two weeks."

"That's good timing," he said, his mouth relaxing. "So what did you learn?"

I reviewed everything I had discovered, both positive and negative, and I didn't leave out the dangers we would be facing if we took on the project.

The woman whom Eddie had mentioned had called me back earlier in the day. Her heart-rending stories made it clear that we needed money, firm commitment, flexibility, a lot of luck, and a strong heart to attempt any rescues out of Iraq. Without having heard her experiences firsthand, I suspected that this project would have been doomed from the start. Forewarned is forearmed, my mother used to say, and in this instance she couldn't have been more correct.

JD leaned back in his chair and folded his hands on top of his head. "In all honesty, now that we know the odds, do you really think we can help Eddie?"

"I don't know. But I sure as hell want to continue trying."

"Then that's what you've got to do. If anyone can make it happen, Terri, it will be you."

"Thanks for the vote of confidence, but I don't feel worthy of it at the moment."

JD thought for a moment. "Getting Charlie out of Iraq will be an expensive endeavor, and we'll have to raise funds to cover the costs. Since Eddie is in Phoenix, let's take advantage of that. Why don't you go there and get an interview with him on tape? Eddie will plead Charlie's case much better than anyone else could. We'll put his video on the SPCA International website and give it the best publicity we can."

"That's a great idea. I'll arrange it right away."

On November 1, 2007, I sat outside a Phoenix recording studio waiting for Eddie to arrive. A car pulled up, and a young man sporting a buzz cut and Army uniform got out and walked toward me, his back straight and his head held high. He was the first soldier I had ever met who was on active duty and serving in a country at war. I stood and smiled as he approached. A handshake seemed too impersonal, so I gave Eddie a big hug.

A short while later Eddie sat in front of a plain blue background as the camera zoomed in on his face and shoulders, recording my questions and his poignant answers. Despite his calm demeanor and a soldier's unemotional expression, the camera had no trouble capturing the incredible bond that had formed between this infantryman and a stray Iraqi dog.

"What will happen to Charlie if you don't get him out of Iraq?" I asked.

"If Charlie were put back out on the street, no doubt about it, he'd never survive," Eddie said with a faraway look in his eyes as if visualizing the harsh life Charlie would have to face on his own.

"This is a dog that has been cared for since he was a tiny pup. He has no idea how to fend for himself. If someone were not there to give him something to eat, he wouldn't know what to do when he got hungry. He's never lived with a pack of dogs, and finding one that would accept him now is unlikely. If Charlie had to depend on himself to survive, there is one thing that'd happen for sure."

Eddie stopped to clear his throat before proceeding. "Charlie would die if he were left on his own. For a dog that has such an amazing personality and is so devoted to us soldiers, it would be tragic to let his life end like that."

"Why is it so important to bring Charlie home?"

Eddie held back for a moment, looked down, and folded his hands in his lap before looking back at me. Letting out a deep sigh, Eddie raised one hand to rub his forehead, as if trying to erase the frown that had suddenly formed. I sensed that he was stalling long enough to compose himself. I will never forget the determination in his eyes when he finally answered my question.

"The reason it's so important for me to save Charlie is that I made him a promise." Eddie paused. His eyes captivated me with their piercing sincerity. "When you're a soldier, every second of every day you stand beside your buddies while your lives are in constant danger. You know these guys will die for you to save your life. And you're just as ready to die for them. So when we make a promise to each other, we keep that promise, no matter what." Eddie pronounced each word distinctly, emphasizing his point.

"We take Charlie out on patrols, and more than once he's proven that he'd lay down his own life to protect us. Charlie is one of us. He's more than just an ordinary mutt off the streets of Iraq. That dog has more guts than most people I know, and he deserves to live.

"In the Army we live by the motto 'No buddy gets left behind.' That motto applies to Charlie, too." Eddie's voice broke on the last word. He stopped for a second, swallowed, and looked straight into my eyes. When he next spoke, his voice came through loud and strong.

"Leaving Charlie in Iraq is not an option. I promised him I'd bring my buddy home."

The recording studio fell silent. Eddie's response brought everyone and everything to a standstill. Relieving the intensity of the moment, I gently cleared my throat and asked the crew if we could take a five-minute break. Then I reached into my briefcase and pulled out a Kleenex.

When the recording session was finished, Eddie took me out to lunch. It was a wonderful opportunity to get to know him better. I couldn't help but like this soldier. After he dropped me off at the airport, I couldn't stop thinking about the incredible devotion Eddie had shown to Charlie. At that moment I vowed that I would not stop until the day I could wrap my arms around Charlie's neck and whisper in his ear, "Welcome home!"

SPCA International put together a five-minute video from our taping session and posted it on the website. Deciding that we needed an official name for the campaign, we considered several until we unanimously agreed on "Operation Baghdad Pups." Striking artwork was added to the web campaign, along with Eddie's story and the video. Almost immediately donations began rolling in.

On this side of the world, progress was being made, but the actual rescue plan was still missing.

Charlie on guard duty *Eddie Watson*

Chapter 3

THE KINDNESS OF STRANGERS

Charlie runs to meet the returning patrol. *Eddie Watson*

After investigating every lead I could find—a person here, a company there—a possible solution was offered by a veterinarian who lived and practiced in Jordan and needed to remain anonymous. I didn't want to tell Eddie this, but the veterinarian was asking for an enormous amount of money; he'd have to pay people to look the other way in order to make the impossible happen. If this person turned out to be our only option for saving Charlie, SPCA International would just have to raise the funds.

I decided to e-mail Eddie now that he was back in Iraq to give him an update and to ask for his reaction to the proffered solution. Over the next few weeks our e-mails became Eddie's lifeline as we brainstormed from a great distance and gave each other moral support.

Hi, Eddie,

I may have some good news. We can fly Charlie from Jordan to the U.S. if we can get him across the border. A Jordanian veterinarian is willing to help us with papers and getting him onto a flight. It sounds like a long shot, but we may not have another option. Do you think you can get Charlie to the border, and if you can, what are the risks we need to consider?

—Terri

As I hit the "Send" button, I imagined what Eddie might feel at the thought of releasing Charlie into strangers' hands for a long cross-country journey. I doubted they could get Charlie to the Jordanian border without traveling through combat zones. With no other feasible solutions, however, a part of me hoped Eddie would agree to this plan. A few days later his reply came through.

Terri,

Regarding Jordan, I believe it's against the law to take dogs from Iraq into neighboring countries due to health concerns. There's a small chance we could get Charlie driven to the border, but I know of a soldier in another unit who went this route, and things couldn't have gone worse. An Iraqi border guard found his dog, dragged him off the truck, and shot him in the head. Then he kicked the body to the side of the road like a piece of trash. Keeping Charlie hidden and quiet could be an issue. If the guards found him, it would be the end of Charlie.

—Eddie

This was really disturbing news. Our only valid rescue plan so far could easily turn into a disaster for Charlie. It sounded as if this option was just too risky to try. I honestly didn't know what to say next other than to encourage Eddie to keep asking everyone he met for ideas and helpful contacts while I did the same. All I could do was pray for something to come through. I had to believe it would; I couldn't let Eddie and Charlie down.

Two days later I heard from Eddie again.

Terri,

One of my buddies told me about a new charter airline that flies between Baghdad and Kuwait. I don't know if they transport animals, but it might be worth looking into. They're called "Gryphon Airlines," and they're an American-owned company. I'm about ready to head out on patrol. Do you have time to check this out? I sure hope you can reach them. Charlie does, too. Time is slipping by fast and still no answers.

—Eddie

I typed "Gryphon Airlines" into the browser search box, and there it was! When I picked up the phone, I couldn't punch those numbers fast enough. After I explained what I needed, my query was directed to John Wagner, one of the founding partners, whose office was in Colorado. John listened to my abbreviated version of Charlie's story, and I could tell by his questions he was intrigued.

"We've flown sniffer dogs for the military, so I don't see why we can't fly this soldier's dog," John said. "I have seen firsthand the gut-wrenching conditions dogs in Iraq are exposed to. If we can give one of those poor mutts a better life, I say let's give it our best shot."

I could hardly contain my excitement. "Boy, you don't know what you've just done," I said laughing through my tears. We arranged to meet in Los Angeles the following week to discuss details.

When we finished the phone conversation, I just sat for a moment. Was this it? Could I dare to hope? The tone of self-assurance in John's voice had made me feel that this guy could do anything. I couldn't wait to share the news with Eddie, and I wrote a quick e-mail.

Gryphon may be our answer! My boss and I are meeting with one of their representatives next week. The airline flies military contractors for the U.S. Department of Defense, so if all goes according to plan, Charlie will be in safe hands. The flight will leave from Sather Air Force Base on the U.S. military side of Baghdad International Airport (BIAP). All you have to do is get

Charlie there. It's beginning to look like you'll get to keep your promise to Charlie.

—Terri

The next morning Eddie called me from Iraq.

"Thank you!" he repeated at least ten times. "After three months of trying everything I could think of to get Charlie home, for the first time I believe it actually might happen." Eddie paused. "There's something I should've told you before," he apologized. "I'm really sorry, but it never came up since we hadn't gotten this far along with a plan."

"What is it?" I held my breath. Any sentence starting out with "I should've told you" usually means bad news.

"I can't get Charlie to BIAP."

"Oh. You can't? Why? Is it too far away?"

Eddie's reply brought another revelation about the extraordinary difficulties of moving around within Iraq.

"It's about twenty miles, but I can't borrow a military vehicle or leave the outpost unless I'm on official military business."

"Isn't there someone local we could hire?"

"I wish there was, but I just don't know anyone I can trust. All the locals I come in contact with would rather have their teeth yanked out with a pair of pliers than get close to a dog, except maybe to kick it. They're the last people we could count on."

This is crazy, I thought. We had finally found a way to transport Charlie over six thousand miles, and now I was being told we couldn't achieve a distance of twenty.

"I'm really sorry," Eddie said again.

"Hey, it's not your fault. We'll get over this hump, too."

I hoped I was right. This new dilemma was too much for me to handle right then. I'd go tackle something I could accomplish and check it off my list. I went to the website of the U.S. Centers for Disease Control and Prevention to determine the requirements for bringing a foreign dog into the United States. I learned that Charlie would have to be vaccinated at least thirty days prior to departing Iraq and would need a health certificate signed by a veterinarian within ten days of departure. I e-mailed this information to Eddie.

The next week JD and I met with John Wagner of Gryphon Airlines. He turned out to be a fascinating man with high adventure stories from his days in Iraq as a Senior Public Affairs Officer for the military during the early years of the war. John was pleased to announce that his partners were on board for saving Eddie's dog.

"Hey, we're happy to do whatever we can to support DOD military operations and help the troops. Saving a soldier's dog at the same time is a double hitter."

John asked us a lot of questions about our specific needs and discussed in more detail what was involved in the transporting of a dog.

"And the plane," I asked. "You're saying that the cargo hold where Charlie will go is pressurized and climate controlled?"

"There's no cargo hold on the plane we use, so the luggage either goes in a compartment at the back of the plane or is placed right behind the cockpit. Charlie," he smiled, "will travel in the cabin."

"Just to confirm," I said, trying to grasp that our miracle really was about to happen, "Gryphon is definitely able to fly Charlie from Baghdad to Kuwait."

"Yes, ma'am, your understanding is correct."

"What will the cost be?" JD asked.

"This one is on us."

Wow. How do you say "thanks" to that?

After a moment of shocked silence, JD and I expressed our heartfelt gratitude to John and his partners for their unbelievably generous offer. At this point I cringed at the thought of begging one more favor. But it had to be done.

"There's one more thing, John. It turns out that Eddie can't get Charlie to BIAP. Any chance you know someone who could pick Charlie up and get him to the airport?"

"As a matter of fact, I do. We've done a lot of work with one of the security companies that operate in Baghdad, and they're a good bunch of guys. I can ask them to help us out."

"Really? No joking?"

"No joking," he grinned. "I'll call them tomorrow and get back to you, but I'm sure they'll step up to the plate. They're always ready to go above and beyond for the troops."

The next morning at work I was giving Matt an account of the meeting with John when my cell phone rang.

"I've got some good news, Terri." John Wagner's confident voice came through like a stream of sunshine after weeks of rain.

"I just got off the phone with the head guy of the security group in Baghdad, and he said it's no problem for them to pick up Charlie since they're not too far from Eddie's location. Gryphon flies between Kuwait and Baghdad three nights a week, so we can get Charlie on whichever flight you pick. All you have to do is let the security team know when and where to pick Charlie up."

"Wow! That's incredible. You've just made my day. I'll let Eddie know right away. Thank you so much, John. You and your partners are an absolute Godsend."

When I wrote to Eddie, I realized that he'd probably be asleep. It was the middle of the night in Baghdad, but he'd be checking his e-mails first thing in the morning, eager to see if our plan was finally coming together.

> Great news, Eddie! We've got transport—door to door! SLG (Security and Logistics Group) will pick Charlie up and deliver him to Gryphon Airlines. Now we have to focus on shots and the health certificate. Can you give me an update on that ASAP?
>
> —Terri

By now I couldn't help but sit back and feel somewhat proud of what we'd accomplished so far. Despite the setbacks, we were moving forward on a mission that many people had claimed was impossible.

If I could put my finger on the most powerful tool I've learned to use over the years, I'd put it on trust. Trusting that everything will work out in the end seems to set the right energy in motion, drawing all the ingredients for a successful outcome toward me. In the few weeks I had been working with Eddie, I noticed that he, too, refused to let setbacks get him down and always focused on the positive outcome.

After waiting several days to hear of Eddie's progress in getting the health certificate, I finally received another e-mail from him.

> You won't believe what just happened. After all the time I spent searching for a vet, I found out the other day that the Ministry of Agriculture is within spitting distance of our outpost. At first I got really excited until I learned I could go there only on official military business. I can't reveal any details, but I can say an official patrol to the ministry was finally arranged. While there I spoke to one of the veterinarians about Charlie. He agreed to help. So guess what? Charlie is vaccinated! He took the shot like a champ and didn't put up a fight at all. The vet said he'd issue his health certificate just before Charlie's flight. I've got to tell you, after all these months of dead ends I really do believe Charlie is going home.
>
> —Eddie

Now it was time to set a date. In order to avoid the upcoming Christmas holiday traffic and major snowstorm delays, we decided on February 13, 2008, for a departure flight from Iraq. Charlie would set foot in America on the following day which happened to be Valentine's Day. What a memorable holiday this Valentine's would be!

Working from my office at home in northern California, I made what I hoped was my final list of tasks still required to put the trip into motion. At the top of the list was a call to United Airlines Cargo. John had recommended them for flying Charlie from Kuwait to Washington, D.C.

"Who will be dropping the dog off at the airport in Kuwait?" the United agent asked.

"No one," I said, beginning to anticipate that this reply was not what the woman needed to hear in order to book Charlie's flight.

"So, how is the dog getting to the airport?"

"He'll be flying from Baghdad on a charter airline. Once they arrive in Kuwait, the ground crew will transfer the dog to United Airlines."

"Okay, that will probably work, but who is going to pay for the dog's freight charge?"

"I am. I can give you a credit card number right now."

"That's not how it works. Cost is based on the weight of the dog and the crate he's traveling in. We can't confirm that information until the dog is actually at the airport."

"I can't pay in advance, even if we overestimate the weight?"

"I'm sorry," she said. "It's the rules."

Oh, my God, how much more complicated could this get? Just when I thought it was clear sailing from here. There had to be another way, but I didn't know what it was.

Needing a break, I let my dogs out for a run around the three acres that surround our house in the Sierra foothills. While they gamboled about, I settled down on the squeaky porch swing, my favorite thinking spot. Usually I find the gentle back-and-forth movement calming, but nothing eased the aggravation I felt at that moment. All I wanted to do was cry.

After chasing each other across the property, my dogs stampeded back toward the house, producing as much noise as they could, tongues lolling, ears flapping, and tails rotating like a collection of giant windup toys. Skyler arrived first, hopped onto the swing, and planted her soft Australian shepherd body next to me. Tabasco, a large spaniel mix, laid his head on my lap, while Millie, a Lab cross, began tapping her black, stubby leg on my foot as she scratched. Luke, our sweet-natured Rottweiler, plopped down on the deck between Morgan, the older black Lab, and Mica, a short-haired terrier cross, each of them vying for the next-closest space to me. They all sensed I was worried.

"So, guys, what am I going to do now?"

I don't know whether it was their collective gaze of trust or just the fact that I sink into a state of contentment whenever the dogs surround me, but something suddenly hit me. The porch swing froze at the back of its arc. As if a tape recording had been switched on by invisible hands, my own words, spoken weeks before, replayed in my head.

"If Eddie is willing to risk everything to save his wartime buddy, I should be willing to take necessary risks as well."

Was this my test? Was I willing to take that risk? Looking at my dogs, I found the answer, but now I needed the approval. It was time to call my boss.

"JD, this is Terri. Sorry to call you after hours, but do you have a minute?"

"Sure. What's up?"

"I came up against another obstacle on Charlie's transport."

"Well, *that's* a surprise."

We spent nearly an hour discussing the options. It was all boiling down to one that left me feeling somewhere between really excited and scared as hell.

"Are you sure you want to do this?" JD asked. All the kidding had stopped. "It *is* a war zone."

Five minutes later I called United Airlines back to book a one-way flight for Charlie and a round-trip ticket for me between Kuwait and Washington, D.C. I then made reservations with Gryphon Airlines and e-mailed Eddie so he could begin to coordinate logistics with SLG.

All I had to do now was break the news to my family that I'd soon be going to Iraq via Kuwait. My husband, Ken, and I had met in 1989 while responding to the Exxon Valdez oil spill in Alaska. And my daughters, Jennifer, Amy, and Megan, had grown up with a mom whose work involved rescuing animals on short notice during floods, fires, and other natural disasters. My family members had long since learned to live with the demands this kind of career can make. Totally supportive when I had to leave home, sometimes for weeks at a time, they would adopt routine B and enjoy hearing about my adventures when I returned. Even so, I had never traveled to a country at war. For the first time they might say, "Don't go!"

When I got up the courage to tell them, they were too stunned to say anything at first. I quickly jumped in with assurances that I would be okay, but it took some convincing, particularly with my oldest daughter. Jennifer also worked for SPCA International, so she was more aware of the kind of dangers I might be facing, whereas my other two daughters were still in high school and less cognizant of the world outside America. Ken knew me too well to even try talking me out of it.

Finally my daughters got down to the nitty-gritty: the most important questions. "What are you going to wear? Do you have to cover your hair? Can you show any skin?" I didn't know the answers, but, thank goodness, John Wagner from Gryphon Airlines did.

"As long as you don't go wandering down to the beach in a bikini, you'll be safe," he laughed. "Just wear normal clothes, and don't shake hands with a man unless he offers his hand first. Rest assured that Kuwait City has everything—you'll feel like you're at home. They

Charlie patrolling the streets of Baghdad *Eddie Watson*

have American restaurants, upscale malls, and they even accept plastic money. What more could you ask for?"

A guarantee that this is going to work? I kept that thought to myself.

Usually when I leave for a disaster, Ken or Jennifer drops me off at the airport, but this time the entire family came and followed me into the airport. After we said our goodbyes, I went through security. When I gathered my stuff again and looked around for one last glimpse of my family, the post 9-11 screens blocked my view, so I took a deep breath, turned back toward the departure gates, and started walking.

Chapter 4

RESCUE MISSION #1

Stephanie, Bev, Jennifer, Barb, and Terri after Charlie's arrival in Washington, D.C.
SPCA International

John Wagner had been right. On February 12, 2008, when I exited the plane from Washington, D.C., and made my way down the crowded Middle Eastern airport concourse, the first thing I saw was a McDonald's. I laughed.

Welcome to Kuwait.

Military backpacks, muscled arms, shaved heads, and sand-colored boots were dead giveaways that the majority of passengers exiting my plane were probably contractors whose final destination was Iraq. The farther into the terminal I walked, the more they dispersed, and the crowd went through a gradual transformation.

Gritty sounds of Arabic chatter began to fill the air. Dark-skinned men wore floor-length, brown or white long-sleeved shirts, perhaps better described as robes. (I later learned that the long shirt is called a *disha-dasha*.) White cotton fabric in red-stitched patterns covered their heads and draped down their backs just past their shoulders. These were held in place with a circular cord crown. Black-robed and veiled female figures also walked gracefully by, some wearing burkas, with only their dark eyes exposed. It was hard not to stare. A cluster of identically shrouded women walked toward me. How could they distinguish one from another?

John had recommended the Safir Transit Hotel, located on airport property, for my overnight stay. Relieved that signs throughout the airport were written in English as well as Arabic, I found my way to the hotel shuttle. When we pulled up in front of the hotel, I was taken aback by its nondescript appearance. Boy, would Martha Stewart like to get her hands on this place!

I had lost track of how long it had been since I'd slept; I hadn't even napped on the plane, despite being in the air for fourteen hours. As long as there was a bed in my room, I'd be happy. Walking down a dimly lit, second-floor corridor, I found the door that opened into my compact sleeping quarters. A twin bed with a gaudy floral bedspread hugged one wall, and a small, outdated TV perched on a rickety wooden table in the corner. One fluorescent light bulb hummed from its wall fixture. Gray light flickered across the hills and valleys of a well-worn carpet that landscaped the floor in various shades of red. Checking the bathroom, I found a shower and was relieved to see a modern toilet rather than a hole in the floor, a common option I had been warned about. I collapsed onto the bed, tour over. What now?

Grabbing my phone, I called home, and my oldest daughter, Jennifer, answered.

"I'm here! I made it!"

"I cannot believe you're actually in Kuwait. Tell me what it's like; I want to hear everything."

Her voice was so clear, as if she were just on the other side of town. Pushing aside the heavy floral curtain from a narrow, dust-covered window, I began to describe the scene outside.

"Well, I'm definitely not in Kansas, but there are similarities. It's flat for as far as I can see. The buildings, cars, and pavement are all covered in sand, almost like a thin dusting of snow. There's no green anywhere. Even the leaves on the trees are tan with dust."

"What about the people?"

"They're not dusty."

"Oh, Mom," she laughed, "tell me, what are they like?"

"In one word? Extraordinary. I've never seen so many types of traditional clothing, and the faces . . . some revealing years of struggle and making you wonder, 'what's their story?' Then there's the blending of sounds and languages that I can't understand . . . it's like a parade of cultures from all over the globe. People are meeting and passing, going to homes and lifestyles totally different from ours. Oh, Jennifer, it feels amazing. This euphoria keeps washing over me—I'm actually here in the Middle East—and I want to run outside and immerse myself in it."

"Just be careful, Mom. Don't immerse too much. We want you back again."

In spite of my exhaustion, I didn't sleep well that night. I was too excited to close my eyes; the anticipation of the next day's adventure kept me rooted at my window, where I spent much of the night gazing at my limited view of Kuwait.

After a breakfast of cucumbers, tomatoes, olives, feta cheese, and flat bread, I returned to my claustrophobic room with seven hours to kill. I was tempted to go back to the airport and get a visa so I could see more of Kuwait but decided to play it safe. I didn't want to risk missing my flight if something were to go wrong.

Meanwhile I was bored. Nothing held my attention. I turned on the TV only to find the movie *My Best Friend's Wedding* playing in Arabic. I tried writing but couldn't concentrate. What really drove me crazy was not being able to communicate with Eddie and the security team. Without Internet or a way to phone them, I had no clue if Charlie had even been picked up.

Only six hours to go . . .

Five hours and twenty-two minutes . . .

Four hours, ten minutes. . . .

Finally it was time to return to the terminal! Once again the shuttle and signs were my allies, guiding me to the Gryphon passenger check-in counter. When I spotted "Baghdad" on the departure board, the realization hit me full throttle. I was about to fly into a country at war.

As I greeted the agent and gave him my passport, my hand was trembling from excitement.

"I need your DOD CAC, please."

"My what? I have no idea what you're talking about."

"You need a Department of Defense Common Access Card in order to enter Iraq."

"I won't be staying in Iraq," I said, trying not to panic. "I'm only flying to the airport to pick up a dog, and then I'm coming right back. I won't even be getting off the plane."

"Oh, you're the Dog Lady!" His reassuring smile washed over me. "I heard you'd be flying with us tonight. Glad to have you aboard."

Promoted from a regular passenger to an expected VIP with the title "Dog Lady," I took my briefcase and my new status, proceeded to the gate, and settled on the plane.

The flight attendant had just finished demonstrating the usual safety procedures with seat belt, oxygen, and flotation device. This routine was one I could deliver myself, having seen it at least a hundred times on journeys to and from major disasters.

"When we begin our descent over Baghdad . . ."

I gazed out the window.

". . . in order to avoid detection from unfriendly forces on the ground . . ."

Now the flight attendant had my undivided attention.

". . . we will turn off all interior and exterior lights."

The next announcement was one I had never heard on any flight I'd ever taken.

"As we enter Baghdad airspace, we will remain at eighteen thousand feet, beyond the range of weapons. Once we are immediately above the airport, the aircraft will begin a corkscrew landing, which involves flying a tight circle while making a steep descent. During the landing approach, which should take approximately ten minutes, all passengers must remain in their seats with belts securely fastened."

As I visualized our plane descending the equivalent of a spiral staircase, I double-checked the tightness of my seatbelt and threw in a short prayer as an added precaution against surface-to-air missiles. "Please, God, if they shoot, let them miss."

As I leaned back against the seat, the thrust of engines lifted us into the sky. It suddenly hit me—I was less than an hour away from meeting Charlie. I imagined that Eddie must be sweating bullets by now. If only he could sense that in the darkness of the star-filled sky above the desert, our souls were meeting somehow and wrapping a protective shield around his beloved dog.

About fifty minutes into the flight, all the lights went out. Even the illuminated "No Smoking" and "Fasten Seatbelts" signs vanished in the dark. The sensation of flying in a pitch-black cabin reminded me of an amusement park ride. I nearly started to giggle, but when the corkscrew descent began, I knew this was no laughing matter.

Only a few hundred feet down I could see what looked like a long stretch of tarmac. Seemingly out of nowhere, a white truck with mounted red lights appeared from the right. It was racing at an angle toward our runway and pointed in the same direction we were going.

Was it planning to attack the plane? Surely this wasn't a suicide bomber. If not, what was the vehicle doing? The truck passed my window and disappeared from view as we came ever closer to the ground. My heart began pounding in anticipation of the impact.

Suddenly the plane's spinning wheels hit the runway . . . *ka thump, thump!* As the reversed engines roared, my body was thrust forward, and the seatbelt strained against me. Tension easing, we slowed until we reached the end of the landing strip, then turned and taxied back past the infamous terminal originally named for Saddam

Hussein. In the almost complete darkness, Baghdad International Airport appeared like a ghost of its former self. What a creepy sight.

The plane seemed to take forever as it taxied first in one direction and then another. When we made a sharp right turn, I caught a glimpse of the white truck that we now seemed to be following.

Oh, so he's not going to blow us up.

Finally we came to a row of hangars, where the aircraft slowed to a stop. The idling engines of a C-17 transport aircraft created a deafening roar outside my window. In the semidarkness, military vehicles circled the monster aircraft as they went about the business of moving pallets, equipment, and other paraphernalia of war.

A wide ramp at the back of the monstrous plane was the stage for a striking scene. Two lines of uniformed soldiers walked single file, up and down the ramp; as one line entered the plane, the other marched out. Side by side, soldiers passed each other in the dark. The strange exchange left one group marching into war and possible death or injury while the other, having survived, was going home. Heavy rucksacks covered their backs; camouflaged helmets and flak jackets protected their heads and bodies, and their arms bore M16 rifles that were held ready to shoot if trouble began. For the first time in my life, war was as close as my window.

A huge, imposing man, wearing a beige SLG security uniform, boarded our plane and spoke to the passengers over the PA system. "In order to get all passengers processed, please stay in your seats and have your DOD CACs ready for checking. We will then clear passengers to deplane."

"I don't have an access card," I said when he reached my seat. "I'm just here to pick up a dog and return to Kuwait."

"Oh, you're here for Charlie," he said with a friendly grin. "He's all ready, so you may as well go and meet him." The man stepped out of the aisle and motioned for me to pass.

When I got to the front of the cabin, I stopped in the open doorway, remembering the instructions given at Kuwait that I must not exit the plane.

It's so dark. Where are they?

As if watching a movie with special effects where objects fade in and out, the figures I was seeking magically appeared into the dimly lit area below the plane. Four well-built men walked toward me, each one grasping a corner of the large crate that was cradled between them.

It's Charlie. There he is. Oh, my God, it's him . . .

I poked my head farther out the door and quickly scanned each side of the stairs to make sure no guns were pointed in my direction. Breaking the rule, I descended the stairs and stood on Iraqi soil, something I never imagined I'd be doing.

Shaking hands amidst hurried introductions and roaring engines, I was unable to catch the names of the SLG guys, but I'll never forget their kind faces. Formalities aside, I squatted down to look at the guy I had flown almost seven thousand miles to save.

"Hey, Charlie." My fingers reached through the metal grate. "It's so good to meet you at long last." He moved closer to me and proceeded to lick as much skin as his tongue could reach. This was one greeting that would be hard to surpass.

"I can't thank you men enough," I said as one of them handed me a large manila envelope containing Charlie's paperwork. "What you've done tonight has made an American soldier extremely happy, and you've saved this dog's life."

"We're glad to see one animal, at least, getting out of this hellhole. Heaven knows, this is no place to be a dog."

Soon the flight attendant signaled for us to get Charlie on board. Two of the men carried his crate into the plane as I followed close behind. After hugs all round and another "Thank you so much," they each said goodbye to Charlie and retreated down the stairs. I found it touching to see how attached these tough security guys had become to Charlie in such a short time.

As I returned to my seat, all I could think was *Holy cow, we did it. If only Eddie could have been here.*

When we completed the corkscrew ascent, and the lights flickered on, the flight attendant came down the aisle.

"If you want to see how Charlie is doing, the pilot said it would be okay."

That was one invitation I wasn't going to turn down! I headed straight up the aisle to the cargo area and sat myself down beside Charlie. His tail thumped on the crate wall when I joined him, and he kept his eyes on me for the duration of the flight. I told him that this strange journey would eventually bring him back to Eddie, but in a country where he'd be safe. Who knows how much any animal can understand from voice and body language? All I knew was that Charlie was glad for my presence. We kept each other company until just before the plane began its descent.

Before I had left Kuwait, I had done a practice run, so I knew exactly where I needed to go after my flight from Baghdad landed. As long as nothing went wrong, I was fairly confident we'd be on time to catch our next flight on United. But there had been a delay just before we took off from Baghdad, so now we'd be cutting it close. If anything caused Charlie and me to miss our connecting flight, we would be in trouble. Dogs from Iraq aren't allowed to enter Kuwait, and the next flight to Washington, D.C., wasn't until the following night. Charlie would be stuck in his crate in the cargo terminal with no one to walk him or give him food and fresh water.

Before landing in Kuwait, I spoke to the flight engineer, who had taken a liking to Charlie. "Now you're sure the ground crew will get Charlie to the United flight okay and not leave him sitting somewhere?"

"Don't worry. I'll personally make sure Charlie doesn't get left behind."

As the passenger shuttle left for the terminal, I watched the airport ground crew load Charlie's crate onto a luggage trolley. This was the last time I would see him until we were reunited in Washington, D.C. I had to fight the urge to jump off that shuttle, much like a new parent who leaves her child in the care of a babysitter for the first time.

When we entered the Kuwait terminal, the transit desk was a hub of activity. Forty of us had arrived on the Gryphon flight, and due to the delay, most were nervous about making their connection. As we stood in line, a United Airlines representative collected our passports and gave them to a man seated at a desk in a small office behind the counter. Working at a snail's pace, the seated man inspected each passport, printed a boarding pass, and then handed both items back to the United representative, who returned them, one by one, to each passenger.

At this pace we'll be here all night, I thought.

The passing minutes on the wall clock seemed to speed up as the time of our departure got closer and closer.

"Terri Crisp!" the United representative called out.

"I'm traveling with a dog," I said as he handed me my passport and boarding pass. "I need to pay the shipping cost."

"All animals are supposed to be here two hours before departure." His voice hinted at impatience, and his eyes betrayed no feelings of sympathy or understanding.

"I know, but our flight was delayed."

He turned to speak in Arabic to the man seated at the desk. I had no idea what they were saying, and their facial expressions were not providing any clues. Being unfamiliar with Middle Eastern mannerisms and body language, I found it impossible to tell whether the agent was a helpful friend or a play-by-the-book foe.

All the other United passengers who approached the desk were told to proceed to the departure gate, while I stood like a penitent sinner at the end of the counter, feeling more helpless than I cared to think about.

The airport PA system announced, "All passengers for United Airlines flight number 981, please proceed to Gate 21 for an on-time departure."

The man with whom I had been dealing returned to the counter. "First we need to locate the dog. Then we'll weigh the crate to determine how much the freight charge is. In the meantime, please fill out these documents."

I was still stuck at "We need to locate the dog." I wanted to scream, "You're telling me you don't know where Charlie is?"

But this was not the time to speak my mind. I filled out the forms while the man went in search of Charlie. I crossed my fingers, hoping he'd be on our side. After completing the paperwork, I paced in front of the counter. The minutes continued to tick by. Once again the voice over the PA system reminded all United Airlines passengers that they should now be boarding the flight for Washington, D.C.

Trying to curb my rising anxiety, I asked myself, "Has anybody died?" The answer was "no" at that point, so everything was still fixable. When I'm faced with challenges, this question has turned more anxiety-filled situations around than I care to count. All I am dealing with is another solvable problem. At the next flight-boarding announcement, I tuned out the annoying voice.

The tap-tapping of the United representative's leather-soled shoes preceded his breathless announcement, "We found him! I've got the weight." He waved a slip of paper in the air as if approaching the finish line of a marathon. He slipped behind the counter, wiping sweat off his brow. For a man whose culture didn't like dogs, he certainly was making an effort to ensure that Charlie and I caught the flight. He had proved himself to be a helpful friend.

After some quick calculations, the agent told me what I owed. I wasted no time giving him my debit card and prayed the woman at the credit union had been correct when she said the card would be accepted in Kuwait. I stared at the small machine, willing the slip of paper to scroll out, confirming that payment had been accepted. Suddenly the machine hummed and began to print, and I expelled one more of the many sighs of relief that had passed my lips that night.

"Now go," the man urged after I signed.

"What about my dog? Is there still enough time to get him on board?"

"They are loading the animal right now," he said. For the first time since we'd met, the agent smiled.

"Thank you!" In America I would have given him a hug or at least a handshake, but here I could only hope that the look in my eyes would convey the depth of my gratitude.

I sprinted through the congested airport, which, thankfully, isn't very large. An airline representative stood at the jet way entrance, her hand ready to pull the door shut. "Wait!" Handing my passport and boarding pass to one agent and my carry-on bag to security for screening, I was the last passenger to slip through and board the plane. I slid my briefcase into the open overhead compartment and collapsed into my seat.

"Hey, you made it," the young man seated beside me grinned. "When I overheard you at the counter say you were bringing a dog from Iraq to the U.S. for a soldier, I was pulling for you. I sure wish the puppy I rescued in Iraq could have been saved and brought home. Leaving my dog behind was one of the hardest things I've ever had to do."

His sad words echoed in my mind, as if foreshadowing that this would not be my last trip to Iraq.

• • •

As soon as we got through U.S. Customs, I pulled out my Blackberry, anxious to let Eddie know we'd arrived.

Eddie, we've landed in D.C.! Charlie is beside me, along with camera crews and news reporters from CNN and other media, waiting for the press conference to begin. Your dog is getting a hero's welcome, and he's loving every minute of it.

Oh, and the guys from SLG wanted me to tell you that even though Charlie howled when they pulled away from your outpost, once they got him to their compound, he settled in just fine. They spoiled him the next day with plenty of treats and affection. He even got a bath. By the time they took him to the airport, they were buddies.

So many people on this journey went out of their way to make sure Charlie had a safe, successful trip. I cannot tell you how full my heart is at this moment.

Rest easy, my friend. Your dog is home.

—Terri

Eddie must have been waiting by the outpost computer. A few seconds later, as I answered questions from journalists, my cell phone rang. It was Eddie. No one could make me ignore this call.

"We did it!" Eddie yelled. His voice was nearly drowned out by the whoops and shouts from soldiers standing around him.

"You'd better believe it! Charlie's paws are on American soil as we speak, and there's not a grain of sand in sight."

A long pause on Eddie's end bore witness to the depth of feeling contained in his next words. "I don't know how to say . . . what this means . . . Thank you."

"Other than knowing Charlie is safe, the only thanks I need, Eddie, is to see you come home."

"I'll be there in six weeks."

An excited group of people waited to welcome Charlie and me amidst the reporters and cameras at the airport. It was such a relief to see the faces of my daughter Jennifer, my boss JD and co-worker Stephanie, plus SPCA International volunteers Bev Westerman and Barb Hartman. Hugs and tears were shared all around, and everyone was in a celebrating mood.

After the crowd of well-wishers and reporters dispersed, Jennifer and Stephanie went to get the rental cars. The only people who stayed behind were JD and the reporter from *The Washington Post*. We had all decided to take Charlie out for a walk along the National Mall and to take his photograph there so I could send it to Eddie. Before Jennifer and Stephanie returned with the cars, JD turned to me. Our eyes met for a few moments in a wordless recognition of what we had just achieved.

On many occasions in the last few months we had sat in JD's office together, sometimes with tears of frustration welling up in our eyes when it looked like Charlie's rescue plan would slip, once again, like dry sand through our fingers. With every obstacle that appeared, the stakes rose, and the price tag mushroomed into frighteningly high figures. That financial burden was always on JD's shoulders. Despite his earnest desire to help Eddie and his dog, I honestly don't know why JD didn't just pull the plug.

"You did it, Terri," JD said. "You kept your promise to Charlie."

"I wasn't the only one; we *all* did it." I replied.

JD looked away, a little embarrassed at the emotions that threatened to spill over in public.

"We actually pulled off the impossible. Isn't it an awesome feeling?" I asked.

"I haven't felt so fulfilled in a long time," JD admitted quietly. Determined to maintain his composure, my boss suddenly changed to a brisk, business-as-usual tone. "I'm going to ride to the mall with the photographer and Stephanie. Do you want me to stay with you until Jennifer gets back?"

"No. You go ahead, and we'll meet all of you there. Charlie and I will just plop ourselves down here and grab a quiet moment."

I sat with my back propped against the wall, legs stretched out in front of me. Closing my eyes, I stroked Charlie, who had lain beside me and placed his head on my lap. Before she left the international arrivals area with JD, the photographer from *The Washington Post* captured Charlie and me with her camera. Above our heads the arrivals board announced only one flight. It read simply, "Kuwait."

For the next few moments Charlie and I sat alone together. I was overcome by the realization that this dog's death warrant was now discarded in Iraq and that his new prospect for a long, healthy life in America was assured. All this happened because one soldier had the courage to ask for help, and we'd had the heart to say, "We'll try."

By the time our party reconvened to walk Charlie past his new country's beautiful buildings and military monuments, our stroll along the National Mall could not have felt more patriotic. Charlie stopped to christen every corner and claimed this country as his own. Eddie would have been proud of his dog. After the memorable photo shoot, Jennifer and I said our goodbyes to all our friends and loaded Charlie into the rental car.

Jennifer and I shared a room with Charlie at the Sheraton. I couldn't wait to sit down with her and let all the details of my journey tumble out. We tried to get Charlie to sit on the bed with us, but he wasn't having it. Shortly after we settled in, someone knocked on our door. I half-expected to see more reporters, but the door opened to the hotel bellman, whose arms bore a huge basket of dog toys and treats. Attached to the basket was a card signed by the hotel staff. It read, "Welcome Home, Charlie."

The hotel employees must have seen the news reports on TV or on SPCA International's website. Perhaps they had been following Eddie's blog. It seemed like the whole world had been following the story.

* * *

Six weeks after Valentine's Day, Charlie's entry into the States, SGT Eddie Watson came home with his unit. Eddie couldn't wait to drive to Bev and Barb's house, where Charlie and I were staying. He left Fort Bragg military base in North Carolina immediately after work and was so eager to see his buddy that he didn't even stop to change out of his Army Combat Uniform (ACU).

When Eddie arrived, Bev, Barb, and I met him out in front of the house.

"Why don't you go around to the back yard?" I said. "Charlie's out there waiting for you."

Sure enough, when Eddie rounded the corner, Charlie was standing by the gate. Having heard the car, he knew that someone was coming; he just didn't know who it was. As Eddie walked toward the gate, Charlie spotted the uniform, and the expression on his face changed. He stared at Eddie for a second and then shook his head as if he couldn't trust what he was seeing.

Eddie unlatched the gate, went in, and took two steps toward Charlie before he bent down to touch his dog. That's when Charlie went crazy. The dog nearly flipped himself inside out before he took off and ran in circles around the yard. Eddie had never seen Charlie act anything like it before. After several rounds, Charlie launched himself from six paces and, airborne, landed in the soldier's out-stretched arms, licking his face and whimpering. He kept repeating his wild greeting as if the only way to release the uncontainable joy was by running. After several spins around the yard, Charlie settled down, and Eddie was finally able to wrap him in the hug he'd been waiting to feel for six long weeks.

The whole scene seemed unreal to Eddie. The dog he remem-bered in Baghdad had lived outdoors at the outpost. That dog had always been covered in sand and filth. To see him like this was a shock. Charlie's fur shone and his tail was now thick and fluffy; he held it up as if waving a victor's flag after the battle is won.

"Look at you! I can't believe it's you," Eddie laughed between choked up tears. "You scrub up good, old buddy."

Eddie buried his face in the dog's fur and gave Charlie a vigorous rub all over as he continued to praise his dog. Charlie leaned against the soldier with his mouth open and tongue hanging out in a wide canine grin, as if he understood every word.

That night Eddie and Charlie stayed at a hotel just outside of Washington, D.C. Charlie slept on the bed and stretched across his soldier's body as if determined never to let him go away again. In the morning the two of them went for a walk around the D.C. monu-ments before they headed back to Ft. Bragg in North Carolina. Eddie walked Charlie past the military memorials and down the tree-lined streets of Washington, humbled by the realization that until he came to America, the only places Charlie had known were the streets of Baghdad's slums. People kept stopping to say hello to the soldier and his handsome dog, and they were intrigued when Eddie told Char-lie's story. The dog loved all the attention he was getting. Any worries Eddie had felt about Charlie adjusting to people in the States were eased. After a couple hours of sightseeing, they returned to the car and began their six-hour journey back to base.

Some of the guys in Eddie's unit knew that he had gone to collect Charlie. They, too, couldn't wait to see their old buddy again. One of the men, named Smith, didn't know that Charlie was in America or even that Eddie had been trying to get him out of Iraq. Smith was one of the guys who had helped to take care of Charlie when the men first found him as a pup. He had doted on the puppy as much as Eddie did.

Back in October, Smith had taken a round through his knee. It was the kind of injury that knocks a soldier out of the war. The Army had sent him back to Ft. Bragg, where he'd been undergoing a painful recovery and grueling physical therapy. But now the soldier from the 82nd Squadron was up and about and glad to be reunited with his platoon. He certainly never expected to see Charlie again.

When SGT Watson got back to the base, he stood in the parking lot next to Charlie, talking with one of the guys from the unit about what a surprise it was going to be for Smith to see Charlie again. Sure enough, when Smith walked across the grounds and saw SGT Watson from the far side of the lot, he caught sight of Charlie, shook his head and his jaw dropped several inches.

"Charlie?" he shouted.

After all that time, the dog remembered Smith as if he'd just seen him yesterday. Charlie started flipping in circles on his leash, barking, and acting as crazy as when he was reunited with Eddie. SGT Watson unclipped the leash, and Charlie sprang forward as if someone had filled him with rocket fuel and pushed the take-off button. Eddie and the other soldier got all choked up as they watched Smith's big grin, and how he kept shaking his head. He couldn't believe it; here was Charlie, the dog that had made all the difference in Iraq, together with his buddies again—together in America.

• • •

Eddie wrote to me after he and Charlie had settled in for a few days. I had been as eager to hear about Eddie and Charlie as a mother who misses her children when they go off to summer camp, and though she's glad her kids were able to go, she needs to know how they're doing.

Relief flooded over me when Eddie's words confirmed that everything I'd worked for had been worth it:

> Coming back from war isn't easy for anyone. In many ways it's as strange as going to war in the first place. But when the dog that smelled fear on your body after you returned from an ambush, and made you laugh when you were war-weary and fed up, comes home with you, it makes a big difference. He knows where you've been and what you've seen. He understands like no one else could. That feeling is too big to put into words.
>
> Charlie earned his place in our unit. All of us just wanted him to be safe and not to think we'd left him behind. Thanks to you, Terri, and SPCA International, this soldier's buddy came home.

Charlie tries to get the hang of baseball. *Terri Crisp*

Chapter 5

A BROTHER'S PLEA

K-Pot on play duty *Matt McDonough*

During the six-week wait for SGT Eddie Watson's unit to rede-ploy, I had hoped to spend much of my time with Charlie, but that was not what fate intended. Three days after Charlie and I arrived in the States together, I received an e-mail that gripped my heart.

To: Terri Crisp, SPCA International
From: Danielle Berger, New Jersey

Dear Terri,
I've been following the news about Operation Baghdad Pups bringing Sergeant Eddie Watson's dog to the States. My brother

has been desperately seeking a way to get the puppy his unit rescued out of Iraq. I can't stress enough how crucial K-Pot's safety is to my brother's well-being.

Matt and I always had a close relationship, and after he joined the Army and became a combat medic, we continued to correspond regularly. As soon as Matt learned he was going to Iraq, though, he distanced himself from me and the rest of our family. Considering what he was facing, it didn't surprise us.

Matt is now stationed in northern Iraq, where heavy insurgent activity is a daily occurrence, and some of the highest casualties have been recorded, so we weren't surprised that the few e-mails he sent were brief, detached, and usually weeks apart. Every day Matt was administering to the bodies of shattered soldiers, often while under fire himself.

Each time I stopped for a moment, I was thinking, what is Matt doing now? Is he okay? Is he even alive? Being almost completely cut off from my brother, I found sleep impossible. Unless people have a loved one serving overseas, they have no idea how hard it is for families back at home.

In August things suddenly changed. It all began with Matt's e-mail saying, "You won't believe what we just did. My unit rescued a puppy. We're still cleaning up after an insurgent attack; I'll write again later."

I received more e-mails from Matt over the next few days than I'd had since he joined the Army. Talk about the crack in the dam; once he began writing about this puppy, he wrote about everything else as well. Immediately the tone of his letters sounded more upbeat, and the wall of silence that war had put between us began to crumble.

Using the webcam, I was able to meet some of the soldiers in Matt's platoon and see K-Pot and another puppy they rescued, named "Liberty." The guys gathered around sharing stories of the puppies' antics. I can't tell you how wonderful it was to hear

Matt's laughter again and to meet his military buddies. It's like my family suddenly grew a lot bigger.

Before K-Pot came into Matt's life, I worried for my brother's sanity as well as his physical safety. But now he has something other than war to consume his thoughts. K-Pot found the weak spot in Matt's soldier-toughened armor, and it's this crack that allows the horrors to drain out while laughter and warmth flow in.

After a few months, one of the military veterinarians responsible for the care of bomb-sniffer dogs, made it possible for Matt's unit to keep K-Pot and Liberty. He got the dogs registered as "force protection canines," but unfortunately the status that protects them from the military's no pets rule also declares them as Army property and, therefore, expendable equipment. K-Pot and Liberty will have to be euthanized when the soldiers leave.

Today Matt e-mailed me saying that his platoon just received orders to report to a fire base and the dogs can't go. Unless Operation Baghdad Pups can transport K-Pot and Liberty to the States before his platoon moves out, these life-saving dogs will die. I hate to think what it will do to my brother and the other soldiers if two members of their close-knit family are destroyed by the same country they have risked life and limbs for.

I am pasting below some excerpts from Matt's e-mails, so you can read, in his own words, how important this little dog is.

Before I moved on to reading Matt's e-mails, I had to sit for a moment. I remembered the troops at Baghdad International Airport marching out of the C-17 transport plane, and I tried to imagine how I'd feel if one of them were my brother. What if he, like Matt, were going to a combat zone where so many had died? Danielle's description of her brother's day-to-day life brought the reality of war into vivid perspective, and a chill ran down my spine. I noticed that Matt's first e-mail had been sent in August 2007.

To: Danielle Berger, New Jersey
From: Matt "Doc" McDonough, Combat Medic, Iraq

Sorry it took me so long to get back to you again. It's been balls to the walls ever since I sent you that flash about the puppy, but things are quiet now, so I can finally tell you our latest story from the sandpit.

We were under mortar fire during a night skirmish, and flashes from exploding shells made it hard to see. Some of the men and I heard the screams, but we couldn't tell who they were coming from, only that the cries of pain and terror were from something small. It probably wasn't a good idea to investigate while rounds were falling, but I was the closest and was just as likely to take a hit wherever I was. The cries led me to a heap of razor wire, where a bleeding puppy had gotten himself tangled up. When I realized it was a dog, I tried to ignore it, knowing if I pulled him out, I'd be tempted to keep him.

You can't afford to get attached to pets when you're in combat. They're a distraction, and distractions get you killed out here. But those screams were louder in our heads than all the firing around us, so we gave up and went back to get him. Once we got him untangled, one of the men slipped him inside his flak jacket, took him to a place where he'd be safer, and then we hightailed it back to the rest of the unit.

When the enemy decided to quit shooting and go to bed, we checked the area, and found the little mutt where we'd left him. He was so young, his eyes had only just opened. He didn't respond to us at first, so I thought he was dead. Then he moved. Dehydrated and covered in cuts from the razor wire, he didn't look like he had much of a chance. We couldn't leave a wounded puppy like that, so, being the medic, I took him back to the aid station, dealt with the lacerations, and got some liquids down him.

Our fire base is situated in a beat-up ruin of a house that overlooks a river valley. Without doors that close, there's no way to keep the puppy inside, and he's so small, he fits through just about any opening he can find. I figured he'd wander off, especially since the enemy is always taking potshots at us. But I guess with all the warm bodies and free food, he decided to stick around.

Every time a skirmish is over, the guys wander around calling, "Anybody seen the puppy?" A minute later someone shouts, "Found him!" A few times we located him curled up in a soldier's Kevlar helmet with all the soft padding. We call them "K-Pots." It wasn't long before the name stuck to the puppy as well. So that's what I wanted to tell you. You've got a new nephew named "K-Pot."

Matt's story made me laugh. I couldn't help but feel delighted for the soldiers who had this new puppy in their lives. The next excerpt was dated a week later.

K-Pot is the most tuckered-out puppy I've ever seen! Guard rotation is every six hours. When men come off duty, they want to play with him. You could say he has been commissioned for around-the-clock play duty. When he gets too tired to hold his head up, K-Pot hides under the blankets in the aid station where I sleep.

In the two months before K-Pot came, we suffered heavy losses and injuries. When your teams are taking hits and you see your buddy going home in a box, it's hard to keep your mind from going to a real dark place. Since the puppy came, we've had something else to think about.

These are some of the toughest guys you'll meet in your life. Friends are dying all around them, and they're still rock solid. But put a puppy in front of them, and they turn into little kids, playing chase and going out of their way to make sure he's fed and taken care of. Someone's always asking me, "Can I play with K-Pot? Can I give him a bath?"

You never know what he's going to do next. Yesterday K-Pot ran up to a big 25-ton Stryker tank with a giant gun on top. One soldier took a photo of him lifting his leg and peeing on it. Man, did we laugh.

The incongruity of men going out, trained to kill and prepared to be killed, and then coming back to play with a puppy, perfectly illustrated how crazy war is and what a source of relief K-Pot must be for those soldiers. The next excerpt gave me more insight to a soldier's life in Iraq.

We've only had K-Pot a month. Last week we nearly lost him and another puppy named Liberty. Someone took a photo of two of us holding up the puppies and they posted it on AKO (Army Knowledge Online). People check e-mails on this site every day. This led one afternoon to our Commanding Sergeant Major yelling, "Those are my men—with pets!" and a few other choice words. We scrambled to get the pups out of here, or they might have been shot. Our Iraqi interpreter offered to take them back to his house.

That evening we asked how the pups were, and he said he'd hidden them in the trunk of his car since he wouldn't bring them in his house. All we could think was they must be dying of the heat. After dark, four of us—a commissioned officer, a noncommissioned officer, an infantryman, and I—snuck outside the wire and found the bullet-riddled car. We pried the trunk open slowly, half-expecting to find two bodies. When we whispered the puppies' names, they jumped up, real glad to see us. The officer grabbed Liberty, I took K-Pot, and we hoofed it back to the fire base.

When we got to the gate, one of the guards came out ready to shoot. "What the hell are you guys doing out here?" he asked, implying either we were up to no good or out of our minds.

You should have seen the look on his face when we held up the two puppies and explained that our "force protection canines" had escaped, and we'd gone to rescue them. "Force protection, eh?" he snickered. It wasn't exactly a lie; we fully intended to get them registered as soon as we could.

The soldier started looking as if he was going to order us to leave the pups outside the gate. Before he had a chance to say a word, the officer in our group stood inches from the guard's face and ordered, "Let us through, or I'll have your ass fried and fed to these dogs." The guard obeyed, but, boy, we were nervous thinking we'd get called in on this. If he reported us, we were looking at docked pay, loss of rank and commission. You can't just go outside the wire in enemy territory during the middle of the night and certainly not for a dog.

When soldiers are willing to risk their lives and their careers to protect a puppy they have befriended, surely there was an important message in this for the military.

Hey, Sis,

It's getting close to Christmas, though it sure doesn't seem like it here. I was thinking about the last time we went to cut down a tree together. I bet K-Pot would be full of Christmas spirit if he was home now. He'd take one look at that tree and mark it as his. K-Pot and Liberty finally got promoted to official Force Protection Canines, buying them some much-needed time. I'd like to get K-Pot to the States if I could. Rumor has it we'll be moving to another fire base soon, and we don't know if the pups will be allowed to come.

I noticed that Matt's next and final email was dated immediately after my return from Iraq. If Matt's sister had spent nearly two months trying to find options for transporting K-Pot, it was easy to imagine the frustration and worry she must be feeling. I knew what kind of obstacles she would have run into.

Danielle

URGENT—Moving out and definitely cannot take pups. We heard SPCA International just saved SGT Watson's dog. Will you contact them? Please move fast, or K-Pot and Liberty will be destroyed.

—Matt

After reading the last excerpt, I was already determined to do whatever I could to save these dogs. I finished reading the rest of Danielle's message.

Terri, my family has been following SGT Watson's website with great interest. He has praised the dedication and persistence you and your organization have shown, a commitment that resulted in Charlie's rescue. When you and Charlie appeared on the news as you arrived in Washington, D.C., my family's cheers must have been heard across the state of New Jersey. Now we are praying that you can bring K-Pot home to us, where he will be lovingly cared for until Matt returns from Iraq. Please, will you help us?

—Danielle Berger

Liberty, Force Protection Canine *Terri Crisp*

It was now clear that Operation Baghdad Pups wasn't just a program that saved a dog. We could prevent one more tragic loss for the men and women who risk their lives protecting what Americans hold dear. They shouldn't have to grieve for their animal buddy when they come home from the war. These dogs were making a difference for our troops, and they deserved to live. I couldn't wait to contact JD and get a go-ahead to give Danielle the news she was hoping for.

Chapter 6

K-POT AND LIBERTY

Camels on the road in Kuwait *Terri Crisp*

During the four days that I had been traveling to rescue Charlie, dozens of e-mails from soldiers in Iraq and from their families in the States had filled my inbox; heartwarming stories of rescued strays followed heart-breaking ones of loss or impending animal destruction. It was a daunting yet humbling task to respond to these brave people. But Danielle Berger's urgent plea required immediate action. Putting everything to one side, I picked up the phone and called JD at SPCA International headquarters.

"We've been getting requests for help here, too," he said, "so I'm not surprised you're reporting the same. I just finished consulting with our board of directors, and they agreed unanimously for the organization to bring additional dogs out of Iraq for U.S. troops. We are well aware that soldiers give everything and ask for so little in return. They deserve our help."

My heart leapt at the sound of those last four words.

"Are we talking about the half-dozen dogs that need urgent transport now, due to redeployments or threat of imminent death, or are we planning to save as many soldiers' dogs as we can?" I asked. "There's a significant difference. Once word gets out about Operation Baghdad Pups, I suspect we will be overrun with requests."

"We'll definitely help the dogs we already know about, and then we'll see what happens after that," JD said. "One of the biggest determining factors for how many dogs we can rescue is whether we can raise adequate funds by donation to support this program."

With approval to move forward, my first action was to phone two of our most reliable volunteers, Bev and Barb. They agreed to take care of Charlie at their home near Washington, D.C. while I scrambled to get our second mission off the ground. Before I knew it, I was boarding another plane to Kuwait.

• • •

Waking up to thunderous revs of passing motorcycles, it took me a few seconds to get my bearings. I realized I was in the Plaza Athenee Hotel as soon as I spotted, high on the opposite wall, the decal depicting a mosque. It was the arrow beneath it, which pointed toward the ceiling that had caught my attention the night before. When the bellman deposited my suitcases inside the room, I had asked him what the arrow signified.

"The arrow points east toward Mecca, for when it's time to pray," Sanjeewa explained.

Prayers were not on my mind when I jumped out of bed and pushed back the heavy, room-darkening drapes. Harsh desert sunlight burst through the window, nearly knocking me over. I squinted against the overpowering brightness to take in a sea of tan. There wasn't even a distinct break along the horizon where the waters of the Persian Gulf ended and the sky began. This could get monotonous real fast.

Because I was planning to be in Kuwait City for one day longer than on the last trip, I got a visa at the airport when I arrived. I had done some research prior to departing to see if there were any animal welfare organizations I could visit, and I learned there was one called "PAWS" outside the city. I sent an e-mail introducing myself, and one of their volunteers, Brenda Nielsen, had generously responded with an invitation to bring me to the shelter. We arranged to meet after breakfast in the hotel lobby.

An hour's drive through the desert is long indeed when the eye has nothing but sand to fall on. Occasional visual relief was provided by dilapidated wooden trailers that were separated by several miles. Situated about twenty feet off the highway, each trailer stood open at one end, displaying shelves filled with what appeared to be an assortment of food and other household products, a Kuwaiti version of 7-Eleven. By the time we reached the animal shelter, it seemed as if we'd found an oasis in the vast desert.

Five adult camels preceded us through the gate. "Oh my gosh," I cried. "They're real!"

Brenda laughed, explaining that the camels were frequent visitors. She gave me a tour of the well-kept shelter, where large, outdoor enclosures and air-conditioned accommodations kept the animals comfortable. Ending our tour in the office, she proudly pointed to a partially completed mural, an ongoing project for Kuwait art students.

"I have to make a couple of calls that can't wait, I'm afraid," Brenda said in her proper British accent. "I shouldn't be more than a few minutes. If you feel like painting in the meantime, you're more than welcome to add a dog or cat to our fresco. The brushes and paints are in the corner."

The artist in me rose to the challenge, and I proceeded to add a black dog to their wall. I had to laugh; here I was in the middle of a desert oasis painting pictures on a Kuwaiti animal shelter wall where camels stroll by on a daily basis. How much cooler could life get than that?

Later, Brenda drove us to the home of Linette Botha, another shelter volunteer who was originally from South Africa. Greeted by her seven friendly dogs and warmly welcomed into Linette's massive house, I found myself among like-minded friends and enjoyed a relaxing afternoon exchanging rescue stories. Before Brenda and I left, Linette told me how much she admired the work SPCA International was doing to help the dogs in Iraq. She handed me her card, saying if there was ever anything she could do to help, she was "just a call away." I put the card in my pocket thinking, you never know when you're going to need a friend.

• • •

Kuwait International Airport was now familiar territory. Loaded down with one bulging suitcase and two large, disassembled airline crates, I maneuvered my trolley through the congested terminal with confidence, dodging people like I was driving in a NASCAR race. I stood in line to clear security, aware of the looks on people's faces when they saw the dog crates. Considering how repulsed these people were by dogs, I hoped the crates wouldn't present a problem.

An elderly man who was two people ahead of me in line pushed a baggage trolley bearing a five-gallon plastic jug filled with liquid.

Despite posted security signs for the liquids-limit of three ounces, his jug was not confiscated, so I was ready to put up a fight if anyone hassled me about the crates. Clearing security without any trouble, I finally pushed my way to the Gryphon Airlines counter.

"Welcome back, Dog Lady," said the Gryphon agent. We laughed, and I felt proud to have earned the distinctive nickname. He looked at my crates. "Before I give you boarding passes, you must take those to the airport superintendent's office for approval stickers." He pointed to a door on the other side of the glassed-in ticket counter area.

"Okay," I said, a little puzzled. I couldn't help but wonder if the old man with the large plastic bottle had to get a sticker, too. My crates were much less of a security threat than a five-gallon container of unidentified liquid.

The open door of the airport superintendent's office revealed five seated men, all chattering in Arabic, smoking cigarettes beneath a "No Smoking" sign, and drinking tea. I stood unnoticed in the doorway. Finally I took a deep breath, put on a big smile, and said, "Hello," as enthusiastically as I could. It worked. All five men turned and stared at me.

"Stickers," I said, suspecting that these men spoke little or no English.

Two of them came over to where I was standing. One cautiously touched the crates as if afraid he might be bitten, while the other man inquired, "Where are dogs?"

"Baghdad," I said. "I take two dogs to U.S. for soldiers."

"You don't have dogs in America?"

"Yes, we do," I replied, trying not to laugh. "But these dogs are special." The other man disappeared behind the office door and opened what sounded like a metal cabinet.

Please, let him be getting the stickers.

He returned with the stickers and looked at me for a long moment. I maintained my composure and kept smiling. He finally bent down and put the stickers on the crates.

"Be careful in Baghdad. That is bad place."

"I will." Gripping the baggage trolley, I high tailed it out of there, before either of the men changed his mind and took back my stickers.

Although the flight to Baghdad was uneventful, when the wheels of the Gryphon plane made contact with the runway, the same excitement washed over me as nine days before when I had picked up Charlie. It struck me again how unreal it all seemed, being back in a combat zone.

The same man from SLG came aboard when we landed, only this time he began his "Welcome to Baghdad" speech by saying over the PA, "Passenger Crisp, please come forward."

He smiled as I walked up the aisle. "Welcome back! Your dogs are waiting. I understand you brought their airline crates with you. If you need any help getting the dogs in them, just ask."

I made my way down the portable stairs and spotted the security team waiting ten yards or so from the plane. I recognized two of the team members from my last trip. Standing between the men and secured with homemade, braided cord leashes were Liberty and K-Pot. Liberty, the older and larger of the dogs, was quickly recognizable with her coat of silver and beige, while K-Pot had a rich walnut brown and sand coloring. They both had charcoal muzzles and at least one 'sock' paw, typical of the mixed-breed dogs from Iraq.

"Hey," I said to the SLG security guys, "I didn't expect to see you so soon!"

"Yeah, we were kind of surprised when we got the request to pick up two more dogs," the man holding K-Pot said. "But we're really glad to help again."

I squatted down to meet Liberty and K-Pot. Wagging tails indicated they were pleased to see me, but their faces registered looks that seemed to say, "We're not quite sure why we're here, so could you fill us in, please?"

"Is there any chance I could borrow two of you to help me put their crates together?"

Eager to do anything they could, the men jumped to it. It wasn't hard to find the crates even in the semidarkness. A mountain of suitcases and duffel bags waited to be transported to the Gryphon office. There, on top of the pile, the two crates stood out like lost penguins in the Iraqi desert. Assembling them felt like participating in a company retreat for developing team-building skills. On the wind-blown tarmac with sand attacking every pore of our bodies, we stood our ground. Using only the minimal light permitted by security rules, we were all but blind as we fitted and screwed the crates together.

After placing absorbent pads, food, and a water dish in each crate, we coaxed the dogs in one by one. It took each dog only two seconds to determine that he was not impressed and wanted back out. Pulling zip-ties out of my pocket, I secured both doors as an added precaution. The last thing I wanted to report to our soldiers was that a loose dog on the runway had been shot by authorities. With Liberty and K-Pot secured in their crates and ready to travel, I thanked the security team members before they loaded the dogs into the plane.

"It's all in a day's work," the man closest to me said, "except helping these dogs is a lot more fun than our usual round of duties."

As my head sank back against the seat, his words ran through my mind. I guess I could say the same thing, I realized with a growing smile. Bringing home a U.S. soldier's dog was one of the most gratifying experiences of my life.

During the return flight to Kuwait, I was allowed once again to visit with Liberty and K-Pot. The Gryphon flight attendants brought me a large bottle of water and helped to fill the dogs' dishes. After the dogs were settled, I joined the attendants in the galley. They treated me to orange juice and stories of their own dogs at home in Spain.

In just two trips to Baghdad, I'd formed a team that I wouldn't have thought possible only four months earlier. With my new friends at PAWS, the Plaza Athenee Hotel staff in Kuwait, the Gryphon Airline folks, and the men at SLG, I felt safe and at home in this foreign place. Operation Baghdad Pups had now transitioned from a desire to save one dog into a program I hoped would save many more.

After landing I approached the transfer desk at the Kuwait airport feeling confident about the next half of my mission. That was a mistake. In a few minutes I would be reminded of how quickly things can change when traveling in the Middle East.

"You're back!" The United counter man, who had run a marathon for Charlie the last time, recognized me instantly. "I assume you have a dog with you tonight?"

"Actually I have two." I handed over my passport.

He glanced up at the clock. His look of relief that he wouldn't have to run another marathon confirmed we had arrived in plenty of time. Everything should go smoothly now that he and I knew the routine.

"Terri Crisp," he called out a few minutes later, holding the weight slip. "The total cost for the two dogs will be 216 dinars." I handed him my debit card. As the receipt began printing, the agent's face fell.

"The card has been declined. I'm sorry."

Having double-checked my online bank balance before I left the hotel, I knew there were sufficient funds in the account. I had also informed the credit union of my travel plans so that it would recognize the Kuwait purchase as legitimate.

"Can you try running it again?"

The man ran the card a second time. Again it was declined.

By the time I could make alternative arrangements for payment, our flight would already be gone. My biggest worry was Liberty and K-Pot. Linette and Brenda had previously told me that bringing dogs through customs into Kuwait wasn't possible due to the government's fear that animals from Iraq would bring in diseases. The puppies certainly could not remain in the airport for twenty-four hours confined to their crates in the cargo area. People here would be too afraid to give them food or water, let alone to walk them.

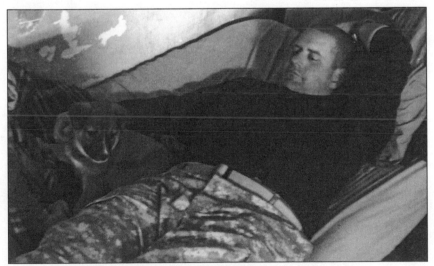

K-Pot and Matt taking a break *Matt MacDonough*

"I assume you want to cancel your ticket and the dogs' reservations," the agent said as he handed a boarding pass to the last remaining passenger.

"Yes, go ahead." My voice trailed off to almost a whisper. He looked at me and hesitated.

"I have to go to the gate now and help board passengers, but I'll show you where the dogs are first, if you like."

I followed him to the baggage claim area, all the while trying to figure out what I was going to do. I kept coming to the same conclusion. Because going back to Iraq was no longer an option, somehow I had to get Liberty and K-Pot through Customs. But if the Customs officers discovered where they were from, the dogs' destruction was a very real possibility.

"I'm so sorry I couldn't do more," the agent said after he led me to the dogs. He surprised me by reaching out to shake my hand, a gesture rarely seen in this part of the world between a man and woman who are not related. After saying goodbye, he hurried off to the boarding gate where I was supposed to be. Even with my two traveling companions, I suddenly felt terribly alone.

Chapter 7

NEW FRIENDS

K-Pot and his new American buddies *Danielle Berger*

Times like these seem to turn on my adrenaline pump, and I shift into high gear. I had to figure out how to handle this particular problem quickly. First I checked to make sure that Liberty and K-Pot were okay. Their bewildered faces peered out from the crates.

"I know you want to stretch your legs, but you'll have to hold on a little longer."

I topped off their water bowls but had nothing to feed the two dogs. "If we clear Customs," I promised, "I'll get you guys two of the biggest, juiciest chicken sandwiches I can buy."

I half-sat on Liberty's crate and finished off the last of the bottled water. Eighteen hours without sleep threatened to fog my thinking, and I needed all my wits to pull this off. As I surveyed my surroundings, I explained our situation to my canine companions.

"Over there is our obstacle. If we can just get through that hurdle, the worst of our problems will be behind us." They tilted their heads and listened, making me feel less alone, as if we were now a team.

It was almost midnight, and the airport still bustled with activity. This might work in our favor. Customs officers would be less inclined to scrutinize the dogs' papers from Iraq when hordes of travelers were pushing through Customs anxious to reach their destinations. I decided not to launch my plan until the next full flight arrived. As I studied from my vantage point how the officers operated, I considered several scenarios.

Considering the lack of compassion that people had for dogs in this part of the world, I decided against playing the sympathy card. There was another good technique I had used while in disaster areas. When approaching a person who has the power to concede permission, you confuse him so thoroughly with distractions that he finally gives up and grants your request just to get rid of you. The key part of this technique is to remain enthusiastic, smile a lot, and exude a genuinely pleasant personality.

Fifteen minutes later weary arrival passengers appeared, forming a human wall around the baggage carousels. "Please," I prayed, "don't let me show any nerves. I can do this. I know I can do this." Then I crossed my fingers and jumped into the fire.

First I needed a porter. When I flagged one down, he wheeled his trolley toward us. After he saw the two dog crates, he enlisted the help of a fellow porter. Two could definitely be useful, I thought. I soon discovered that neither one of them spoke English. Their accents sounded as if the two men were from Sri Lanka or possibly Bangladesh, meaning they probably weren't Muslim and wouldn't, therefore, be afraid of the dogs. On their royal blue uniforms, the porters each wore badges that showed the numbers 128 and 314 instead of their names. This was typical of how poorly paid foreign laborers are treated in Kuwait, the role being considered more important than the person behind the badge.

While they loaded the dogs' crates onto the trolleys, I pulled out K-Pot's and Liberty's paperwork from my briefcase. I made sure that any pages with the word *Iraq* on them were placed at the bottom of the stack, and then I tucked the envelope under everything in my suitcase.

"I sure hope I haven't forgotten anything," I mumbled. "If I have, it's too late to fix it now."

Just before we reached the Customs checkpoint, I directed the porters to follow me over to the side, out of the flow of traffic. For a few minutes we stood there, giving me a chance to more closely observe the individual officers. Six of them worked the night shift, increasing the odds that one would fit perfectly into my plan. I studied each man carefully, hoping to find an officer whose actions revealed that he hated his job and who displayed an "I don't care" attitude. A stickler for rules would be a disaster for us.

One officer paid as much attention to his line of passengers as a bored child pays to the preacher in church. He was exactly the type I sought. I nodded to my porters, and we stepped into the apathetic officer's line.

Inch by inch our line moved forward. My skills at reading body language would soon be put to the test. When we got to the security checkpoint, I motioned for my porters to push their trolleys off to one side with the dogs still in their crates. If all went as planned, I would go through Customs and then have the porters slide along behind unnoticed. It was a long shot, but given how inconsistent security procedures in this airport had already been, I thought it might just work.

I smiled at the middle-aged officer, and he half-acknowledged my greeting. The baggage handlers placed my suitcase and briefcase on the conveyor belt. While the baggage rolled slowly toward the X-ray machine, I walked to the other side of the scanning unit to wait. Just then the officer demanded, "Paperwork!" He pointed to the dogs.

"Oh, crap," I said under my breath.

Earlier I had peeled the "Operation Baghdad Pups" stickers off the crates to remove any evidence of where we had just been. Scrunching the wadded stickers tighter in my hand, I made my first move.

"Garbage?" I showed the wad to the officer, trying to stall for time without being obvious. He pointed to the nearest trashcan. I ambled slowly over to it and stopped along the way to retrieve a discarded candy wrapper which also needed to be thrown away.

Returning to the security area, I explained that the dogs' paperwork was in my suitcase, which had now passed through the X-ray machine. I pointed across to my luggage.

"Can I go there?"

The man nodded his head and followed me.

Unzipping my suitcase, I pretended to forget exactly where I had put the paperwork. I made small talk with the officer while rifling through pockets and layers of clothes. Because he knew about as much English as I knew Arabic, I'm sure it sounded like gibberish to him. Several times I stopped rummaging, straightened up, and smiled at him while my hands made grand motions to emphasize whatever elusive point I was making. All the while the porters watched me as if we had rehearsed our getaway plan a million times.

The officer's face began to reveal what I wanted. He was looking at me as if thinking, *this woman is crazy.*

What happened next was completely unexpected. Another passenger came through Customs, and traveling with her was a large orange tabby. The woman, who looked like she was an American, took the cat out of its carrying case so the empty carrier could go through the X-ray machine, just as they do in the States.

As fast as I turned to look at Liberty and K-Pot, they had zeroed in on the cat. Both of them began barking aggressively, silencing everyone and drawing attention to them. I realized this might turn out to be the lucky break I needed.

The cat struggled to get out of the woman's arms, while the terrified baggage handlers who worked the X-ray machine quickly abandoned their posts, putting as much distance as they could between themselves, the cat, and the dogs. In the commotion, the cat's carrying case got caught in the scanner, slowing its exit. Now the woman holding the cat was dripping blood and yelling, "Where is my carrier? Get me my carrier! I can't hold onto this cat forever. Ouch! Hurry up!"

I froze and stared at the woman. The Customs officer glanced quickly back and forth between me and my suitcase, the screaming woman, and the scanner that was releasing strange noises. Every animal-fearing Muslim in the area would soon be shrieking and running to avoid contact with the equally panicked cat if he managed to escape. The officer made a lunge toward the scanner; then he turned and looked at me. With a flustered wave of his hand he said, "You go."

Those were the words I was waiting to hear!

I motioned for my porters to quickly follow me. There was no language barrier now. They got my message loud and clear and acknowledged it with a thumbs-up gesture. I closed and zipped my suitcase, then grabbed my briefcase and headed straight for the exit. Porters 128 and 314, in their bright blue uniforms and hats, followed me closely and pushed the barking dogs as fast as they possibly could.

When the automatic security doors opened, my cohorts and I headed straight for the closest terminal exit without looking back. After we were out of the Customs officer's sight, I put up my right hand to give my partners a high-five, exclaiming, "We did it!" The porters knew immediately how to respond, and they understood we had just accomplished something, though they weren't quite sure what. I couldn't have found two better men to help execute my plan.

My victory, however, was short-lived. Standing outside the airport with two hungry dogs, waiting for a flight that wouldn't leave for twenty hours with no place to sleep did not sound appealing. On my second trip in nine days, halfway across the world and miles from family and friends, I had reached the point of exhaustion. This was no good; I couldn't succumb now.

Looking at the dogs, I pulled myself together and motioned to one of the porters to follow me back into the terminal and for the other porter to stay with the dogs. Thank goodness those men didn't abandon us but showed instead that they were willing to do all they could to help.

Earlier that day when I had entered the terminal, I had passed an entire row of hotel counters and noticed a sign for the Sheraton. This gave me hope, considering how kindly the staff at the Sheraton in Washington, D.C., had treated Charlie. My porter and I approached the hotel agent.

"Excuse me."

The sleepy man, slouched in a desk chair behind the counter, stubbed his cigarette in an overflowing ashtray, slowly rose to his feet, and shuffled toward me as if it pained him to do so.

"How can I help you?"

"Does your hotel allow pets?"

His puzzled expression was accompanied by, "What are you asking?"

"Does the Sheraton allow dogs?" I rephrased my question, sensing he didn't know what the word *pet* means. This was not a good sign.

"No, no, no, no, no!" He emphasized every word each time he blurted it out. "Dogs are dirty."

One down, seven to go.

My next stop was at the Radisson counter. This man didn't even get up from his desk, but his response was the same. Strike two.

Working my way down the row, I asked the same question. JW Marriott, Hilton, Holiday Inn, Crowne Plaza, and Four Points all responded in the negative until I reached the young man who represented the Courtyard Hotel.

"No, we do not allow dogs, but let me call the hotel, and I'll see what I can do."

Porter 314 had been listening intently to each of the conversations between the hotel representatives and me, and I think he now understood what I was trying to do. He smiled encouragement.

"This is Ahmed," the young man said into the phone. "I have a good friend of mine here at the airport. She missed her flight, and she needs a room for tonight."

I looked at this man in amazement. He was making up a story to help me and what he thought was my one dog. I hadn't broken the news to him yet that there were two. We'd cross that bridge when we got to it.

"Great. She'll take that room. Oh, one other thing, she has a dog with her. It's just a small, well-behaved one. I know he won't be any problem."

I held my breath and watched my new friend's face.

"Are you sure we can't put her in the old wing, in a room at the end of the hall? There is the entrance no one uses. She could take the dog in and out from there."

Finally, as he hung up the phone, his defeated expression preceded the words, "I'm so sorry; they just won't allow a dog."

"You were the only person here who went out of your way to help me find a room. I can't tell you how much I appreciate that you tried." I reached out to shake his hand and, remembering the taboo, started to draw it back. "I'm sorry," I said. Once again he surprised me and offered his hand, so we shook. "You're a kind man. Thank you for everything."

My search may not have resulted in my getting a room for the night, but I did meet a Muslim who went the extra mile to help me and my dogs. He had indeed acted like a good friend, and he proved that not all Muslims hold the same attitude toward dogs.

As my porter and I walked back to where his colleague and the dogs were waiting, I came up with another idea. Searching through my briefcase, I found the business card that Linette had given me. Calling someone in the middle of the night can be a real test of a friendship, but I was desperate. I phoned Linette two times, only to have someone pick up the phone and immediately hang up again. The person at the other end probably thought it was a crank call. I phoned her several more times but no one picked up. All I got was a recorded message in Arabic. Now what was I going to do?

As we stood outside, I couldn't believe how busy the airport was at this time of the night. Car horns and exhaust fumes gave me a nauseating headache. Loud music from the open windows of passing vehicles reverberated against the concrete buildings and buzzed through my tired bones. Never-ending groups of shrouded, robed, and uniformed people said their greetings and goodbyes in a stream of Arabic and other foreign languages. The taunting aroma from a nearby vendor's stall reminded me I hadn't eaten since lunch. A yawn escaped me. Tired, hungry, and desperately wanting to be somewhere safe with the dogs, I tried ringing Linette's number one more time.

I couldn't believe my ears when a sleepy voice answered, "Hello."

"Linette, this is Terri, and I'm at the airport." I talked fast, afraid she was going to hang up again. "I have Liberty and K-Pot with me." There was a long pause.

"Is your flight delayed?"

"No, it left without us. My debit card wouldn't work, and I couldn't pay the dogs' freight charge."

"Where are the dogs now?"

"We're standing outside the airport in the baggage claim area."

"You got the dogs through Customs? How in the world did you do that?" Linette was now wide awake.

"With timing, a bit of psychology, and divine intervention in the form of a cat. But we desperately need a place to stay. We're exhausted."

"I'll come and pick you up. It'll take about forty-five minutes."

"Thank you, my friend," I said in relief.

It was time to celebrate. I looked at the porters and pretended to sip from a cup. "Coffee?" They both nodded yes.

Motioning for them to stay with the dogs, I went back inside the terminal and purchased an assortment of pastries and three Starbucks Grande White Mochas, with an extra shot of espresso in mine. While the coffees were being made, I went to KFC and bought Liberty and K-Pot large chicken sandwiches, grateful I could finally keep my promise to feed them.

When I returned, we sat on the trolleys and ate our picnic, making what small talk we could while learning a little bit about each other.

When Linette finally pulled up to the arrival area, I stood and waved. Amazed to see me there with the dogs, she forgot to brake and nearly drove over the curb. By the time my porters pushed the trolleys to the waiting vehicle, Linette was standing by the open rear door of her SUV.

"You really did it," she said, giving me a big hug.

"And I hope I never have to do it again! I was so afraid I was going to lose the dogs." The sight of her was such a relief that I would have cried if I had not been too tuckered out.

It was time to say goodbye to my Sri Lankan porters, and I handed each of them a generous tip. The money seemed inconsequential in comparison with what they had done for me and the dogs. I would never forget their kindness and the comfort it bestowed. Looking both of them in the eyes, I placed my hand against my chest as a gesture of my deepest thanks. Their responding smiles revealed that we had left an impression on each other's lives that would not soon be forgotten.

When I slid into the comfort of Linette's car, my exhaustion took over. I closed my eyes for just a few seconds only to open them and discover that we had reached our destination. Linette's dogs, along with her husband and their two daughters, were asleep upstairs. As quietly as we could, we released Liberty and K-Pot into the court-yard. They wasted no time sniffing out the best spot to pee. Each one stood in the grass for at least a full minute while relieving a ready-to-explode bladder.

A few minutes later, when the dogs and I were snug in Linette's guest room, she stuck her head in to wish us goodnight.

"Sleep as long as you can, and once you're up we'll plan how to get the export documents you need."

"More documents? I had no idea we needed more. How difficult will that be?"

"Go to sleep and don't worry. You three are safe for now, and that's all that matters."

Giving Linette a grateful goodnight hug, I did as I was told. Worry could wait for tomorrow. I sat down on the bed; both dogs came over and leaned against my legs. Liberty gently licked my hand as if to say, "Everything is okay."

Pulling out my Blackberry, I sent a short message to the soldiers' waiting families and to JD and my family, saying that the dogs and I were fine and that we would be arriving a little later than originally planned. I promised to send our new flight information as soon as the details were confirmed.

Liberty and K-Pot were already stretched out on the cool tile floor. One of them let out a long sigh. As I lay down in the dark, my weary mind and body began to relax. Drifting back over the strange events and the people who had helped along the way, the thousands of miles that separated me from home and family seemed to dissolve into nothing. By the time the clock struck three, the dogs and I were fast asleep.

The nasal-toned call to prayer, broadcast on loudspeakers throughout Kuwait, woke me at 5:00 a.m. I dozed on and off for about an hour, and when the dogs began to stir, I got dressed and took them into the courtyard, where I found Linette and half of her menagerie.

"How about some breakfast?" Linette asked as she herded her dogs back into the house. Later, over coffee and croissants, Linette cast her eyes over Liberty's and K-Pots' vaccination records that I had fetched from my bag while she made the coffee.

"These look good. We shouldn't have any problems."

The "should" part of that sentence hit me like a hammer.

Please make this go easy, I thought. *I don't know how much more I can stand.*

Linette took one look at my worried expression and suggested I should stay with the dogs and rest while she ran the paperwork to the veterinary clinic.

"Once I've got their health certificates, I'll take them to the Ministry of Agriculture to be stamped. I should be back in two hours if there are no delays."

I spent the time throwing tennis balls for K-Pot and Liberty and playing with Linette's dogs. Every once in a while my two would come and lie beside me as if confirming I was their protector. Nothing is as gratifying to me as the look in a dog's eyes that says, "I trust you" and "thanks." No matter how difficult my two journeys to Iraq had been, the dogs' faith-filled faces erased all the stress and worries. I understood a little better how much the presence of such dogs helps our soldiers.

When Linette returned with the official paperwork, I made reservations for the United flight leaving that night. I asked about the previous day's problem with my debit card and was told that a computer glitch that had caused the error had been corrected. Even so, we took no chances. Not only did Linette drive us to the airport that evening, but she also came inside to the counter and stayed until my card was authorized and the receipt was in my hand.

"Travel safe, my friend," she said with tears in her eyes. Already the adventure had bonded us two women, each of whom, only two days before, had not known that the other existed.

"You saved us last night, and I will never, ever forget that."

K-Pot and Matt's sister, Danielle *Danielle Berger*

"Anything for the animals," she laughed.

Liberty, K-Pot, and I left Kuwait just after 11:00 p.m. on February 22. We arrived at Dulles International Airport the next afternoon to find Danielle Berger and Amanda Byrnside already waiting to greet us among a crowd of reporters, cameras, SPCA International staff, and volunteers.

Having family members who were dog lovers and who served together in Iraq made for an instant friendship between Amanda and Danielle. They had supported each other with e-mails, phone calls, photographs, information, and anything else they could to ease the worry of having a loved one at war. Whenever Amanda heard from her husband, she'd pass on the latest news to Danielle, and when Matt wrote to Danielle, she would do the same in return. Not only did keeping in touch help minimize the sleepless nights, but their common goal of saving the dogs sealed their friendship. When I agreed to take on K-Pot's rescue, leaving Liberty behind was out of the question.

Although we hadn't met in person, my greeting with Danielle and Amanda was as warm as if we were reunited sisters. "I can't believe the blizzard I drove through to get here," Danielle laughed with tears rolling down her cheeks. The atmosphere was full of jubilation. But now it was time to let these women properly meet their loved ones' dogs.

Without being prompted, everyone moved back and watched in silence while two women —a soldier's sister and another soldier's wife—squatted down to open the crate doors. After the women clipped on the leashes, the dogs stepped out of the crates, sniffed the new faces, and wagged their tails. Everyone remarked that the dogs seemed to understand that they were carrying the hearts of the men they had left behind.

As much as it hurt to say goodbye to my traveling companions, the satisfaction I got from watching the puppies bridge the physical gap that separated U.S. soldiers from their family made it all worthwhile.

Chapter 8

GUARD DUTY

Socks looking for his buddy at the Welcome Home ceremony *Terri Crisp*

The dogs of Iraq come from a gene pool of animals that have learned to survive in some of the world's harshest conditions. They have to be resilient and sharp witted. Those that are born sickly, deformed, weak willed, or mentally slow are quickly weeded out by nature and by man. Time and again soldiers' e-mails mentioned the all-too-common sight of lifeless animals strewn along roadsides and rotting in neighborhoods. Carcasses lay where the animals had died from culling, torture, starvation, or disease.

The U.S. military had implemented sanitation practices for collecting and disposing of the dead animals, but with the thousands of additional animals struck down by vehicles every day, there were just too many.

"One day I counted 286 dead dogs in just the sector we were patrolling," a Marine wrote to me in disbelief. "These animals are definitely the uncounted casualties of this war."

I was shocked when another Marine wrote, "We are forbidden to provide any kind of assistance to an injured animal we come across. The enemy discovered Americans can be real softies when it comes to animals, especially dogs, so they use that knowledge to their advantage. They have been known to purposely injure a dog, making it unable to move, and then they place a booby trap underneath its body. When a kind-hearted soldier sees the animal, feels sorry for it and goes to help, guess what happens next? *Boom.*

Wow. I never realized. So that's why the military has these rules.

Witnessing culturally based attitudes that showed little compassion or respect for animals was especially hard on Americans who came from a different background. Although soldiers rarely went out of their way to befriend a stray, many found themselves adopted by one that had come to their compound for food or protection.

Stray animals are not part of military veterinarians' mission in Iraq, but when these animals start living with the troops, the spread of disease becomes one of their concerns. Veterinarians responsible for the care of American working dogs in Iraq sympathize with soldiers whose befriended strays come under threat of destruction or abandonment when the soldiers redeploy. One veterinarian introduced a program for classifying a select number of stray dogs. These animals were registered as "force protection canines," which allowed them to be micro-chipped, vaccinated, spayed or neutered, and given parasite-prevention medication. The animals got access to better-quality dog food as opposed to MREs, and they received full veterinary care at no cost to the units.

According to one veterinary officer I talked with, "The job of a force protection canine is to hang out with the troops at some of the more remote military installations and bark when intruders, human or animal, come around. In addition, the dogs provide much-needed companionship. We now find that instead of hiding potential carriers of disease, the soldiers can take action to make sure the befriended dogs are healthy. This has taken up a lot of our time, but it has been well worth it, not only for the animals but for military personnel as well."

In February 2008 I learned about one stray dog that had gained the respect of both Marines and Army soldiers thanks to an e-mail sent to me by SGT Andrew Bankey, asking for help to get the dog to the States. Andrew was stationed at an outpost in an Iraqi province west of Baghdad. I asked Andrew to explain why it was so important to rescue this dog, and here is his response:

Socks is about three years old, which makes him an old-timer by Iraq standards. When I met him, he was already a permanent fixture at this outpost. No one really knows how Socks actually got here. When my unit took over the outpost, the Marines who were leaving recommended that we keep Socks around. His sixty-pound presence was a good deterrent against intruders, and they said his courage was especially appreciated at night.

Our purpose here is to train Iraqi soldiers so they can take over the job of protecting their own country. Although there are 1,500 Iraqi soldiers at this outpost, there are only twenty Americans. We don't know how many of the men we train are enemy infiltrators, but we do know they're here. So, although most Iraqi soldiers are allies, at any given moment U.S. soldiers could be sabotaged by one of the men from this outpost.

Socks has always been fed and cared for by Americans, so he considers us his family, and all Iraqis potential enemies. He doesn't trust any of them. Whenever an Iraqi approaches our section of the outpost, Socks won't let him in until one of us has checked him out and said, "He's okay, Socks."

The bathrooms on our outpost are some distance from where we sleep. During the day, a trip to the john is no big deal, but at night, you have to be pretty desperate to make the trek.

In spite of our efforts to keep stray dogs away, there are still packs that prowl around at night. Our base is a long way from the city, and the closest villages are a few miles off, so we're out in the middle of nowhere, and the nights are eerie and quiet. Sometimes you go outside, and in the moonlight, you'll see them—

feral dogs—filthy, scarred, and mean, scrounging for garbage and hunting. You have to remember, these aren't friendly pooches; they're wild carnivores, ready to kill for food. Sometimes only a dozen or so are out there, but I've known nights when there must have been a hundred. They howl like wolves, and when you hear that low, steady growl, the hairs on your neck rise up.

Although most of these dogs steer clear of people, if a guy made the mistake of getting between the pack and the morsel of food they're fighting over, the dogs could get downright vicious.

Other than stray dogs, the second-biggest threat we face is coming up on one of those camel spiders. Looking more like a scorpion on steroids, some of them grow to nearly a foot long. If you run into one of them when you're half-asleep, it definitely wakes you up, and when those spiders feel threatened, they chase you. They're not afraid of anything.

The first time I had to make the middle-of-the-night hike to the john, I was not looking forward to it. When I stepped out the door, there was Socks lying in the dirt. He wasn't asleep, but wide awake, as if he had orders to be on duty.

"Hey, boy, what're you doing here?' I asked, wondering if he'd be friend or foe after dark. That's when I found out—Socks considers it his job to guard the men. He sits outside our barracks every night, waiting for soldiers to stumble out the door on their way to the bathroom.

Well, Socks took his job real serious. He stuck to me like a president's bodyguard, his eyes and nose at full alert, until we reached the john. His head went down and hackles stood up; he was one mean looking guard. Socks stayed outside manning his post until I was done and escorted me back to the barracks. After that he lay down waiting for the next person who couldn't hold it until morning.

The other awesome thing Socks does is that he leans against us. It's not just a dog planting himself against your leg; it's like he senses when you need contact with another living being. He'll just come over and lean. If you move away, he'll follow and reattach himself until you feel better.

In the time that I have been stationed here, Socks and I have grown real close. He sleeps in my hooch now and follows me everywhere. Seems like he decided I was his. When my unit re-deploys at the end of March, we'll be handing full control of this base over to the Iraqi Army, and there won't be any more Ameri-can soldiers replacing us. Socks will be surrounded by people he considers his enemies, and they don't trust him either.

Considering that Socks has been on duty 24/7 for over three years, I don't think he deserves to be left behind when we go. If there is anything you can do to help me get him back to the States, I'll take good care of Socks for as long as he lives. He's fought off several gangs of dogs that tried to attack me, and prob-ably saved my life. I can't just walk away from him now.

—SGT Andrew Bankey

I agreed with Andrew—any dog that served the military in such an important way did not deserve to be left in Iraq. Andrew's unit was getting ready to redeploy in a matter of weeks, so we'd have to act fast. Socks had not been vaccinated, which created a dilemma, but he did have one advantage. Socks had been serving as an outer perim-eter guard for quite some time, so it wouldn't be too difficult to have him classified as a force protection canine. This classification would enable him to get the veterinary care and health certificate required for travel. Andrew promised to get onto this task right away.

Socks was not the only dog that needed immediate transport to the United States. I received several urgent requests for help, includ-ing one for two puppies named "Oreo" and "Bags." Bags had been rescued by a soldier who saw a group of kids kicking a bag around the street like a soccer ball. When the bag yelped, he realized what was inside.

The SLG operations manager coordinated the collection of the dogs from each owner. The animals' exact locations had to be confirmed and a movement request submitted to U.S. Military Central Communications (CENT COM). Approval came back, along with directions for the route that was least likely to involve skirmishes. Other arrangements had to be made, such as fueling locations, food for the security team, and a safe place to grab a few hours' sleep.

The SLG security team drove throughout the night in two Ford Excursions and two Ford gun trucks, one with a 360-degree turret on top. Their mission was to collect the dogs and transport them to the airport. The hundreds of miles they covered were fraught with danger.

When the team arrived at Andrew's location in March, ready to load Socks, the dog took one look at the armored vehicle and decided he was not going into it. I received an e-mail from Andrew describing the scene.

> I drove to the convoy meeting place today, and all went smoothly until we got there, and I tried to put Socks in the truck. He got really upset, even growled at me, his buddy, and fought like hell not to go in that vehicle. He was so scared, I nearly called it off. How could I tell him this was for his own good? I guess he thought I was a traitor, because he sure was mad, and I worried about the safety of the transport team.
>
> One of the men, named "Jerry," said, "Don't worry. I'm fine with taking him." They got a dusty old blanket and wrapped Socks in it. It took five men to hoist that dog into the truck and slam the door before he fought his way out of the blanket. I sure hope he calms down. This is all very new and scary for Socks. He's a good dog, and I know he's in good hands. Thanks.
>
> —Andrew

I replied to Andrew, "I'm glad you didn't cancel. Socks will calm down, and I'll take good care of him, I promise."

• • •

On March 13, 2008, I landed at Dulles International Airport with Oreo, Bags, and Socks, three of the five dogs we had attempted to save on mission 3. This was the first time that we received, upon arrival in Iraq, tragic news from SLG of a dog's death or loss before the animal could be picked up. In this case the two other dogs had been shot. Sometimes the animals were culled by contracted companies called "vector control;" other times they were killed by locals or even members of the U.S. military. Whenever this happened, it was devastating for the soldiers, their families, and for me. All I could do was contact the soldiers as soon as possible and express my deepest sympathy. Then I got back to work saving the dogs I could.

Considering the odds that were against us, each time my flight landed on American soil and the rescued dogs were taken to Bev and Barb's house or united with their families, I felt a million sighs of relief sweep over me and a renewed sense of determination to carry on the mission of Operation Baghdad Pups.

I kept in touch with Andrew by e-mail to let him know how Socks was doing. Again, just as with Eddie, it seemed almost as if Andrew and I were parents separated by distance and as if Socks was our child. I knew how important it was for the owners to receive my updates. A few days later I sent the following report:

Hi, Andrew,

Today Socks came with me while I ran some errands. He sat in the front seat, taking in all the new sights, and he behaved so well, I treated him to his first McDonald's cheeseburger minus the ketchup, lettuce, and pickles. Your dog is now a real American.

Socks learns everything so fast. The first few nights he slept for only short periods, but after he realized there are no threats here or a need for him to escort anyone to the bathroom, he started to sleep through the night. Socks is thoroughly enjoying his retirement from the Army, and I believe he dreams of becoming a couch potato!

—Terri

Andrew's unit was due to arrive at Ft. Stewart, Georgia, on March 29. It turned out that the best way to deliver Socks to Andrew was for me to drive south from Washington, D.C., on Interstate 95. Once again I would be spending more time with an Operation Baghdad Pups dog during his first weeks in the States. Doing this gave me further insight into the dog's perception of a totally different world as I witnessed his fascinating and often entertaining reactions. Whenever we drove under a bridge or an overpass, for example, Socks ducked. His fascination with windshield wipers made me laugh as his head mimicked a metronome and followed the wipers' blade movement until I turned them off. Every time a semi-trailer roared up alongside our rented PT Cruiser, Socks backed away from the window, and I had to rest my hand on his back, assuring him it was okay.

Socks and I arrived at Ft. Stewart in plenty of time to see the military "Welcome Home" ceremony for Andrew's battalion. As we got closer to the base, hundreds of homemade signs and banners began to appear on the route:

WELCOME HOME, DADDY

YOU ARE MY HERO

PROUD OF OUR SOLDIER DAUGHTER

Attached to fences, staked in yards, taped on streetlights and store windows, they all welcomed home the troops.

At the main gate a guard gave me a temporary pass and a map to the field where the ceremony would take place. I knew that Socks would not be allowed in the bleachers, and even if he had been, the reaction of an emotional crowd might be too much for him. When family members spotted one another, it was going to get loud and crazy.

Working our way across the ceremonial field, I found a quieter place to sit with Socks. I pulled out a red, white, and blue bandanna and tied it around his neck. A row of flowering redbud trees was planted beside the walkway where we waited. At the base of each young tree, a small American flag cast its shadow over a plaque, each one engraved with a soldier's name. Excited families waited for their loved ones' return on the opposite side of the field while Socks and I stood beside these memorials to soldiers who would never return. We took a stroll along the solitary row of trees and stopped to read the name on each plaque.

My thoughts were soon interrupted as a crescendo of cheers emanated from the crowd. On the road that approached one side of the field, a white school bus turned the corner and headed toward me and Socks. This bus was immediately followed by one white bus after another. The buses were full of soldiers just off their home-bound flight. With hardly any time to transition, they still carried the smell of desert dust in their nostrils and the battles of war in the forefront of their minds. Looking out the bus windows and passing the welcome signs as they approached Ft. Stewart must have seemed like a dream.

This was the moment we'd all been waiting for. The buses slowly passed by, and uniformed men and women hung out the windows. Shouts and cries of soldiers and their families filled the air as they called out to each other. Socks raised his ears, wondering what all the excitement was about.

Suddenly a voice cried, "Socks!" Instantly Socks let out a sound unlike anything I'd ever heard. There was no mistaking the joy in his voice. He barked and strained at his leash, and a look of intense yearning filled his eyes. He just couldn't figure out where the voice came from. He kept looking toward the passing buses and then back at me as if to say, "So where is he? Let's find him!"

For the next twenty minutes, the buses were out of our view while the unloading took place in a parking lot down the street. It's common knowledge in the military that you have to prepare for a whole lot of hurry up and wait. It seemed to take forever. Finally, without warning, the first row of marching soldiers appeared from behind the tree line. A deafening cheer burst from the crowd as row after row marched across the field. Before long, several battalions had gathered in formation, and the soldiers stood at attention. I couldn't help but marvel at their self-control. If that were me, I'd have jumped over the fence and run straight into the arms of my loved ones, but these men and women held it together, like always.

People in the bleachers finally began to sit down, and a restrained quiet replaced the exuberant outbursts. The longer families took to settle, the longer their soldiers would have to wait. Socks stopped pulling as well. He seemed to recognize the command to stand at attention and knew it was time to be still, but his eyes continued to scan the field, searching for Andrew.

Speeches from high-ranking military officers claimed no one's attention. Words were wasted at this point. Not a single person in that crowd could have focused on a speech when a loved one stood only a few hundred feet away. At last we heard the words everyone waited for, "You are released," and a happy pandemonium ensued. Streaming out of the bleachers, a landslide of people ran onto the field while the soldiers ran toward them. The scene resulted in a mass collision of embraces, laughter, and tears.

I knew that members of Andrew's family had come to greet him and would want their moment together, so I didn't cross the field but instead waited for him to find us. Sure enough, after a few minutes, a soldier broke from the crowd and headed straight toward us. Socks began to strain on the leash again. I never let these dogs run loose. It would be a tragedy if they ran out and got hit by a car or disappeared, but this time there was no chance of Socks wandering away. He aimed his nose toward his buddy, and when I let go of the leash, he took off like a bullet. That dog flew—literally flew—into Andrew's arms. In a second they were both on the ground rolling and wrestling.

I thought back to the day when Andrew and four other men had wrapped Socks in a blanket and shoved him into a strange security vehicle, and Andrew questioned whether to call the whole thing off. I wondered, as the SLG team had driven away, if Socks thought he'd ever see Andrew again. What a huge relief it was to see these two buddies reunited.

After a while I approached Andrew and Socks, and they stopped their roughhouse play. Andrew stretched out on the ground, and Socks lay on top of him, covering Andrew's chest and body. For a long moment one soldier and his dog embraced in a wordless conversation. From now on Andrew and Socks would remain together, bound by memories, love, and a soldier's commitment to his buddy.

SGT Andrew Bankey reunited with Socks in the USA
Terri Crisp

Chapter 9

FINDING FELINES

Hope—all grown up *Pam Bousquet*

Before an animal could be accepted by the Operation Baghdad Pups program, I had to consider a number of factors. First the soldier had to have a reliable home for the animal to go to in the States, either with the soldier or with a family member. SPCA International had no intention of adding to America's overcrowded animal shelters. Soldiers also had to establish their commitment to the animal and show that anyone who was going to care for the animal until the owner arrived home was also on board.

In the first two months of Operation Baghdad Pups, all the rescued animals were dogs that belonged to soldiers. Cats had also worked their way into people's hearts, however, and not all of the owners were active military. Many of the Americans living in Iraq are there as contracted workers. They also contend with war-zone challenges that affect soldiers. Separation from family, limited access to after-work distractions, depressing surroundings where infrastructures are unreliable or unavailable, and the constant awareness of danger make life in Iraq stressful and intense.

I was contacted in April 2008 by a woman named "Pam Bousquet" regarding her husband, who was desperate to save his cat. I asked her to have him send me an e-mail explaining his situation. The very next day, Bruce's e-mail arrived.

Dear Terri,

In October 2007 I was hired by a private company to be lead technical advisor for the installation of a new power plant near the northern city of Erbil. It is one of the many reconstruction projects coordinated by the U.S. government to rebuild an infrastructure for this war-ravaged country.

On most days in Erbil, there is electricity for no more than a couple of hours. Can you imagine getting through a day without air conditioning when it's 120 degrees outside? This new power plant represents hope for people who have little else to hang onto.

My home away from home is in a construction camp not far from the plant. Some mornings I'm tempted to walk to work, but working in a war zone means I can't do a lot of the things we take for granted in the States. Instead, an armed driver from Olive Security Group takes me wherever I need to go. My driver is a Kurdish man who commutes 18 miles each morning from his home in Erbil.

One morning, as his car pulled up, I saw something fall from the engine and land on the ground. Considering how many cars in Iraq are rigged to blow up and kill people, I didn't know whether to investigate or run. That's when the howling started. As I bent down to get a better look under the car, the most pitiful calico kitten I've ever seen stared back with frightened eyes. I figured she couldn't be more than seven weeks old.

I wasn't real sure what to do next, and my driver wasn't offering any suggestions. The stray cats that hang around camp are mean suckers, and I had yet to see a friendly one. So trying to pick her up was not a good idea. While I was trying to come up with a plan, the kitten moved, exposing part of the reason she was crying. She wasn't just scared. Her front leg was badly burned.

She must have come in contact with the hot engine while she hitched the ride from Erbil. There was no way I could just leave her there. That burn looked nasty. I slowly reached my hand toward the kitten, and she never took her eyes off of me. Fully expecting her to fight or run away, I was relieved when she allowed me to gently pull her into my arms.

Going to work was out of the question. I sent my driver back home while I took the kitten to my room to get a better look at her leg. Not only was the fur gone, but the skin had melted away as well, leaving the leg muscles exposed. I was not equipped to take care of something this serious. My only option was to take her to the camp medic. Helping a stray cat was prohibited, but what else could I do? Without proper medical care, the kitten would not survive.

It turned out the medic liked cats. He cleaned the kitten's wound, applied some antibiotic ointment, and bandaged the leg. With another week of antibiotics and bandages, my feline roommate was well on the road to recovery. I was amazed she was going to pull through. Miracles in Iraq are few and far between.

The day she literally dropped into my life, I didn't expect the kitten to live, but she made it clear she wasn't giving up. By proving me wrong, she filled me with hope. She was a lot like the local people. In spite of the difficulties in their lives, they hadn't given up either. As the power plant got closer to completion, it gave the local people hope for a better future. That's why I decided to name the kitten "Hope."

I used to sit and watch her, wishing my little friend would let me pick her up again but didn't want to push my luck. She had already made it clear that keeping some distance between us made for better living arrangements, so I went along with it. Then one night that changed. Startled awake by something that felt like a warm wig draped across my head, I suddenly realized what it was. Hope has been sleeping there ever since. I call her my "cat hat."

I never planned for Hope to enter my life, but she did, and now she is a part of me. We have a strong bond between us, and I'm her only family and provider. If I left Iraq without her, it would be like abandoning my own child. I want her to be a part of my family in the States, not just another dead cat in Iraq.

I'm no soldier, and Hope is definitely not a pup, so I don't know if she qualifies for your program. I have worked hard to help this war-damaged country build a future and made many Iraqi friends. In that sense, I have played an important part in the peace process in the Middle East. If there is any way your organization can help me to bring Hope home, I will be forever grateful.

—Bruce Bousquet

Until I read Bruce's story, I hadn't really thought about what it must be like to live and work in Iraq as a civilian. I felt bad that people such as Bruce weren't recognized enough for the important role they play in promoting democracy and providing services that help citizens recover their lives after their country is torn apart, especially when much of the destruction was done by American military weapons. Soldiers enjoy the camaraderie of their buddies, but often contractors such as Bruce are terribly alone. My heart went out to him, and I e-mailed Bruce back, saying I'd be glad to put his cat on the active rescue list.

On the same day that I received Bruce's request for transporting Hope, I also got a call from Matt Kincaid of Pet Relocations with our second cat. Matt explained that his company specializes in transporting animals all over the world, but one of the few countries where it cannot operate is Iraq. Matt asked us to help a U.S. Marine who had contacted him, and was desperate to get his cat to Virginia. I told Matt to tell the cat's owner to send me an e-mail. Two days later Captain Thomas Liu's e-mail landed in my inbox and told a remarkable story of love and commitment.

My platoon was originally stationed at a forward operating base about 50 miles west of the Iraq–Iran border. We provided security for convoys, cleared IEDs, and patrolled the area surrounding our base, always on the lookout for insurgents. We had over 230 Marines in six platoons, and I commanded one of those platoons.

The terrain in that part of Iraq is harsh, and the people are dirt poor. Iraqi farmers migrate into the area at the beginning of the rainy season to plant crops. They live in small huts built out of mud bricks. After harvesting their meager crops, the farmers return to where they came from.

During one of our patrols, we came upon one of these abandoned huts where the walls and roof had collapsed. I certainly didn't expect to stumble upon a kitten there. A scrawny little thing, she was sitting in the rubble all on her own. Her pitiful meows confirmed that life at that moment couldn't get much worse. I gave the rubble a quick once-over, and there were no signs of any other cats.

It was a tough call to make. Do I leave the kitten behind, knowing she's too young to survive on her own? Or do I break the rules and take her back to camp? I'm a Judge Advocate, meaning I advise and enforce military regulations, including General Order 1A, which prohibits military personnel from befriending stray animals in a war zone. If I flouted the very regulations I make others uphold, I could get into serious trouble.

No matter what a Marine's specialty is, we are all trained to kill if that's what it takes to protect our country. No training can replicate the carnage of war, however, and prepare men for what they'll face on the front line. In Iraq, life is as cruel as I've ever seen it. When I found that innocent kitten, it tore me apart realizing one more life was about to be wasted. I didn't want to add to the brutality of her world. Maybe I just wanted to make reparation for all the horrors that war brings. I couldn't turn my back on her and let the poor thing die.

That was the beginning of my covert operation. I snuck her into my trailer and gave her some tuna from the chow hall. I was determined to keep the other platoons from finding out I had a cat. But keeping secrets isn't easy, especially when you need to find kitty litter. People started noticing me wandering around in the middle of the night, carrying my little shovel and a trash bag, looking for patches of sand. They must have thought I was really strange.

I refused to name the kitten at first. I'd push her out the door In the mornings, hoping she'd learn to fend for herself, but every night when she heard my boots coming, she'd beat me to the door and wait to be let into my room. Over time the Marines in my platoon got to know her. Eventually I gave in and named her "Jasmine." She knew the difference between my Marines and the ones from the other platoons, and she stuck to her own men, doing the rounds every day, accepting everything they offered.

Rivalry between platoons is a part of life on a military base. Jasmine became the target of a prank instigated by some of the Marines from the 4th Platoon. They were on a mission to kidnap Jasmine, but her feline instincts foiled their repeated attempts. After two weeks of dodging their traps, she had a moment of weakness and walked up to them purring. They nabbed her.

The next day I was the last of six Platoon Commanders to give a status update during a staff meeting with our Commanding Officers. Using a PowerPoint presentation, I stood in front of the room and detailed our operations. When I was almost through, I got hit with a surprise that I thought would cost me my job. Somebody had slipped a video into my presentation.

Two Marines, dressed up like jihad fighters in a classic Al Qaeda ransom video, held Jasmine up in the air and were dancing around chanting, "Allah akbar, Allah akbar, Mohammed Jihad! Durka, Durka, Mohammad Jihad!" Her legs dangled as they swayed her around, proving she was totally relaxed and enjoying the experience of being held captive. The video ended with a ransom message, demanding me to pay two cans of Copenhagen Long Cut chewing tobacco to the 4th Commander and to deliver it to the Sons of Allah if I wanted Jasmine back.

My secret was out. I didn't know whether to plead ignorance or beg for forgiveness. It turned out I didn't need to do either. When the video started, the Commanding Officers were curling over themselves chuckling behind their hands, but by the time it ended, the whole room had erupted in guffaws of laughter. I let out a sigh of relief. I think the prank actually worked in Jasmine's favor because every time she crossed paths with the Commanders after that meeting, they smiled and looked the other way.

I couldn't stop thinking about taking Jasmine home. I asked around to see whether anyone knew how I could get her out of Iraq. Master Gunnery Sergeant is one of those crusty old Marines who can figure a way through just about any predicament, and he's tough as hell. I was reluctant to admit to him how attached I had become to a kitten, but in my desperation I decided to ask him anyway.

He was the first one who gave me any hope. "Don't be ashamed about loving an animal," he said. "You may be surprised to hear it from the mouth of this old salt, but back in the days of the Beirut war, I befriended a dog. He followed me everywhere I went; the best buddy I've ever had. I tried to send him home, but before I could, somebody shot him. If I knew who the bastard was, I'd probably have killed him."

Master Guns said that Baghdad was our best bet for getting Jasmine out of the country, but our camp convoys didn't go anywhere near there. He suggested taking her up north to where we were soon scheduled to move. From there we might find someone willing to smuggle her to Baghdad on a supply convoy. There was only one problem with his plan. We were going to our new location by helicopter. I'd have to find a way to hide Jasmine in the bird.

It took some doing, but I managed to locate a cat carrier. While I was carrying it back to my room, one of my Commanding Officers (CO) belted out from behind, "Liu, you are *not* bringing that cat when you move out!"

I couldn't disobey a direct order. Now I had a problem that required more help. I was tutoring a First Sergeant in statistics at the time, so during one of our sessions, I explained my dilemma to him. He works for the Commanding Officer who caught me with the carrier. I asked him if he would talk to his CO and explain that I had grown real attached to Jasmine and that I had a plan to bring her home, but in order to carry it out I had to get her up north first. It was her only chance to survive.

First Sergeant had a word with the CO and reported back to me that my request was being considered. The only hitch was that I had to be present for the verdict. We have several Commanding Officers, and most of them are pretty reasonable. This one wasn't too bad, so I hoped for a good outcome. I had never begged for anything until the day I stood in front of that CO, but beg I did.

"Which night are you and your men leaving?" he asked. When I gave him the date, he said, "Just make sure I don't see anything."

I wasn't out of the woods yet. There was an Executive Officer (XO) on the base who worried me because he hates cats with a passion. There was no way he would ever allow Jasmine to fly with us, especially not in a troop helicopter. I had to be extra careful not to let him get wind of my plan.

So, picture this: It's a cold night in March, and thirty Marines in full body armor, wearing backpacks and carrying weapons, run head down like charging bulls toward the landing zone. It's lights-out. Copters are coming in with their engines roaring so loud, the noise is deafening. Sand is blasting from a whiplashing wind that nearly knocks you over. I'm shouting at my men, "Get on! Load up! Quick!" While doing this, I'm carrying all my gear, with my weapon in one hand and Jasmine's carrier in the other. She, in the meantime, is going berserk, fighting to get out of her carrier. Suddenly she rips a hole in the mesh, and I'm scared she's going to escape. Before she can get away, I grab her and hang on, while she's fighting me for all she's worth. All the time I'm praying we don't get caught by the Commanders. God knows how I managed to get Jasmine safely stowed away on that helicopter.

A good Commander always sees his men off. Ours were no exception, including the one I was hoping to avoid. My CO and the cat-hating XO always made a point to stand together and watch the Marines deploy, making sure the men got off safely. In all the time I was stationed there, they never missed a single departure. All I can say is, that night, my Commander really stuck his neck out for me because he and the XO were conspicuously absent when our helicopters loaded up and took off.

By the time we reached our location to the north, the war was heating up. Recently there have been increased ambush attacks and IEDs on the Baghdad road, and Mother Nature has been throwing in some blinding sandstorms to make matters worse. Getting Jasmine to Baghdad is getting less likely, and our time for redeployment is getting closer. I'm worried sick about Jasmine. At our new location, there are packs of wild dogs and jackals. They will hunt Jasmine down if she is left behind. I've been so desperate to find a solution, every day I go to the chow hall and ask all the contractors if they have a way of getting her out, but so far no luck.

To complicate matters more, Jasmine went into heat. She has been yowling, and every time the door opens, she tries to escape. Sure enough, we lost her for two days. My men and I looked for her everywhere.

I printed up one of her photographs and took it over to Vector Control. They are privately contracted to keep the base free of all animals. I walked into their office with Jasmine's photo, and this slack-jawed guy was sitting at the desk, half the buttons on his shirt missing. I showed him her picture and asked, "Have you seen my cat?" He said if one of his guys had seen her, they'd have shot her. Spitting on the floor, he laughed and said, "She's probably meat by now."

I was carrying my weapon and had grenades and my knife hanging from my belt. A feeling of rage filled me and it took a lot of self-control to walk out of there and leave that unsympathetic, dim-witted jerk behind.

A few hours later a familiar voice crackled on my two-way radio. "We found her! We've got her cornered."

I ran to their location. When I got there, four Marines guarded each corner of the small building, looking as if they'd caught the enemy.

"She's under here!"

I got down on my knees and had a look.

"Sorry, guys. It's not Jasmine. We have to keep searching."

Next to our base is a fenced construction area belonging to a private contractor. My Marines found a weak spot in the chain link, and a hole appeared as we stood there. We crawled through and began a reconnaissance of the construction property.

Angry yowls started coming from behind a huge pile of cement blocks. I went to investigate, and there she was, filthy with matted fur sticking out all over. In the midst of cavorting with a big Iraqi tom, Jasmine was obviously enjoying herself. Much to her annoyance, I broke up the party and brought her back to base.

Jasmine has survived this long only because my senior officers and my men have stood by me. They joke around, calling me out for being a cat lover, but if it weren't for them, she wouldn't be here now. Marines aren't cold-blooded. There is a compassionate, caring side to these guys. We're like brothers, and when one of us needs a hand, we give it—no matter what. My men would do anything they could to help me get Jasmine out of here, but no one has a way. It has been driving me crazy.

> When I contacted Matt Kincaid of Pet Relocations and received his message from you at SPCA International, I almost couldn't believe it. What an amazing relief—an absolute miracle—to learn that Operation Baghdad Pups is prepared to help me get Jasmine home. You are truly an answer to this Marine's prayers.
> —Capt Thomas Liu, USMC

At some point, I hoped, SPCA International would be able to persuade the military to amend General Order 1A, making it possible for troops to have a mascot under certain conditions, but for now I had to direct my energy into getting Hope and Jasmine home. The desperation in Thomas's e-mail was echoed in more than twenty requests from other Americans in Iraq, all in similar situations. Having added the first two cats to my active rescue list, I found myself thinking about the old saying that things happen in threes. Sure enough, one of the next urgent requests was for a very pregnant cat named "Miki." If we waited much longer, Miki's kittens would be born. Airline regulations forbid transport of animals younger than twelve weeks. By then this soldier's unit would have redeployed.

I had already promised to bring home a dog named "Kujo" with the double-feline rescue, and I was limited to three animals per flight. Each mission required approximately thirty hours of actual time spent in the air if I traveled from the east coast. From my home in California, however, I'd be adding another twelve hours. At this rate I could bring home only three animals a week.

The summer travel embargo, when airlines refuse to transport animals during extreme heat, would begin in about six weeks. But I had forty anxious owners desperate to get their buddies out of the country before they redeployed.

I envisioned scenes from war movies in which medics and nurses mark the foreheads of incoming wounded soldiers—*This one can be treated; this one hasn't got a chance*—virtually sealing their fate. I had to come up with another plan of action.

My oldest daughter, Jennifer McKim, was aware of Operation

Baghdad Pups from its inception. She had been working with SPCA International's administrative team. I talked to my boss and discussed the possibility of asking my daughter to run a mission under my supervision. JD agreed that as long as Jennifer was willing to go, he would release her from her work commitments. As soon as we hung up, I called Jennifer from D.C.

"Hi! I've got a question for you. Remember the day I told you guys I was going to Iraq?"

"I'll never forget it. When you're really quiet, Mom, I know you are hanging onto something big. That day you hadn't said a word all morning, so I was thinking the worst. While several possibilities crossed my mind, it never occurred to me that my mother would announce she was flying into a war zone. I just wasn't prepared to lose you to a suicide bomber or hear on the news that you'd been killed by an IED."

"Well, thank goodness it didn't turn out like anything you imagined. I've been quite safe on every trip."

"So what's brewing now? You said you had a question."

"How would you feel about going to Iraq?" A long silence filled the air. "Jennifer? Are you still there?"

"I'm thinking."

"With two of us going, we'll double the number of animals we bring home in a week, and the place where we'll be staying is not that dangerous. It isn't like the reports you've seen on TV. Just think, the very first stamp in your passport would be from Kuwait, and other than people in the military, how many Americans can say they've been to Iraq?"

"Okay. I'll go."

"Way to go, Jennifer," I said with all the pride a mother could possibly feel in her heart.

• • •

I checked dates with John Wagner from Gryphon Airlines, hoping we could arrange the two missions for the week of April 23. Recent air restrictions due to increased war activity were having an impact on Gryphon, causing some flights to be rescheduled. After John confirmed my requested dates, I contacted SLG security and the animals' owners. As usual, there were last-minute scrambles to find airline travel crates and to get the animals from point A to point B, ensuring they all arrived at BIAP on time. Because Miki was so close to giving birth, I arranged for Jennifer to carry her in a soft-sided carrier inside the passenger cabin of the Kuwait to Dulles flight. The three dogs she was accompanying would stay in the pressurized cargo hold of the plane.

I flew into Kuwait two days before Jennifer to finalize the two mission plans, but before I left, I went over the whole routine with my daughter. I assured her that I'd be waiting at Kuwait International Airport when she arrived, would accompany her on the round-trip flight into Baghdad to pick up the animals from the SLG security men, and would make certain that she and her charges successfully boarded the final flight from Kuwait to Washington. I would then go through the same routine on the following day for the animals I was accompanying, and I'd meet Jennifer at Bev and Barb's house the day after she returned.

When I finally landed at Dulles International Airport with Hope, Jasmine, and the dog named "Kujo," Pam Bousquet was eagerly waiting in the arrivals lounge to meet the cat her husband had befriended. Pam was dressed in one of Bruce's T-shirts that he had worn for several days and then mailed to Pam, presuming that Hope would recognize her as part of Bruce's family.

Pam gasped. "She's even more beautiful than her photo," she said, her eyes glistening with tears. Hope's kohl-rimmed eyes captivated anyone who gazed at her, and she instantly won Pam's heart. The moment Hope picked up Bruce's scent she rubbed against Pam's chest and expressed herself in a surprisingly loud Siamese-like voice.

"Bruce warned me how vocal she is," Pam laughed with delight. "Apparently she runs around his room at night, about a hundred miles an hour, growling all the way. He calls her his 'Indy 500 race car.'"

I could already see that this was a match made in heaven.

After gathering Thomas Liu's cat, Jasmine, and Kujo the dog, I drove to Bev and Barb's house, remembering the day I had received Adela's e-mail. Adela was engaged to Matt, the soldier who had befriended Kujo. The e-mail began:

> Matt is a U.S. Marine currently serving in Iraq. This is his first tour, and already he has made several amazing friends. His best friend is a little pup he found and named "Kujo."
>
> Matt and his team were out on a mission and came across two puppies, one of which had been shot and the other, no older than five weeks, was probably next in line. Despite the rules, Matt took the dog with him, fearing he'd be killed if left to fend for himself. And he brought him back to his hooch, where he fed and bathed the puppy, and he has potty-trained him as well. Kujo is now a couple of months old.
>
> Matt will be leaving his base in about thirty days and then a week or two after will come back to the States. He is worried that if the puppy is left behind, Kujo will slowly starve since he doesn't know how to fend for himself.
>
> Matt does not know I am writing to you because the chances of Kujo being brought home are probably slim to none, and I don't want to get his hopes up only to let him down again. But if there is ANYTHING you or anyone else can do, Matt's family and friends would appreciate your help and will do whatever it takes to bring this puppy home.
>
> —Adela Vodenicarevic

It had taken me all of two minutes to read the e-mail, and I immediately responded by calling Adela's phone number. Bev and Barb had been sitting at the table with me and were caught in the anticipation of listening to the good-news phone call.

"Hello," a sweet voice answered.

"Is this Adela?" I asked.

"Yes," she replied hesitantly. I wondered if she thought I was trying to sell her something. Bev and Barb watched me with big grins on their faces, eager to hear the young woman's reaction to news that would surely be an answer to many prayers.

"This is Terri Crisp from . . ." I didn't even complete my sentence before Adela interrupted with an oh-my-God outburst.

"I can't believe it. You called!" she cried into the phone. "Please tell me you are calling to say there is a way to get Kujo home for Matt."

Never had the word "yes" felt so good coming out of my mouth.

Now that I had returned from Iraq with Kujo, as soon as we got back to Bev and Barb's house I would call Adela and make plans for uniting her with the dog her sweetheart loved so much.

Jennifer greeted me with a big hug when I entered Bev and Barb's house.

"How did your flight go?" I asked, eager for my daughter's first impressions of her incredible journey.

"I wouldn't have admitted it before," Jennifer laughed, "but when I first agreed to go to Iraq, I secretly began to wonder about saying my goodbyes to family and friends. I know that sounds over-dramatic now, but images of CNN news reports kept flashing across my mind. Once my plane began the approach to Kuwait City and I saw that it looked a lot like Phoenix, I realized everything was going to be fine, just like you said. The whole trip was great. I'd do it again gladly."

"What about Miki? Did you manage okay with her? Did she have the kittens yet?"

"No, thank goodness. When I saw her tummy swollen to the size of a melon, knowing we had a thirteen-hour flight ahead of us, I thought for sure she would give birth at thirty-five thousand feet. I was seated beside a woman wearing an abaya, and she made it quite clear she was not happy about sitting next to someone with a cat tucked under her seat. Each time I pulled the carrier onto my lap to see how Miki was doing, a look of disgust crossed her face, and she

Jasmine just after her arrival in the United States *Terri Crisp*

Miki enjoying the good life in the United States *Terri Crisp*

insisted that I mustn't unzip the carrier. It was a reaction you warned me to expect from people over there, but I was totally unprepared for the intensity of the woman's prejudice. I kept praying Miki wouldn't start having those kittens. Oh, Mom, it was the longest thirteen hours of my life."

Bev and Barb's house had become the unofficial staging area for the animals' arrival in the States. At their cozy home with the fenced-in backyard, animals had a chance to recover and adjust. As soon as the animals arrived, Bev or Barb took each one to Tyson Corners Animal Hospital for a thorough examination and afterward took the dogs upstairs to Waggin Tails grooming salon for a much-needed bath. Barb said the dogs always had the same look on their faces when they came out wearing fancy bandannas: *If only those mutts in Iraq could see me now.*

The saying that "you win some; you lose some," never held so true, as the number of requests for assistance from Operation Baghdad Pups continued to increase. I had a scorecard in my head that recorded the winners as well as those that lost. By the time Jennifer and I finished our missions, a total of eleven dogs and three cats had, in less than three months, beaten almost insurmountable odds to make it safely out of a combat zone and into the arms of loving families in America. Little did I know then, how many more animals would walk through the door of victory before the summer travel embargo slammed it shut.

Chapter 10

HEROES IN THE MAKING

Tiger in the mountains of Afghanistan *Jessica Walker*

Iraq wasn't the only Middle Eastern country the United States was occupying when our rescue missions began. Back in October of 2001, the United States had launched Operation Enduring Freedom in Afghanistan after the terrorist attacks on September 11. I wasn't surprised, therefore, when we received, in March 2008, our first plea from a soldier stationed in Afghanistan.

I am desperately seeking help to get my dog, Tiger, home from Afghanistan. He was about four weeks old when friendly Afghan soldiers found him on a military firing range outside our camp. They brought the puppy around to show everyone, and when they handed me the fluffy white bundle, I took one look into his piercing blue eyes, and it broke my heart. How could we leave this poor thing out there to die? I gave him a bath and fed him his first chow. From that day forward, he became the camp dog, and now he's a big part of our lives, impacting more than twenty-five soldiers.

Tiger is such a clown and doesn't even realize it. When he sits with us, and someone tells a story, he looks at them and listens as if he understands what they're saying. When we start laughing, he barks along with us, as if he got the joke. It cracks us up every time.

Tiger's temperament is as soft as his body. When I see him, it knocks the chaos of war down several notches. He's my little piece of sanity in the middle of an insane country. Tiger sleeps in my room, and he eats breakfast, lunch, and dinner with the soldiers. He makes us laugh and raises our spirits in this desolate, harsh place.

I exercise Tiger every day. Even though he's just a pup, his long legs are already navigating the rocky mountain terrain above camp, where I let him off the leash.

Tiger is the best thing that has happened to me since I got to Afghanistan. When we redeploy in the middle of April, if I don't find a way to bring him home, Tiger will think I've abandoned him. He won't understand. I can't do that to the best friend I've ever had.

—SSG Jessie Walker

With no Afghanistan contacts and so little time to arrange another miracle, I called a friend who, facing enormous obstacles, had managed to get her brother's dog, Cinnamon, out of Afghanistan. Her recently published book, *Saving Cinnamon,* chronicled the dog's adventure and was making more people aware of the plight of animals in this particular war zone.

"You'll never guess why I'm calling," I said. "I need your help to get a dog out of Afghanistan."

"You're kidding."

My friend's words had already painted an image of Afghanistan that made it sound as dangerous and uncivilized as a place could possibly be. It was definitely not a country I envisioned entering, except perhaps, to rescue some animals.

"What's his name?"

"Tiger. He's an adorable puppy; I'll send you a picture. The locals say he's an Afghan Koochee Mountain dog. By the time he's full grown, a small child could ride him."

"He sounds beautiful. Where does this big boy live?"

"I don't know. The camp's location is classified. But the owner says she can get Tiger to the airport in Kabul if we coordinate logistics to fly him from there. That's the part that makes me nervous. I can imagine a hundred different reasons why this is risky."

"You're right. The risks are off the chart," she said. "I've recently learned of an organization in Kabul that might be able to help." Her next words were slow and deliberate. "The only thing is, they must, and I repeat *must,* remain completely under wraps."

I was getting really good at keeping secrets.

"I can't emphasize enough how important this is," my friend reiterated. "If certain people in Afghanistan find out this organization exists, a lot of animals would be killed, and I'm not just talking about dogs and cats that belong to the troops. A few brave individuals who have dared to help save other animals would also find their lives in jeopardy. The bad guys in that country do not play nice."

All of a sudden Iraq looked pretty darn tame.

The absence of a functional infrastructure in Afghanistan would make the logistics of transporting animals a nightmare. Without roads in many parts of the country, a security company would be unable to reach most pickup destinations. This was a whole new ball game, one where the playing field was downright ugly.

"So, can I contact this organization?"

"Let me get hold of the director, and she'll get back to you," my friend said and told me to be patient because the woman traveled a great deal and was often in parts of the world with no Internet and computers.

I heard from the mysterious woman almost a week later by e-mail. It turned out the director was an American who spent part of her time in Washington, D.C. How much more perfect could that be?

When she asked if I wanted to meet for breakfast in D.C., I was thrilled, even though it dispelled my fantasy of engaging in espionage and hiding notes in dark alleys late at night. We met at a cozy ma-and-pa diner in Arlington, Virginia, on April 1. The woman looked like she might scare at the sound of "Boo," but I suspected that hidden under her fragile exterior was the determination of a bronze star Marine. As she told her stories about animal rescues under some of the most difficult and dangerous conditions in the world, I was astonished that she had accomplished any at all. Knowing what she had to do, she just did it, defying anyone or anything that got in her way. It was indeed an honor to spend time with someone of her resolve.

Before we left the restaurant the director gave me an e-mail address and phone number for a man in Kabul. "Tell the dog's owner to contact this man, and he'll get Tiger to a safe house. Don't worry; he will be in good hands."

I could hardly wait to e-mail Jessie and give her the good news. She replied almost immediately.

Hi Terri,
I can't begin to tell you how thrilled I am to hear this. Now Tiger will get to live the good life with me at the beach and leave this barren country behind. I gave him a shower today, and he's so dang pretty! He's all ready to go traveling.
—SSG Jessie Walker

An hour later I received a phone call that made the day even better. Dena DeSantis, a guidance counselor at Fair Lawn High School in New Jersey, was moderator for the Animal Rights Club, a group consisting of twelve girls. Her students were looking for a project that would benefit animals. When Dena saw the news story about Operation Baghdad Pups rescuing K-Pot and Liberty, she asked the girls if they'd be interested in raising enough funds to bring a soldier's dog home from Iraq. The entire club agreed it was a cool idea.

Tiger seemed to be the ideal dog for the girls' project. When Tiger entered the States, he would land at John F. Kennedy Airport in New York, close enough to the girls' school for them to greet Tiger on his first stop in America. That sealed the deal.

"How much money do we need to round up?" Dena asked.

"On average, it costs SPCA International about four thousand dollars to get one animal out of the Middle East."

"Wow," she said after a pause. "That's a lot of money, but the kids' hearts are set on helping a soldier save his or her pet, and I'm determined to help them succeed. If they aren't able to raise the whole four thousand, I'll pitch in whatever is needed to cover the shortfall."

This was one rare guidance counselor.

"Dena," I told her, "before we agree to go ahead with this, there's one thing you and your students need to understand. I can't give you any guarantees when it comes to getting an animal out of a war zone. Any number of things could go wrong, in spite of our best-laid plans. If that happens, it will be a terrible blow for those kids."

"My students know that when you care about animals, it's not always easy," Dena said. "We'll be praying Tiger makes it out safely, but if something goes wrong, we'll just have to deal with it as one of life's learning experiences. They'll be willing to take the risk, I'm sure."

Later I e-mailed Jessic to ask if she was willing to be the students' pen pal.

"Are you kidding?" she responded. "I can't believe they'd do this for a complete stranger. I'll gladly correspond with them, and I'll send photos of Tiger, too. This is incredible news. I just can't get over it. You have no idea what this means to me."

The students were thrilled to hear from Jessie and see pictures of Tiger. They fell instantly in love with the pup that was growing like a weed in the mountains of Afghanistan. Every day they checked to see if Jessie had e-mailed any more updates on Tiger's antics.

Dena sent me regular reports on her students' progress for their Bring Tiger Home project. One of her e-mails chronicled the girls' accomplishments and contained an amazing announcement.

When I told the faculty and staff that my students were going to raise $4,000, everyone said they'll never do it. But those girls got together and brainstormed, leaving no stone unturned. Since then they have been doing bake sales, car washes, can drives, and even a massive community-wide garage sale. At least two girls have attended every PTA or school event where there's an audience and talked about their project, asking for donations and help.

Our local newspaper ran a story about the club's mission to save a soldier's dog. They included Tiger's picture and even gave a plug for donations. Community response has been unbelievable. One person donated a coveted pair of Broadway show tickets to raffle; another sent a check for $1,000. A neighboring high school's tennis team made a donation, and dozens of heartfelt letters of praise for the girls and our soldiers have accompanied checks. Each week at our meeting we pass the letters around, along with the tissue box, as we read. I am so proud of these" kids. Today the girls reported they have raised $8,000 and *are still counting.*

—Dena

The plans to get Tiger home moved forward quicker than I expected. Jessie had made contact with the person in Kabul, and they agreed to hand over Tiger on April 21, just before she left Afghanistan. "A driver is coming from Jalalabad to pick up Tiger," Jessie wrote, "and will take him to a safe house in Kabul. They'll keep him there until arrangements are made for his flight to the States from Islamabad."

My first thought was "*Where the heck are Jalalabad and Islamabad?*" I wished now that I'd paid more attention in my school geography class. Grateful for Internet maps, I quickly located Jalalabad in eastern Afghanistan, and learned that Islamabad is the capital of Pakistan. Apparently Tiger would remain in the capital for five days, enough time to arrange his transport and health documents. Then he would fly on Pakistan Airways to England and from there to New York. This would be one hell of a long journey for Tiger, but it was his only option. What concerned me the most was that Tiger would be flying the whole distance alone.

When the day for Tiger's pickup arrived, I got an e-mail from Jessie.

> Two of our guys took Tiger this morning and brought him to the driver in Jalalabad. When they took my dog away, it felt like I was losing a part of me. During my Army career, I have learned to overcome my feelings, so I don't often show my emotions, but when that truck drove away from the base, I cried. I have been fighting the tears and losing ever since.
>
> —Jessie

Within days Jessie redeployed and made it safely home to the American base where she was stationed. Tiger in the meantime waited in Kabul, probably confused as to what was going on.

As the Afghan pup's arrival date approached, Dena's students grew more excited. Diligent efforts to bring Tiger home had ultimately resulted in their raising a total of $11,000, far exceeding anyone's expectations. Not only would Tiger get a ticket home, but the rescue of two other animals from Iraq would also be covered, thanks to a group of kids who believed they could make a difference and proved it big time. Dena sent me another email that showed once again how eager people were to help the girls in their effort to save Jessie's dog.

> Terri, my kids have been plain unstoppable. Everyone said they couldn't possibly do it, even our school principal, Jim. But he also promised that no matter what the kids decided to do, he would support them. So, I went in yesterday and said, "Jim, I need a bus to take my kids to the airport, and I'm not going to take no for an answer." Finding an extra bus around this town is like looking for

a lost contact in the snow, but Jim bent over backwards to get one for us. This means all the girls will be able to meet Tiger at the airport and welcome him to the States.

—Dena

It was indeed an honor to finally meet the twelve students and their dedicated advisor. On May 6, 2008, when my colleagues and I drove into the Pakistan Airlines cargo area at JFK and saw the school bus, I was even more excited than I had expected. With me was Jean, the mother of a soldier whose dog, Dusty, had been rescued from Iraq two weeks earlier. Jean had met my flight and driven me to the train station to pick up JD on our way to meet Tiger. My boss was so impressed with the girls' commitment and fundraising results that he wanted to be there to thank them personally.

Dripping wet from the torrential rain, the three of us climbed onto the bus. Loud music accentuated a celebratory party atmosphere. Dena lost no time in greeting me with a big hug.

"I'm so glad to be here and even more excited to finally meet all of you," I said after the music had been turned down. "You guys are absolutely amazing!" Wide smiles appeared down the rows of seats. "What you have done for Tiger and Jessie proves that every little effort made on your part makes a huge impact on someone else's life. Not a single moment of your time was wasted. You should be very proud of yourselves."

The kids began to talk all at once. Their excitement and energy were beautiful. JD took his turn to praise the girls and to tell them how everyone at SPCA International had agreed that they were a force to be reckoned with. "That's another way of saying you guys rock," JD said, followed by the girls' cheers and high-fives.

"Any word on Tiger's flight yet?" I asked. Dena had been following the flight's progress since they had reached the airport an hour earlier.

"His plane should be touching down in about forty minutes. The freight agent said it will take another forty-five minutes to get Tiger unloaded and moved to this building."

We helped to pass the time by sharing stories. The students were animated as they talked about their fundraising experiences and the other activities of the animal rights club. It did my heart good to know that kids like these would be the future guardians of animals. The girls also wanted to hear more about the soldiers' dogs and cats in the Operation Baghdad Pups program. While my stories unfolded, tears trickled down faces, and occasional bursts of laughter drowned out the sound of pummeling rain on the school bus rooftop. As we took refuge together from the storm, I knew this was one afternoon none of us would ever forget.

"Tiger's plane has landed!" Dena had just returned from the agent's counter and now stood at the front of the bus. "Okay, it's time to go and greet our Afghan friend. Bring the posters!" The kids had rolled them up inside garbage bags. Their homemade signs read: WELCOME TO AMERICA, TIGER!

We huddled under umbrellas and made the dash across the parking lot to the Pakistan Airways cargo office. When we entered the building, the poor man at the cargo counter must have thought he had been invaded. The students couldn't wait to tell him about their mission, and he was visibly moved. As the big moment got closer, the noise level escalated. The anticipation was intoxicating.

The sound of an approaching forklift gave us the first clue that Tiger was in the building. When a passing cargo employee gave us a thumbs-up, we knew our wait was just about over. The kids lined up, holding their posters proudly in front of them. Dena took pictures of them—not an easy feat since no one would stand still. The building contained as much energy as a high school pep rally for a league title football game.

One of the students suddenly screamed, "There he is!"

I spun around to see a forklift driving toward us, carrying a large airline crate on a wooden pallet. No doubt about it, Tiger was home.

The students were sensitive enough to realize that surrounding Tiger might overwhelm him, so they generously refrained from showing him how glad they were to meet him. One could only imagine what he had been through over the last couple of weeks and what was going through his head right then. He had to be scared, tired, and desperate for a potty break.

After the forklift operator lowered Tiger's crate to the ground, I cut the zip-ties that had secured the crate en route. Before opening the door, I kneeled down and greeted the world traveler in a quiet voice. "What do you think of all this?" I asked while Tiger stared back at me. Once he began to wag his tail, I knew he was ready. Speaking softly, I opened the crate door and carefully clipped a leash onto Tiger's collar.

Jessie wasn't exaggerating about Tiger's size. Although he was still just a puppy, the long-legged Afghan dog filled the height of his crate. He was glad to leave the confines of his travel container and trotted happily beside me as I took him out for a potty break. Tiger didn't seem to mind the rain; he was more interested in finding just the right place to lift his leg. As soon as Tiger found the spot, he peed and peed and peed. The look of contentment on his face made me laugh.

For the next hour we stayed in the cargo warehouse, out of the interminable downpour, and we slowly became acquainted with the giant puppy.

"Oh, look," one of the girls said. "He held up his paw when I asked for a shake."

Tiger looked around at the girls, wagging his tail and panting as if waiting for another command. He liked being the center of attention.

"See if he knows how to sit and lie down," another girl coaxed.

"Sit, Tiger. Now lie down. Good boy! You're such a smart puppy, aren't you?" The dog's whole body wiggled in response.

No matter what Tiger did or didn't do, the girls praised him. After the long hours spent in his crate, this must have seemed like heaven. He enjoyed their affection most of all and responded to their requests for a cuddle by leaning against the girls' legs and looking up with innocent puppy eyes directly into theirs.

Fair Lawn High School animal welfare club welcoming Tiger home *Terri Crisp*

Tiger and one of his many new toys *Jessica Walker*

"Aw, he's so sweet. He's such a softie. I wish he was mine."

After Tiger seemed comfortable with his new star status, I stood back and placed a call to Jessie.

"He's here," I said as soon as she answered. "And he's just fine."

Jessie began to yell, and everyone could hear her voice as I held the phone away from my ear. By then there wasn't a dry eye among the group. The moment we had all been working toward was even better than we had imagined. It was a grand day indeed.

"Thank you, thank you, thank you," Jessie said when she was finally able to talk. "And please tell the students how much I appreciate everything they did. They are *awesome*. I will never be able to repay all the people who made it possible for me to keep my dog." She paused to catch her breath. "How do I ever thank you?"

"By coming home alive and well. People here are just glad to do whatever they can to support our heroes."

When this American soldier, who had risked her life every day in the middle of Afghanistan, said to me, "You are all my heroes," it took my breath away.

My eyes scanned the group of girls and landed on Dena, who was animated and laughing. It was her suggestion, after seeing the Operation Baghdad Pups story on the news that resulted in this wonderful scene. Dena's support of the kids' club project had shown them they could achieve miracles. What a gift to give to a youngster. What a gift to give Tiger and Jessie.

As I stood there marveling at all the outstanding people around me, I had no inkling of the important role that Dena was going to play a few weeks later, when Operation Baghdad Pups took on the most challenging rescue it had yet to pull off.

Chapter 11

REACHING OUT

Tom in Iraq, soaking up the sun *Kevin Connors*

It was the beginning of May 2008, and all over Iraq things were heating up—literally. Although the airlplanes were climate-controlled, during the animal-loading process and long waiting periods between flights, air conditioning was not a certainty. Death by heat stroke was a real possibility—a risk that neither the airlines nor I was prepared to take. The travel embargo for animals would go into effect on June 1 and end on September 30.

My number one priority was to transport the animals on Operation Baghdad Pups' active list halfway around the world before the June 1 embargo began. Using our current method of operation, we'd be lucky to rescue half of them before the end of May. If my daughter Jennifer and I, plus one more person, accompanied groups of three animals each, we'd have to make ten trips. Gryphon planes flew only three days a week, and with mounting attacks in Iraq, there was no guarantee they'd even be able to fly.

I boiled it down to two solutions: SPCA International either had to raise enough donations to pay for a charter flight or find someone to lend us a plane that could fly from the Middle East to anywhere on the U.S. east coast. We had less than a month to make this happen. I began to feel like I do when I fill my pressure cooker with vegetables and water and screw the lid onto the pot. Placing the steel weight on the lid, I turn the stove up to "High" and wait for things to start rocking. It's kind of exciting.

I started living Operation Baghdad Pups nearly twenty-four hours a day. Sleep and my seat at the dining room table became strangers to me. On one day alone, I received 586 e-mails, and there was only me to answer them all. Most of my days and nights were spent in front of the computer or on my Blackberry, often answering frantic e-mails from thirty understandably nervous owners. Because of the eleven-hour time difference, correspondence from Iraq reached me late at night or in the early morning. When pressing issues came up or an overly worried owner needed attention, I stayed awake until we worked things out, tapping into all my resources.

Although I was the only person at SPCA International managing the Operation Baghdad Pups program on the ground, a growing team of other people worked hard to muster the support and funds we desperately needed to make the next missions possible.

Stephanie Scroggs, SPCA International's Director of Communications, began a media onslaught, trying to alert the public to our soldiers' need. She flooded the desks of newspaper editors and radio and television news producers with press releases. The name "Operation Baghdad Pups" buzzed around the country like a military march gathering soldiers to war. We soon began to reap results from her effort.

My first encouraging contact came in an e-mail from David Dean in Florida.

**From: David Dean, Pensacola Naval Hospital Health
and Wellness Clinic
To: Terri Crisp, SPCA International
May 3, 2008**

Dear Terri,

As a counselor to veterans returning from war, many of whom suffer from post-traumatic stress disorder (PTSD), I was particularly
glad to read about the Operation Baghdad Pups program. It's
great to see animal lovers who are willing to override the system
in order to ensure our soldiers' animals get the care they and their
GI pals deserve. Good for you!

Pets are unquestionably beneficial therapeutic aids for soldiers with PTSD and for those who struggle to transition into the
life of a civilian. While applauding your efforts, I also hope we can
help you drum up support for your program.

My colleagues and I would like to extend an invitation for you
to attend our May 8–9 symposium entitled "The Hidden Casualties of War: Promoting Healing and Resiliency for U.S. Service
Members and Their Families." This is a joint effort of the Univer-
sity of West Florida's Center for Applied Psychology and Pensacola Naval Hospital's Health and Wellness Clinic. The event will
be attended by professionals from military, medical, and political
echelons. Perhaps you will meet someone at the event who can
solve your transport and funding problems.

I hope you will come, and I look forward to hearing from you
soon.

—David Dean

In all my years of doing rescue work, soldiers, more than any
other group I'd previously encountered, had a deeply embedded fear
of losing their animals, especially of seeing them intentionally killed
by someone who was enforcing military rules. The soldiers' desperation was often intense. I knew that if my efforts to save a dog or cat

failed, the resulting tragedy could have a much greater impact on a soldier's mental well-being.

With each plea for help, my life became more deeply entwined in the lives of those who counted on me to keep their wartime buddy alive. I was often afraid of saying or doing the wrong thing when communicating with a person whose animal had died or disappeared. Handling the situation badly could leave an even deeper scar. Determined to maintain the good reputation that SPCA International had earned so far by handling the requests of animal owners with caring humanity, I gratefully accepted David's invitation and looked forward to improving my skills for responding to people who had suffered psychological trauma.

Unfortunately, the symposium did not introduce me to anyone with access to a plane or the funds to charter one, but it did give me a great deal of insight into what men and women returning from Iraq and Afghanistan were dealing with emotionally as well as the strains placed on families during their loved ones' deployment. I didn't walk away from the symposium a certified therapist, but I certainly had a better idea of how to ease some of the pain and worry. Listening turned out to be the best thing I could do.

The skill of listening was needed over and over again, particularly when one of the animals on the growing active rescue list never made it home. The following e-mail arrived on my last day at the symposium. It was sent from a soldier I had been working with, planning to transport her dog home before the summer embargo began.

Dear Terri,

This morning Misfit was just fine. But this afternoon he started salivating at the mouth, and he's been trying to puke. It's so sad, Terri. Even though he's obviously in distress, he is still just as sweet as ever. He wags his tail when I walk up to him, but he can't stand up. He won't eat his tuna or beef jerky.

I discovered a dish of food outside that was mostly eaten. I suspect by the smell that it was laced with antifreeze. Someone obviously gave it to Misfit on purpose. People are trying to save him right now, but we are not veterinarians. Do you have any suggestions?

— CPL Crystal Barrows

As soon as I read this, I contacted a veterinarian friend. She warned that the odds of Misfit pulling through were pretty dire but gave some suggestions for treatment. Before I could send them along, Crystal's next e-mail arrived.

Our beloved Misfit died. He was still just a puppy. We took everyone's suggestions on what to do, and we Googled like hell, trying to find a way to help him, but all of our efforts failed. According to what we read, alcohol helps when an animal has swallowed antifreeze, but alcohol is not allowed in Iraq, so we were missing a crucial remedy.

What is really difficult now is that there are four other dogs living here on the base. Jenga is one of them, and he's Misfit's brother. The four dogs were all buddies. Anyway, they've been sniffing around our area all day looking for Misfit. It is so sad to watch them. Thankfully, the other dogs are fine. Misfit was a specific target, so we are keeping a close eye on the rest of the dogs. We've got Neighborhood Watch going big time. We think we know who did it. They were other U.S. soldiers. I just can't believe it; how could they do this to a puppy?

I may want to bring Jenga home. He acts a lot like Misfit, and he's the only one still alive from that litter. But right now, I am too exhausted emotionally to think about it. I'm afraid to get close, knowing someone could do the same thing to Jenga. Our Battalion Commander said a lot of people have heard about Misfit, and whether they're dog lovers or not, they all think this was just plain dirty. We're all so upset. One soldier even asked if we were going to hold a memorial service for Misfit. Thanks for all your help trying to get Misfit home. I'm so sad we didn't save him. It makes this war stink even more.

— CPL Crystal Barrows

My heart could not have sunk lower. After all this soldier had gone through, the last thing she needed was to lose her dog in such a horrible way. I wouldn't be surprised if, when she returned to the States, she needed counseling to deal with the emotional trauma of her war experiences. Grateful for the insight I had gained from the symposium lectures, I wrote back to Crystal.

Crystal, I cannot begin to tell you how truly sorry I am. I know there is nothing I can say to ease the pain. However, it is my hope that maybe the story of what happened to Misfit may be used in such a way that this won't happen to other animals. We will not forget Misfit and all the joy he brought to the people who knew him. I hope you will be able to find comfort knowing that Misfit's days were filled with your love. This is more than many dogs in Iraq ever experience. Please know that my heart and thoughts are with you.

—Terri

More determined than ever to get these animals home, I went back to work. Correspondence still took up a major part of each day as I worked out the logistics of each mission.

On May 12 I received an e-mail from a soldier I'd not heard from before. Usually I had to ask the soldiers to write me a letter explaining why we should consider their animal for the program, but this particular soldier gave me all the details from the start.

To Whom It May Concern:
I am writing this with the intent of seeing an important member of my team make it to the United States. Back in November 2007,

a stray cat began hanging out around our compound. Someone had tied a piece of cord around his neck. Over time the cord got tighter and was slowly strangling the cat. We wanted to get it off of him, but he'd never let us get close enough to help.

A member of our team had an idea. We lured the cat into a vehicle with some tuna, and with a lot of hacking and gasping, he began to eat. SFC Jackson then grabbed him and the fight was on! As the cat connected with a few well-aimed claws, I took a pair of scissors and managed to sever the cord from his neck. When we let him go, the cat scampered off, madder than hell and hissing just to make sure we knew he was pissed. We didn't expect to see him again.

The next day there he was outside the door, looking at us with a "How about some more tuna?" expression on his face. The old Chinese adage came to mind: Once you save someone's life, they become your responsibility for the rest of their life. Over time Tom proved the adage true; he became a permanent resident outside our building.

We are an eleven-man team. Since our arrival in Iraq, four of our team members have died. I was in the vehicle during the IED strike that killed two of our teammates. I was physically wounded, but those injuries healed up fine. Mentally, however, I was distraught, to say the least.

For several weeks I couldn't get much sleep and was consumed with worry over when I would ever start feeling better inside. I'd go outside at night so I wouldn't wake my roommate with all my tossing and turning. After Tom adopted us, every time I went out, he would appear, hop up onto my lap, and look at me with an expression that said, "Hey, buddy, wish I could help, but what I really need is some tuna."

This one cat has given me more reasons to smile. Just having him hang out with me helped to pull me out of a dark funk that pervaded my existence ever since the IED attack. I owe an awful lot to my four-legged buddy.

> We are getting close to redeployment, and Tom must come
> back to the States with us. He has certainly done his part for
> me. The other individuals whose lives he touched all have stories
> that mirror my own. Whoever has the power or authority to make
> this happen, please help us. We don't want to lose another team
> member. There is no other option but to succeed!
>
> —CPT Kevin Connors

The space freed up by the death of a puppy named Misfit opened the possibility of rescue for a cat named Tom. I couldn't help but think of the old saying that when one door closes, another one opens. I wrote back to Kevin and began the process of getting Tom onto our list.

Shortly after replying to Kevin's e-mail with the news that we would try to help, I received a call from Stephanie Scroggs, our director of communications. Her relentless efforts to reach out to the media had just paid off.

"Terri, I had a call from the producers of Laura Ingraham's national radio talk show. Laura wants to interview you on her program." Stephanie's voice bubbled with excitement.

As the good news filtered through my brain, a light seemed to fill the darkness of the deep well that the morning had become.

"This is big, Stephanie; it's huge! Surely someone with the means to help us will be listening to Laura's program. Good work!"

"I think it would help to convey urgency if one of the soldiers whose dog is already home joins you on the show," Stephanie said.

"I agree." My mind was already going down the list of possibilities.

"Who would you suggest?" Stephanie asked.

"Andrew Bankey. We rescued his dog, Socks. Andrew is home for good now, unless he gets called up for reserves. The last time I phoned to see how Socks is doing, Andrew said he's been missing his unit. I bet he'd be more than happy to put in a good word for other soldiers in need of help."

After Stephanie hung up, I called Andrew. The embargo date was not far away, so there was no time to waste. It was a relief when he answered on the first try. When I explained what we needed him to do, Andrew agreed.

"Are you sure you're okay with this?" I asked. "A lot of people will hear this interview. I wouldn't want it to get back to the military and result in your getting into trouble."

"Hey, if I can help to get these thirty animals home, that's what matters right now," he said. "I doubt the military will get on my case, but if they do, I'll deal with it."

Immediately after listening to the broadcast, Stephanie sent a memo to the staff, board of directors, and volunteers who were closely following the ever-changing saga of Operation Baghdad Pups.

Tom and Francine in Iraq *Kevin Connors*

From: Stephanie Scroggs, Director of Communications
To: SPCA International Staff, Board Members, and Volunteers
May 14, 2008

Terri and SGT Andrew Bankey just ROCKED a nationwide interview on the Laura Ingraham radio show. The program is syndicated to over 230 stations nationwide. Terri mentioned our website at least three times, and Andrew was a pro. They nailed it. Now let's see what happens.

—Stephanie

I had to believe that because we were doing the right thing for these animals and soldiers, our work was destined to succeed. People were putting a lot of faith in me, and along with the responsibility of each new animal added to our list, I took on the weight of another human being and his or her family.

At the end of the day I received an e-mail response from an exultant Kevin Connors. He and his men were so excited, he said. They couldn't believe we had added Tom to our active list. Our news was the best thing that had happened to them since they'd arrived in Iraq. "There's just one thing I forgot to mention," Kevin wrote. "I also have a dog named Francine."

Once again the list grew.

Chapter 12

PATRIOT PETS

Dusty—One of the dogs anxiously waiting for a ride to the USA *Joan Mathers*

May 14, 2008, began at 5:15 a.m. with a logjam of e-mails, a lengthy to-do list, and follow-up calls. Twelve hours later I stepped away from my computer to play with Army Specialist Michael Payne's dog, Coke. He was the tenth dog that we had successfully rescued from Iraq and was one of the many that Bev and Barb fostered while waiting for the soldier to come home. When I tossed Coke's ball for the umpteenth time, my phone rang.

Stephanie had called me less than an hour earlier, so I was surprised to hear her voice again. She had been expressing concern that the looming embargo deadline of June 1 was approaching crisis level for all those involved. On this call, however, her voice jumped several points on the optimism scale.

"Terri," she bubbled, "I just got an e-mail from a man named 'Dave Lusk.' He's one of the senior managers of global operations at FedEx. Listen to this . . ."

Stephanie proceeded to read his message:

"Over the next two weeks, we will be repositioning some of our aircrafts, routing them from Dubai through Frankfurt and finally ending up at McGuire Air Force Base in New Jersey. The next departure is this coming Sunday. Since we are operating these flights from Dubai, would you be able to get the animals there? If you can, we'll fly them home at no charge."

As Stephanie continued to read, my eyes closed. There it was—that voice inside—reassuring me the universe was ready to line up for something spectacular to occur. I touched the top of Coke's head and let go of the worry. It was time to get down to business.

After we hung up, I ran back into the house. Bursting with adrenaline, I returned to my computer and e-mailed Dave, while an exhausted Coke followed me indoors, curled up, and fell asleep. Asking Dave how he knew about our predicament, his reply came back, "Deborah Amos, a FedEx employee, heard you on the radio. She sent an e-mail to Lisa Daniel in the FedEx department that handles charitable requests. Everyone agreed; we want to do our part to support the men and women willing to go off to war. We've even given this project a name: 'Operation Patriot Pets.' I will be your primary contact at FedEx and will do everything I can to get things rolling."

The one thing Dave asked in return was that we keep FedEx out of the spotlight. "The company does not ship dogs and cats," he wrote. "In this case, and this case only, we're making an exception. If word got out, we wouldn't be able to handle the anticipated bombardment of requests to ship other domestic animals. That's just never going to happen, so for now, we'd like to keep this operation quiet."

Once Dave laid out the rules, I had an even greater respect for the decision makers at FedEx. I wrote back to him, "What FedEx is doing is the kind of act that renews people's faith in the human race.

Twenty-eight dogs and two cats will live because of your decision. For the anxious soldiers and contractors, this news could not be any better. I can't wait to tell them. I suspect you'll hear their hurrahs all the way from Iraq."

Morning could not come fast enough. I got up before dawn to write a group e-mail and pressed the "Send" button with a huge smile on my face. I wished I could be a fly on the wall as each of the anxious owners read the news.

From: Terri Crisp, SPCA International
To: Operation Baghdad Pups Owners
May 16, 2008

On Wednesday morning, Laura Ingraham invited me and SGT Andrew Bankey to be guests on her radio show. She gave me plenty of air time to explain the urgency of your animals' situation. After that, Andrew went to bat for all of you, explaining how important it is to get these dogs and cats back to the States . His dog, Socks, was one of the first we transported, so he was well qualified to speak. Laura's show was broadcast nationwide.

Now . . . here's the GOOD NEWS. Are you ready?

Thanks to the show, a company that is willing *and able* to transport your animals offered to help. WE ARE FORMING A PLAN! There is still much to organize, and I'll need to stay in regular contact with you. Please stand by and keep checking your e-mails daily.

—Terri

As I typed, one soldier on our active list came to mind. In a combat zone where his life was under constant threat, you would think that this guy's biggest worry would be about going home severely wounded or in a body bag. But it wasn't. He said the hardest thing of all was worrying over how to get his dog out of there. Boy, did these animals matter.

The number of people working worldwide to pull off this mission was growing rapidly, and I was blown away by the level of commitment from each team member. Even so, I knew from experience that in the next few days seemingly insurmountable obstacles would raise their ugly heads to test that commitment. When faced with all the logistical and bureaucratic nightmares, it would be easy to forget who we were doing this for and how important it was to succeed against all odds.

I decided to send some photographs I'd received from the soldiers, along with excerpts from their e-mails. The poignancy of soldiers' words, combined with their buddies' appealing faces, worked like a double injection of motivation.

From: Terri Crisp, SPCA International
To: Dave Lusk (FedEx); John Wagner (Gryphon); Doug Crowe (SLG);
May 18, 2008

In case any members of your teams wonder why we are crazy enough to even attempt this mission, let them read the following passages, all excerpts from e-mails sent to me by owners of the dogs and cats we'll be transporting:

> We are in Fallujah and have an orange tabby that has been part of our unit for the past two years. He's lived in our offices since he was a kitten. Burt has been passed down from each Marine expeditionary force that comes in. We are shutting this base down fairly soon, and I cannot leave him here by himself knowing he is used to living with us. He is a complete doll baby. He loves people, and he lies upside down in our arms, getting tummy scratches. Until recently, he had his sister with him. That was until KBR, the company hired by the military to euthanize stray cats, showed up. Our boy is safe for now because he lives with us where the "cat-napper" can't get

him. My home in the States will provide Burt a safe place, and he'll be spoiled beyond belief. I just need to get him there. Please help us. He is one of the sweetest cats I have ever met; he deserves a good home and not to be left behind.

On behalf of Burt (short for "Burtuqaalli," "orange" in Arabic), thank you.

—CPL Erin A. Kirk

This is about Beatrice Kiddo. We have cared for her for so long; I cry when I write this. She is the most loving, sweetest dog I have ever known, and she is a part of our Army family here. She loves being loved, as she has probably never been treated this well. She has five puppies now, and all have been claimed by soldiers ranking from Specialist all the way to Captain. I can't imagine leaving them here when we go. They would not know how to fend for themselves. Beatrice is spoiled, and she would starve to death on her own. Please help us get her and the pups out of Iraq. They will be almost twelve weeks old in June and able to fly.

—SSG Roberta Green

My husband, SGT Gary Dobbs, is currently serving his third tour in Iraq. While driving back from an exhausting mission, the driver of the Humvee, who is not allowed to stop under any circumstances for our own soldiers' safety, hit a pup that darted out in front of them. Fortunately, they were not far from the FOB (forward operating base), and this puppy had such a fight for life. He actually followed the convoy back to the FOB.

My husband immediately went to the puppy's aid. He got their medic to come and see him. After an extensive examination, it was apparent he had some minor and some possibly serious injuries. My husband went to work fetching all the supplies needed to disinfect the wounds and to brace his back leg for support. He fed him and gave him a warm bath.

When Gary called and told me the story of what happened, he asked me to send supplies for Dodger and begged me to see if I could find some way to help get this precious little guy out of Iraq. Dodger has since healed of all his injuries except for a minor limp on his back leg.

This dog is just what Gary needed to pull his morale back up. Dodger has become my husband's best friend and a focus point that helps Gary deal with being away from his family and in the middle of a war. My husband's buddy deserves a loving home where he can be taken care of without the fear of abandonment.

—Susan Dobbs

I am an international police advisor working at the Ministry of Interior. We have a small pup, approximately four months old. The Iraqis where we work had abused him, kicking and throwing rocks at him, until we intervened. The pup has adopted us now. I would like to get him home to Texas where he will never experience cruelty again.

—Michael Hughes

I am an Air Force mental health technician assigned to a FOB combat stress control unit with the Army. Our team of mental health professionals consists of five Air Force and one Army member. We recently adopted a four-week-old puppy that was found at the motor pool and would have been put to sleep if no one took him. Patton has quickly become a loved member of the team. I see the joy he brings to the soldiers we come in contact with on a daily basis. Many of the soldiers who wouldn't come for counseling before now willingly come to visit the puppy. Without their realizing it, we establish therapeutic relationships while the soldiers hold the puppy and talk. He's the best mental health technician on the team!

With tours lasting up to eighteen months, it's grueling on the soldiers and their families. Our records show that 50 percent of them have relationship difficulties as a result of separation. Without skilled listeners, soldiers suffer alone with depression as well as war-related trauma.

Our team members work twelve-hour days listening to and feeling the same emotions the combat soldiers feel, so it's incredibly draining, and we need an outlet for release. Until Patton came, we didn't have that outlet. Patton never stops giving unconditional love. At the end of his workday of comforting soldiers, the little guy comes and sits on our laps, with no idea he's putting in overtime. His tail is like a paintbrush that sweeps sorrows away while he makes us forget the harsh reality of war for a little while. I have two daughters at home, and when I miss holding them in my arms, I hug Patton.

Patton has played an extraordinary role, and now that our deployment is about to end, we want to get our co-therapist to the United States. Any assistance in this matter would be greatly appreciated because we cannot leave him behind!

—Major Jennifer Mann

My company made a great friend on this deployment. Our dog Stubbs deserves so much more than what this country can offer. When an Iraqi walks by, Stubbs stands his ground and barks. He is willing to protect us, no matter what. He sits at the gate all day and night keeping the guards company. When we soldiers go running, Stubbs is right there with us, motivating us to run farther or just darn right making us look bad by doing circles around us, showing what a PT stud he is. A few times when we came off missions, we found Stubbs beaten up by other dogs, with blood from teeth marks on his head. I would sit down beside him, thinking he wouldn't make it through the night, and he'd just fall asleep with his head next to my leg. That's the great thing about Stubbs, he'll sit next to

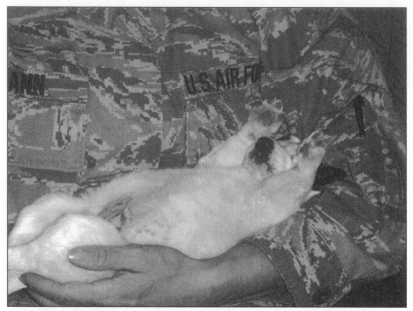

Patton hard at work during "talk therapy" *Jenni Mann*

Puppy with an Iraqi version of a dog toy *SPCA International*

you as you pet him, and soon he'll be asleep, so peaceful after an exhausting day. Stubbs is the greatest sight in life when there's little good to see here.

—SSG Darlene Jones

I understand that being on your list means our girl has a one-way ticket to the States. You have no clue how happy we are to hear this great news. We just came off of patrol and to tell my people that Diwo is going to the States, I wish you could see their faces. If there is anything else you need between now and then, don't hesitate to let me know. Again, thanks for everything you have done for us. You have made our day.

—SSG Carole Cooper

After reading the soldiers' testaments, Dave Lusk sent a reply that summed up what everyone on the FedEx, Gryphon, and SLG teams felt.

"Bringing these animals home is not a question of *if* this will happen, Terri. It is a matter of *when*."

Chapter 13

TEAM EFFORT

Ralphie after another long day in the war zone *Amber Daigle*

The next few days churned into a whirlwind of communication, activity, hard decisions, and international teamwork. The newly assembled FedEx team was headed by Dave Lusk, whose office was in Memphis, Tennessee. Dave worked nonstop trying to find a feasible air route from Dubai to New Jersey as well as an available aircraft with a pressurized and climate-controlled cargo hold. In order for FedEx to move the animals at no cost to SPCA International, the plane we'd be on would be carrying a full load of cargo as well. Delivery stopovers in more than one country would have to be made on the route to New Jersey.

Another issue for Dave was meeting the regulations for unloading cargo in each of the countries where we'd stop. Having animals on board altered all the rules. Even though they weren't going to leave the plane, government paperwork and certifications for each animal needed to be presented for inspection upon landing.

The FedEx ground crew in Dubai also needed extra time to design and build three platforms that would support the animals' crates while preventing them from toppling over during air turbulence. The crates would be strapped onto the platforms in such a way that equipment could quickly maneuver them when cargo was being loaded or unloaded. The platforms also had to be configured so that every animal's crate faced outward and was easily accessible for giving food and water and for cleaning.

The other major challenge was determining how to get the animals from Baghdad to Dubai since FedEx did not fly this route. Once again John Wagner jumped in to offer Gryphon's services for transporting the animals on this leg of their journey. Gryphon Airlines had never landed at Dubai, however. The pressing task for John was to get permission from Dubai Civil Aviation Authority. First-time approval normally took thirty days. We had less than two weeks. Gryphon also had to coordinate flight crews and available aircraft while ensuring that the company's regular service wasn't interrupted.

Doug Crowe, one of the SLG Operations Managers in Baghdad, focused on logistics. He needed to know the location of every animal and to work with the owners to agree on a pickup time and location. Only four dogs could be delivered to BIAP by their owners. That left twenty-six animals for the SLG team to collect while logging hundreds of miles in armored vehicles. Before his men could even leave the gates of the SLG compound, Doug had to submit movement requests to the U.S. Military Central Command (CENT COM), giving full route disclosure seventy-two hours in advance. Pinpointing the animals' location became one of Doug's greatest challenges. Soldiers weren't always available to correspond, yet they were the only people who could relay the animals' specific whereabouts.

Whereas FedEx was able to cover the cost of moving the animals, Gryphon was a much smaller airline and could not afford to fly the animals at no charge to SPCA International. It would cost approximately $35,000 to charter the Gryphon plane. Inevitably many other expenses of such a huge undertaking would also have to be covered. The team challenge for SPCA International, therefore, was to bring in donations. Public awareness was paramount, and individual response to each offer of fundraising projects or volunteer help was essential but also incredibly time-consuming. SPCA International staff and volunteers were giving it their all.

Another equally important matter was what we would do with the animals after they landed in New Jersey. We couldn't just unload a bunch of crates on the tarmac and hope someone would take over from there. An arrival team was needed. While trying to resolve this problem, I thought of Dena DeSantis, the high school guidance counselor whose animal rights club girls had raised $11,000 for Operation Baghdad Pups missions. Dena lived close to Newark Liberty International, and she had proven herself to be another "can-do" person. Her challenge was to locate a holding facility on or near the airport.

While Dena worked on the shelter, I got busy gathering a team of volunteers who had worked with me in disasters and had the kind of specialized experience needed to care for the Iraqi animals until every one of them was picked up by its owner or transferred onto another homeward-bound flight.

My next task involved shopping. Only two of the owners had crates in Iraq that were suitable for their animal's journey, so I quickly placed an order for twenty-eight airline crates from Drs. Foster and Smith Pet Supplies and asked for shipping to Bev and Barb's house. The crates would have to fly as checked baggage. I couldn't begin to imagine how hefty that charge would be.

Difficult decisions also had to be made that would involve exposing another person to potentially devastating circumstances. This wasn't something I could take on without consulting my boss. On May 18, I called JD with my latest update.

"I can't do this alone, JD. Someone has to go with me. The other person needs to have the right kind of experience and a good head on their shoulders. You see, this time we won't be going in and out of BIAP on the same flight. We'll have to stay in Baghdad for three days."

"Where? At the airport?"

"No, we'll be at the SLG compound in central Baghdad."

JD went quiet while he digested this news. "Isn't that in the Red Zone?"

The Red Zone was any part of the city that was outside of American fortified boundaries and was considered a high-risk, no-go area. People who lived in the Red Zone spent most of their time indoors; many were afraid to go to work, attend school, or do their shopping. Countless numbers of stores and businesses had been closed; schools had been taken over by coalition forces or destroyed. Being kidnapped, injured, or worse were risks that had to be seriously considered. Just recently, ninety-nine people had been killed in a central Baghdad market when two women with bombs strapped to their bodies committed suicide.

"Yes, it's in the Red Zone," I said. "I will admit, JD, the realization that we'd have to stay outside the confines of the U.S. Air Force base at BIAP took some getting used to, but we can't avoid it. With the number of animals SLG will be transporting to its compound, I have no choice but to go and take care of them, and that's going to be a job one person couldn't possibly handle on her own." I waited several seconds for his response.

"Who are you thinking should go?" JD asked. "Although the more realistic question is probably, who is *willing* to go?"

"Bev Westerman. She's had years of animal rescue experience. I've worked with her during disasters, and I know I can depend on her."

"She agreed while knowing the risks?"

"Yes, with SLG security looking out for us, we'll be well protected. After all, that's what they do when they aren't rounding up animals for SPCA International."

JD let out a loud sigh. "To be honest, Terri, I'm nervous enough about *you* going into a Red Zone, let alone asking a volunteer to take that risk as well. I'd never be able to live with myself if anything happened to either of you. Is there no other way?"

"Not if we want to bring these animals home before the embargo, and that means certain death for most of them. I know it sounds potentially dangerous, JD, but believe me, if I wasn't sure that the guys at SLG could keep Bev and me totally safe, I wouldn't risk it. It's a hard decision to make, I know, but I need you to back me up."

I waited what seemed like an eternity until JD finally made his decision. "Okay," he said, "in the few months we've worked together, I've learned to trust your judgment. Go ahead and make your plans, but make sure you come back safe and sound." I appreciated my boss's confidence more than he would ever imagine. Before we finished our conversation, I briefed JD on the other details. We had three target dates for departure from Iraq. So far they were May 28, 29, or 30. Dave was still working on this part of the plan with FedEx employees in the Middle East. We had less than two weeks to succeed or fail. Thank God, none of us were quitters.

Another critical task came up on May 22, 2008, in an e-mail from Dave Lusk that he'd flagged as "urgent." His message arrived on the morning I was planning to fly home to California for my daughter Amy's graduation.

> Terri,
>
> How soon can you get ten-year federal background checks done on you and Bev? They need to be accompanied by a digital photograph and two government IDs, then returned with the attached FedEx form fully completed. We need these ASAP for Transportation Security Administration (TSA) as well as internal FedEx security or you can't fly aboard our plane.
>
> —Dave

I called Bev at work. "Guess what we have to do now?"

"Hard telling," she laughed, considering how many times I had called her with addendums to plans we thought were already set. Thank goodness for Bev's easygoing manner.

The first thing I did was postpone my flight to Sacramento. Bev and I immediately initiated background checks online through USSearch.com. By the next day we were relieved to discover that neither of us had dark secrets lurking in the closet, and I was able to fax the required documents to Dave.

· · ·

On May 24 I flew to California and made it to Amy's graduation ceremony just in the nick of time. Our youngest daughter, Megan, sat between Ken and me as we waited for the graduating students to walk in. "It's a good thing you made it home, Mom. If you hadn't, Amy would have been really disappointed. She was so worried you weren't going to see her receive her diploma."

Her words struck my heart, thinking about the number of times I had missed out on important dates for my girls, but I couldn't help comparing the relatively small sacrifices my family made with those of the soldiers' families. Their loved ones went away for months or years at a time, missing all those special family days. All too often when soldiers finally came home from the war zone, they seemed like strangers or were damaged in some way.

That evening, before I boarded the last flight out of Sacramento, I thanked my family for their support and told my girls how proud I was of them.

· · ·

The next morning Dave e-mailed to say he was fairly certain that FedEx's requested stopover in Paris, France, would be possible, provided the animals remained in the crates, on netting-wrapped pallets, and would stop at Charles de Gaulle Airport for less than twenty-four hours. All veterinary paperwork would have to be up-to-date and accompany the animals. Dave then recommended that I ask John to arrange the Gryphon flight from Baghdad (BIAP) to Dubai for June 2. I should have been excited to settle on a date, but I was still somewhat gun shy at that point. There had been too many ups and downs to tally in the previous days.

I walked to the window overlooking Bev and Barb's back yard. Eight rescued Operation Baghdad Pups dogs had left a circular trail in the grass where they had become acquainted with the new sights, smells, and sounds during their first days in America. Seeing that path made me believe there would soon be twenty-eight more dogs doing the same thing. It was time to get this show on the road.

Immediately I e-mailed the owners to announce we would be departing from BIAP on June 2, leaving at midnight and arriving in Dubai at 3:00 a.m. Flying during the coolest time of the day would avoid the problems associated with hot temperatures. Bev and I would travel with the animals all the way and bring squirt bottles for cooling them down if necessary. They would also have plenty of food and water for the trip. I ended the e-mail with our planned itinerary for the rest of the flight with stops in France and England and our final destination of Newark Liberty International Airport in New Jersey at 11:00 p.m. on Tuesday, June 3.

"Do you know what we're going to do with all the animals when we arrive in Newark?" Bev asked.

"Dena has made progress. This morning she sent me this." I read Dena's e-mail out loud:

> We have been given the use of a heated/air-conditioned ware-house by the Port Authority of New York and New Jersey. The facility is located on the airport property. There will be volunteers standing by to pick up the animals once they land and transport them to this location. In the morning, a veterinarian will come to examine each of the animals and issue domestic health certificates for those that are flying the rest of the way home. When the vets are finished, there will be several mobile groomers arriving. They offered to get the animals all spruced up for the final leg of their journey home.

"That's wonderful news! I can't wait to meet all the animals," Bev said. "I'm getting really excited thinking about them now and wondering how it's all going to pan out. How many did we have at last count?"

"A second ago I thought we had confirmed twenty-six dogs and four cats," I said after glancing at my next e-mail. "But wait a minute . . . it looks like the number has changed *again.*"

Although Dena's accomplishment had been a huge relief, the universe seemed determined to keep testing us in a wide variety of ways. The e-mail I had just finished reading arrived from a soldier whose cat named "Dexter" was one of the animals on our list.

Hi Terri,

I think we have a problem. It appears that my cat Dexter also belongs to someone else trying to get him to the States. I have attached his photo above. I believe the other soldier calls him "Burt." What are we going to do?

—John Norris

In a combat zone where teams work on rotation and soldiers are continually on the move, mix ups like this could happen. I require, as part of the Operation Baghdad Pups application process, that a current photo of each animal be sent to me. Until that afternoon John had not sent one. Rules are rules, but I was learning with this program that I had to know when to bend them. Holding up a rescue for lack of a temporarily unobtainable photo made no sense. It wasn't until that afternoon that I received a picture of Dexter and could compare the two pictures.

"Bev, can you grab my active file and pull out the print of Burt's photo? It seems there may be one less cat to transport."

Sure enough, as Bev and I studied the photograph that Erin had sent a few weeks before, we agreed that John's orange tabby shared the same markings as Burt. We looked at each other and started to laugh. Out of all the things that could go wrong, this was perhaps the best kind of mishap we could possibly have. Before I did anything else, I had to write back to John and deal with the awkward dilemma.

> Hi, John,
>
> Yes, Erin Kirk is trying to get a cat she calls "Burt" to the States as well. I just looked at the pictures of her cat and yours. It appears that Burt and Dexter are one and the same cat. If that's the case, which one of you will give Burt/Dexter a home? Both of you have become attached to this cat and want him out of Iraq, so you two will need to work out what you are going to do and get back to me as soon as possible. For the time being we will keep Burt/Dexter on the list for the upcoming mission. I can't wait to meet this two-timing feline who has stolen so many hearts!
>
> —Terri

By now most of the owners had received the updated e-mail I'd sent that morning, which was starting to generate more questions from them.

Kevin Connors, owner of Tom, asked if any of the cats would be placed in shared crates and explained that Tom was a well-known scrapper, ready to fight for his territory.

Amber Daigle expressed her worries about Ralphie, who had never been confined in a crate and panicked whenever they tried to put him into one of the vehicles. "He just loses it," she wrote, "so I haven't had the heart to confine him. I hope this won't prevent him from being sent home."

"Please be careful with Patton," Jennifer wrote. "He's so little he can fit through just about anything, and he's used to being with lots of different people, so he'll follow anyone he takes a liking to."

"Let me know if you need me to send food along with Mama Leesa and her pup," wrote her owner. "She's had such a rough time up to now. Her condition is poor, and I'm concerned that she gets plenty of food on her long journey."

Oreo peeks out at his new world *Bev Westerman*

Beatrice and puppy *Bev Westerman*

What many of the owners really needed was reassurance. I continued to sound positive, stopping short of using the words "I promise." Several asked about making travel arrangements after the animals arrived in the United States. My response was, "Let's get them out of Iraq first."

Little did I know how difficult "getting them out of Iraq" would be.

Chapter 14

COUNTDOWN TO BAGHDAD

Terri Crisp and Bev Westerman embarking on their adventure to Iraq
Bev Westerman

On May 26 I had a make-or-break conference call with JD and Dave Lusk. This was it. We would decide whether to go with our plan as it was or conclude that it just wasn't feasible to get thirty animals out of Iraq in time.

After taking plenty of time to air our concerns and listen to our hearts, we made a decision. Despite the fact that several key issues regarding French regulations had not been resolved, we agreed that it was time to get Bev and me onto a plane. If we remained in the States until every detail for Operation Patriot Pets was ironed out, we would never leave.

After our meeting, I made airline reservations for two. The e-tickets landed in my inbox with the weight of reality. Any details I overlooked now could cost an animal its life.

I was relieved to see that John and Erin had come to an agreement regarding the two-timing cat. John had just befriended another cat named "Molly," so we decided to work toward getting her home in the autumn, whereas Burt would be a part of the upcoming mission.

Although it always felt good to add an animal to the active list, I dreaded having to take one off. That night Susan Dobbs called with news about the puppy named "Dodger." Her husband, Gary, had nursed him back to health after the puppy had collided with the soldiers' Humvee and had followed them back to camp despite his injuries.

"Dodger won't be coming home." Susan's voice broke before she could say anything more.

"Oh, Susan, I'm so sorry. Can you tell me what happened?" I waited several seconds as she tried to compose herself enough to talk. The image of an IED explosion flashed across my mind. I hastily wiped it away. Finally Susan took a deep breath and began to speak.

"He loved that dog. Dodger was like his own child." She took another deep breath and held onto it. I knew you can't rush people; you just have to listen and let it come out in its own time.

"Gary went out on patrol. While he was gone, one of the Iraqi soldiers at the base said Dodger attacked him. Oh, Terri, he was just a puppy . . ."

Given what I knew about Iraqis' all-too-frequent mistreatment of dogs, I could imagine the scene. Many of the soldiers I'd dealt with reported that their dogs loved Americans but feared Iraqis. When American soldiers worked with Iraqi civilians or soldiers during the day, the chance that one or more of those workers could be an enemy infiltrator was always a possibility. People had been wounded or killed by undercover insurgents who came on base with suicide bombs hidden under their clothing, and the dogs sensed the threat. Dogs had also learned to distrust a population that, by tradition, had kicked, stoned, tortured, and shot them. Unless Iraqis earned a dog's trust by showing that they weren't a threat and demonstrating kindness, dogs saw local people as potential enemies, even when they lived and worked at the base.

"Dodger wouldn't attack unless he was provoked, Terri! The soldier never even gave Gary a chance to intervene. Before he got back from patrol, the Iraqi shot Dodger. Every day my husband risks his life, and now this . . . it's ripping him apart."

We had come within days of bringing the puppy home only to have his life extinguished. I couldn't find a way to reconcile the tragic situation. So many things about war and rules and other countries' customs seemed brutally unfair. Although I could do nothing to make Susan's and Gary's pain go away, I could grieve with them and remind them that Dodger's last days had been filled with knowing he was loved.

I began to fear that another tragedy might happen before we got these animals out of Iraq. Each time I opened an e-mail, I held my breath, hoping it wasn't sad news. Losing Dodger meant a replacement dog or cat could be added to the mission. Was there enough time to make this happen? I'd have to try.

On the morning of May 27 I shuffled out of bed knowing this was the last full day I had to prepare for the mission. My first caller of the day was John Wagner from Gryphon.

"What are you doing up so early?" I asked. It was barely 5:00 a.m. in Colorado, where John's office was based.

"Good morning to you, too," he laughed. "I've been on the phone with our guys in Kuwait. They're still working on getting our landing permits for Dubai, but they say the FedEx people over there have been terrific, pulling out all the stops to help speed things along. We should know something today."

"If the answer is no, I'll be spending the summer in Baghdad, babysitting animals."

"We'll make sure you get home long before then," he laughed.

My next e-mail was from Doug at SLG security in Baghdad. The day before, CPT Kevin Connor's dog, Francine, and his cat, Tom, had been collected and driven to the compound. Tom was the cat found with a cord tied around his neck, and John's team saved him from death by slow strangulation. Tom had been a great source of comfort after the unit lost several men to IEDs while training Iraqi Army soldiers.

According to Doug's e-mail, Tom wasn't eating, and he walked as if he was in pain. Searching for a local veterinarian with cat experience had proved fruitless so far. When I e-mailed Kevin to see if he knew what might be causing the problem, he replied that Tom had been fine up to the time SLG collected him. Kevin ended his e-mail with, "Please try to save him."

By mid afternoon the twenty-eight airline crates had not been delivered to Bev and Barb's house, and I was starting to get nervous. I took Bev up on her earlier offer to call her at work if I needed help. She immediately got on the phone and chased down the crates.

"It's a good thing I called," Bev said. "For some reason they never got loaded onto the truck this morning. They're still sitting in a warehouse in Virginia."

"Well, that's doing us a lot of good, isn't it?" I said, shaking my head in disbelief. When I had placed the order I had stressed how important it was for the crates to arrive on time, and the woman assured me they would get here in time. "At least the warehouse is in Virginia. Did you ask where they are exactly?"

"Yes. I've got the address. I called them to say we're coming, and the man at the warehouse said we could pick them up tonight around 9:00 p.m. It won't be busy then, and there will be someone available to help us load them. We'll have to take them out of the shipping cartons first and stack them, or they won't all fit in my car and Barb's truck."

"Okay," I said, laughing with relief. "One more thing I can add to our to-do list."

As I slapped together a quick peanut butter and jelly sandwich for lunch, the phone rang again.

What now? I thought.

"We got it," John blurted out, bypassing his usual greeting.

"Got what?"

"The landing permit."

"Are you serious?" I asked, almost choking on my first bite of PB&J.

"Yep, you're going to Dubai."

John's news made me feel as if all the red traffic lights had suddenly turned green.

When the long day should have been winding down, Bev, Barb, and I headed out the door and drove through the dark until we found the warehouse where our carton-packed crates were stacked nearly to the ceiling. We broke down the cartons and managed, after some reconfiguring, to get all the crates stuffed into both vehicles. Finally, by 10:30 p.m., we made it back to the house, tuckered out and ready to call it a day.

Being a seasoned traveler, I usually get to the airport with just enough time to check in, but the next afternoon I was taking no chances. We went to the airport four hours before departure in case any check-in problems arose. The airport porters were more than accommodating as they pushed three baggage trolleys bearing the weight of the crates through the bustling terminal. When we approached the ticket counter, I wished I had my camera handy to capture the looks on the airline agents' faces. Apparently they hadn't seen anything like this pull up to their counter before.

"Where are you flying to?" an agent asked in a guarded voice.

"Kuwait first; then on to Baghdad, Iraq, in a couple of days," I replied.

"And you're taking all these crates?"

I resisted the temptation to say, "No. I'm taking one and leaving the rest with you." Instead I said, "Yes. We'll be using them to transport dogs and cats to the States for U.S. soldiers."

The agent exchanged looks with her manager. This didn't look good. I was prepared to pay a hefty charge if I had to; I was not leaving these crates behind.

The manager turned to me and asked, "Did you say these are for the dogs of American servicemen and women?"

"Yes," I replied, hope rising. "They have no way of transporting their wartime buddies home when they redeploy. If SPCA International doesn't help them, the animals will be left to starve to death or worse."

"Don't charge the extra baggage fee," she said to her agent. "We're happy to do what we can to support our troops."

Another red light turned green.

After we reached the departure gate, I checked my e-mails one last time.

One of the pressing issues that Doug had been dealing with was locating a place for the animals to stay during the two-hour wait before loading them onto the Gryphon plane that would fly them out of Baghdad. Being surrounded by U.S. military traffic, it would be extremely difficult to remain off the radar.

Just before we boarded, Doug e-mailed me with instructions as to where we should gather at BIAP. The location was about as discreet as we could get. With one more problem solved, my faith in the universe's intention to keep things rolling was strengthened.

Bev and I landed in Kuwait just after 9:00 p.m. on May 29. Ahmed, from the Plaza Athenee Hotel, stood outside Customs waiting to greet us with his wide, welcoming smile. Knowing how much baggage we were bringing, he had driven the hotel's catering truck. With the help of three porters, we soon got twenty-eight crates loaded onto the truck, and we made it to the hotel without any holdups.

I enjoyed watching Bev's face mirror the same excitement and intrigue I had experienced when I arrived in Kuwait for the first time only three months before. Exhausted and grateful to have made it this far, when we reached the hotel, Bev and I looked forward to a good night's rest. It might be our last for quite a while.

A neighbor's crowing rooster woke us in the morning, fooling me into thinking for a moment that I was at home. From the air-conditioned room, I stepped onto the balcony where a wall of desert heat hit me. The temperature would reach 113 degrees by noon, but already we were melting. I could see now why the airlines had a heat embargo restricting animal cargo. It should have applied to people as well.

The day passed quietly. Bev rested, and I checked last-minute e-mails. We went out for a huge meal at TGI Friday's since we didn't know what the food would be like in the security compound in Baghdad. After our late lunch, Bev and I made last-minute phone calls home.

"Remember, don't do anything stupid or heroic," my oldest daughter, Jennifer, warned.

My husband, Ken, yelled from the background: "And if you hear any shelling, keep your head down!"

"Be safe, Mom," Amy shouted.

"Go get those animals, Mom," Megan, the youngest one, called out.

Their voices reached across the miles like a warm group hug. Knowing I had their love and support made my job so much easier, especially when the danger stakes were raised.

John Wagner had already forewarned the Gryphon counter staff that Bev and I would be on the flight to Baghdad and that we were not traveling light, so when we returned to the airport at 2:30 p.m., they were ready for us.

"The Dog Lady has returned! I hear you are embarking on a big adventure this time," the familiar agent said as Bev and I approached the counter.

"That we are. A thirty-animal big adventure," I responded with enthusiasm.

"I'm glad Gryphon was able to help you to save these animals," he said. "It is a good thing you are doing."

Hearing these words from a Muslim was so heartening, and the sincerity in his voice was unmistakable. I wanted to give him a hug, but all I could do was look him in the eyes and say, "Thank you. You have no idea how much I appreciate your kindness."

Instead of waiting for us to push the heavily loaded trolley across the busy concourse, the sticker man from the airport administration office came to the ticket counter. He greeted me with a smile, and the whole time he was slapping stickers onto the crates, he shook his head in disbelief. I glanced at Bev, who looked like she was trying not to giggle. Before the sticker man returned to his office, he repeated the warning from my first trip, "You be safe. Baghdad is bad place."

This time, as Bev and I boarded with one-way tickets, the sticker man's warning took on a whole different meaning.

Forty minutes into our flight, the cabin went pitch black.

"Is this when the fun begins?" Bev asked.

"Yep. Hold on tight for the ride of your life."

This was my seventh trip into Baghdad, and the excitement was still there, only this time, a smidgen of fear was present. Doug and John had both assured me that Bev and I would be well protected during our three-day layover in the city. I trusted these men, and I knew that the entire SLG team would do everything necessary to keep us safe. Even so, no one is exempt from danger in a war zone.

Neither Bev nor I spoke as the plane made its steep descent. I think we were both trying to absorb the enormity of what we were about to do. When the Gryphon plane finally came to a stop, I stood up and pulled my briefcase out of the overhead compartment.

"Are you ready for Baghdad, my friend?"

"You'd better believe it," Bev said, grinning.

While finalizing this part of the journey, I had asked John what Bev and I should do about visas because neither of us had the proper credentials to enter Iraq. The last thing we wanted was to have the Iraqis arrest us for entering their country illegally.

"Don't worry," John had assured me. "SLG is doing all the credential checking for the Gryphon flight, and they will treat your situation as an extended layover."

"Are you sure?"

"Trust me."

When we stepped out of the plane, it felt strange not to be picking up animals and heading back to Kuwait. This time my familiar muscled friends stood there empty-handed, ready to escort Bev and me to the SLG compound.

"Good to see you guys again," I said.

"Yeah, welcome back, Terri," said the team leader. "I understand this time you're staying. That has to be somewhat unnerving."

"Hey, who says it's fun to always play it safe?"

Introductions to Bev were made in the dark as we walked over to where the twenty-eight crates and our two suitcases were unloaded by the ground crew.

"Boy, you sure don't travel light," one of the SLG men commented. "Did you leave anything at home?"

While the SLG drivers went to get their vehicles, Bev and I sat and waited on a cement barricade, dwarfed by our heap of baggage. We had not been there five minutes when, out of a nearby hangar, a line of about two hundred soldiers who were exiting Iraq paraded past us.

I had seen similar processions on previous trips, only this time I was close enough to see the expressions on the young men's and women's faces and the effects of war in their eyes. At first, relief and excitement covered the battle-weary lines, but under the surface of desert grime, hints of emotions, as dangerous as any planted IED, lay waiting to explode.

Just then four heavily reinforced, black SUVs pulled up like a scene right out of an action movie. Armed and dressed in bullet-proof protection, the SLG men jumped out, nudging me slightly outside of my comfort zone. Once we began moving the crates, however, the ominous feeling about where we were going slipped away.

A thick, protective metal lining on the SUVs' interior walls had reduced carrying space to such a degree that, no matter how many ways we tried to cram the airline crates into the vehicles, we could not fit them all in.

"We'll have to stash some of these at one of the outbuildings until we can come back for them tomorrow," one of the men concluded. Harry, the SLG medic, stayed with Bev and me while the rest of the team went to deal with the crates.

When the men returned, we followed them to the armored cars, and as we reached the second vehicle, one of them instructed us to stand next to it. The driver then reached into the back and produced two bullet-proof vests and helmets.

"Put these on," he said. The body armor was big, black, and incredibly heavy. As Bev and I donned our protective gear, that comfort zone began to melt away. We glanced at each other for a moment with looks that clearly said, "What have we gotten ourselves into?"

Some of the men climbed into their vehicles, while Harry checked our vests and began his safety briefing. "You two will ride in the middle seat. Make sure you stay in the center and sit as close to each other as possible. If we should run into trouble, get down on the floor as quickly as you can and don't move until we tell you."

The floor? That doesn't sound like fun.

"Any questions?" Harry asked.

Bev and I shook our heads.

Twenty-eight airline crates headed for Baghdad *Bev Westerman*

The car's tinted windows were made of glass at least an inch thick, a bonus for safety, but it made sightseeing at night impossible. It seemed a shame to come all this way and not have at least a few stories to tell about our first sights of Baghdad.

During the drive to the SLG compound, we stopped at three heavily guarded checkpoints. At each one a U.S. soldier cautiously approached our vehicle and asked what our business was. The driver answered the questions, showing some kind of document he removed from the visor above his head. After the guard inspected the paper, he handed it back and waved us on.

After we cleared the third checkpoint, Harry turned around in his seat to inform us, "We have now left the Green Zone."

Despite the heat, a chill crept down my spine. There was no turning back now.

Chapter 15

IN THE RED ZONE

A sign that definitely gets your attention *Bev Westerman*

Bold red letters on the large white sign facing our vehicle read, "All Weapons Red at This Point. Lock and Load." This was no place to stop for a picnic.

Although Bev and I had been doing our best to see out the windows of our armored vehicle, after we entered the Red Zone we decided the floor looked pretty darn attractive. When your senses are on high alert, mortality becomes your only concern and time becomes distorted. The trip from BIAP to the SLG compound took less than twenty minutes, but it seemed as if an hour had passed before Harry announced we'd reached our destination.

Surrounded by fifteen-foot cement blast walls, miles of razor wire, and dozens of well-armed men, the block-long SLG compound was a dimly lit fortress. Four men stood with guns at the ready as we drove through the main gate. When we parked, I could just make out a garden courtyard to our left that led to the front door of a massive house. A single light bulb illuminated the entryway.

"We have a total of five villas," Harry explained as we followed him to the house. "They belonged to government ministers who worked for Saddam Hussein. When the war began, they either fled Iraq or were captured. The furnishings you'll see are what they left behind. If your taste leans toward ornate and oversized, you'll feel right at home."

Harry wasn't exaggerating. We entered a huge foyer with shining marble floors, walls, and a sweeping marble staircase outlined with gorgeous carved railings. The scale of everything symbolized the wealth of a chosen few who overindulged at the expense of less fortunate people during Saddam's regime. We followed Harry up to the third floor, where our room was located at the end the hall. We were relieved to discover that it came with air conditioning and had a modern bathroom right across the hall.

"Just a heads-up," Harry cautioned. "Don't drink the water out of the tap, and keep your mouths shut when you shower. When you brush your teeth or need a drink, we have plenty of bottled water downstairs, so help yourself."

Dropping our suitcases onto the beds, I asked Harry if we could see Tom, the sick cat. The last e-mail I had received from Doug said that Tom still wasn't well and had no appetite.

While Bev and Harry checked on Tom, I poked my head through the adjoining door to the operations center where Doug was communicating with one of the teams out on the road. He motioned for me to come in. As soon as Doug got off the phone, he jumped up from his desk and greeted me with a big hug.

"You made it!"

"Of course! Why would anyone pass up the opportunity to hang out in Baghdad for a few days? I've heard it's a great place to work on a tan."

"You ladies better keep your skin covered," Doug laughed. "We've got enough to worry about here without you two getting arrested for immodesty."

"Darn! And I just bought a skimpy new bikini, too." In a war zone, sharing a few laughs is just as important as getting down to business.

"If you need to check your e-mails," Doug offered, "feel free to set up your computer in here. In fact, you can have that desk in the corner." He stood up and cleared some things from the dust-covered surface. "Heads up, though; the Internet here is slower than a one-winged mosquito. Between that and the power going on and off all day, you'll be doing good to get one e-mail sent. That's what happens when you pick a war zone for your vacation."

Before I could make a comeback comment, Bev called me from the other room.

"How's he doing?" I asked. Doug followed me through the door looking just as concerned as Bev and I felt. Bev was seated with a very sorry-looking Tom on her lap.

"He's really dehydrated," she said. "Harry just went to get some IV fluids."

After Harry got the IV drip going, Bev coaxed Tom into eating several bites of tuna that Doug had fetched from the kitchen. This seemed to perk him up, giving us hope that our patient would be okay. Bev stayed with Tom while I retrieved my computer and returned to the ops center. While the Internet took its time, I took in the layout of the all the equipment Doug used to communicate with the teams while they were out on missions.

So this is where all the planning happens.

As I sat waiting for my Outlook e-mail program to open, Doug maintained radio contact with the men on the road. In the midst of a sentence he said to the guy, "Hold on," then reached for the wastepaper basket and proceeded to throw up. He put the basket down and carried on with his conversation as if nothing was amiss.

When he finished that call, I asked, "Are you okay?"

"Yeah, it's nothing. I just picked up the stomach flu. I'll live," he said, then grabbed the waste basket and puked again.

"Don't you think you should be in bed?"

"There's only one person to sit in this seat at any given time," Doug explained patiently. "And the guys out on the road depend on whoever is here. It's the difference between them coming back in one piece or not showing up at all. Don't worry, Terri. One day and a wakeup, and I'll be on R&R; I'll get a chance to rest up then."

Talk about dedication, I thought.

When Outlook finally opened, I began scanning e-mails that had come in since I had left Kuwait. I stopped at one from Dave Lusk that he'd tagged as "urgent."

May 30, 2008

Terri,

I hate to hit you with this, but the list of requirements for transitioning animals through Paris is attached, and frankly, it's a bureaucratic nightmare. Please correspond with Lynda Baumann, our bilingual coordinator at FedEx, ASAP. It is better if you work directly with her so she can pass the requested information on to the French veterinary officials. In the meantime, I don't think we should move the animals until we get this latest hurdle resolved.

—Dave

That last line of his e-mail stopped me in my tracks. As I read through the list of questions and requirements, my heart began to pound. One of the items—an Iraqi sanitary certificate—I'd never heard of. I researched it on the Internet, and when I learned the purpose of this document, I couldn't believe the French were asking us to submit it. This requirement made no sense.

Just then Bev walked into the ops center. "What's wrong?" she asked.

"The French have sent a list of requirements in order to get the animals through Paris."

"What are they?"

"Each animal has to have an Iraqi sanitary certificate, written in French, a vaccination certificate, a tattoo or microchip, and a rabies antibody test, completed by a certified laboratory. Here is the clincher—they want to unload the animals in Paris and take them to the animal holding area for veterinary inspection, which will take several hours and means our flight would have to leave without us."

Bev was speechless.

"Not only that, but the Iraqi sanitary certificate turns out to be a process for verifying that the animals have been raised in sanitary conditions, making them suitable for human consumption."

"But we aren't using them for food! That's ridiculous."

"I know. I'm not even going to waste my time on that one. Luckily FedEx has Lynda Baumann liaising on our behalf with the French. I'm sure she'll make them see how unnecessary that demand is."

"What about the microchips?" Bev asked.

"Some of the animals already have them. For the ones that don't, I'll call Linette to see if she can deliver microchips to the Kuwait airport in time for tomorrow night's Gryphon flight." Linette had come to my rescue before when the problem with my debit card had left me stranded with two dogs at the Kuwait airport.

"When the SLG team goes to process passengers on tomorrow night's incoming flight from Kuwait, the Gryphon flight attendant can hand over the microchips, and the SLG men could bring them back to us. All we'll need to do then is find someone to inject them."

"How are you going to handle the antibody test?" Bev asked. "If I'm not mistaken, in the States, it takes as long as twenty-one days to get the results back. Should we have to stay in Iraq for that long, it will be too hot to move animals by the time we get the results."

"That's why we need to go to Dubai," I said. "We have a much greater chance of getting the test done there, and if we do have to stay in the Middle East through the summer, there are more resources at our disposal in Dubai than here in Iraq."

"That makes sense."

"Let's just hope everyone at FedEx agrees and lets us go."

I put aside thoughts of French demands while Bev gave a report on all the animals she had just been introduced to. So far eight dogs and Tom the cat had arrived at the SLG compound. When Bev finished her update, she asked about Mama Leesa's history.

"Never have I seen a dog as beaten down and ready to give up as she is. It breaks my heart to imagine what she must have been through. I wonder what happened to her."

"I've got some of her story here," I said and searched on my computer for the e-mail that Mama Leesa's owner had sent. A Captain had submitted one of the most riveting appeals I had ever received. "Here it is, Bev. Read this."

In March 2008 I was assigned to be an advisor at the Iraqi Police Training Center. Outside the employee housing units and the nearby dining facility, a river of waste runs from the drains and flows through a junkyard situated beyond the compound. That junkyard was where I came upon a filthy, emaciated Saluki-mix dog that had given birth to beautiful puppies. Over the next few days, my interpreter and I managed to sneak food from our dining facility and left it for her. He named our new friend "Mama Leesa."

She had a hard job taking care of those pups. On no less than five occasions, I witnessed her wading chest-deep into that watery effluence to retrieve a puppy before it drowned. Each time I went out with a tub of clean water to wash the disgusting filth off her and the pups. Finally I located some fencing material and built a barrier to keep the pups confined until I could devise a plan to get Mama Leesa and her family somewhere safe.

A vet tech at the K-9 center suggested giving the pups to various farmers he had become acquainted with while treating their livestock. A few of them expressed interest in acquiring a pup and training it to protect their livestock. Unfortunately, no one was interested in taking an adult female dog. When I told my wife about Mama Leesa, she agreed without hesitation to keep her if we could find a way to transport her home.

Because of the no-strays policy at the training facility, once word got out about what I was doing, a privately contracted animal-kill team was dispatched to the camp. I couldn't let the vector control group kill Mama Leesa and her pups. With the help of a former British Special Forces Sergeant nicknamed "Rocky," I devised a plan to save them. Rocky supervised the gate guards, so he knew when the contracted killers were expected to arrive.

As soon as he saw the vector control trucks approaching, Rocky called my cell phone. The vet tech, my interpreter, and I grabbed the pups and loaded them into cardboard boxes. We had just enough time to hide them in the bushes, and Mama Leesa stood guard over them until the kill-team passed through the gate. On Rocky's signal, we each picked up a box of pups and casually strolled out the security checkpoint and down toward the vet tech's waiting vehicle, with Mama Leesa bringing up the rear of our fugitive party.

Something caused the kill-team supervisor to turn around before we got out of sight. He called out and ordered us to stop, but Rocky told us to keep going and turned to ask the supervisor what the problem was. We stepped up our pace, but Mama Leesa kept looking over her shoulder at the ensuing argument with a worried look on her face.

Suddenly, without warning, Mama Leesa galloped back through the gate, past the kill-team on a dead run, barking all the way. The kill-team forgot about us and pursued the decoy mother, giving us time to run down to the vet tech's vehicle and whisk the pups off to safety.

After we delivered all but one of her pups to their new homes, we returned to the training facility, expecting to hear bad news about Mama Leesa. When we got back, however, Rocky told us she had escaped the kill team. I searched all her old haunts, but there was no sign of her. By now the temperature had risen to one hundred–plus degrees. I had to go to the K-9 facility, some five miles away, to check on the police dogs' water, so I took the last remaining puppy and drove off.

As I turned into the K-9 facility, I couldn't believe my eyes. A wobbly Mama Leesa appeared in my rear-view mirror, trailing behind my vehicle. I jumped out to assist her, and she collapsed in the middle of the road. Carrying her into the K-9 facility, I bathed her and got her rehydrated. I have been taking care of her and the pup ever since while searching for a way to get them out of the country. That is, until I found SPCA International.

Knowing that Mama and Baby Leesa are going stateside is the best thing that's happened since I've been here. Even Rocky, the supervisor who was subsequently fired for assisting me, told me it was well worth it!

—Capt B

Bev and I sat in silence for a moment. These stories never failed to touch our hearts. People who went the extra mile to save an animal, often at personal risk, reminded us to keep believing in the goodness of people. And Mama Leesa's extraordinary courage and determination to save her pups inspired us to keep going despite all the challenges ahead of us, no matter how exhausted we were.

After checking on Tom one last time, Bev went to our room while I sent my last e-mail of the day to Linette, asking for microchips. Finally, at half-past two, I collapsed into bed.

The chattering of birds stirred me awake just before 5:00 a.m. How strange their sweet songs sounded in this city where war had torn apart so many lives, both human and animal.

"You awake?" Bev asked after a long yawn.

"I haven't decided yet. Do you want the shower first?"

"You go ahead. And don't forget to keep your mouth shut," Bev warned.

As soon as Bev and I dressed, our first priority was to take charge of the nine animals that had arrived at the SLG compound in the previous two days. The group included Tippy, Pooty, Francine, Diwo, Mama Leesa, Baby Leesa, Crusader, Patton, and our ailing cat, Tom.

There were no kennels or dog runs at SLG. By the time we arrived, the dogs had already scouted around the compound, picked the places where they wanted to hang out, and no one had argued with them. Diwo and Crusader were the smart ones. They resided in the office of Dutch, SLG's fleet manager. This room, lined with spare tires and assorted car parts, was air conditioned. I'd have to remember that later when the heat was taking its toll. It was not quite 7:00 a.m., and already I was sweating.

Tippy had chosen territory outside the kitchen where Bandola, the Filipino cook, prepared meals for the entire SLG staff. Doug said Tippy had taken less than ten minutes to locate where the food was prepared, and he was not budging from his station. Tippy earned the nickname "Houdini" after several attempts to lock him away resulted in his quick reappearance outside the kitchen door. Out of mutual respect, Bandola the cook and Tippy the Houdini soon became fast friends.

Francine resided in our villa's courtyard, where a good-sized swimming pool offered high-class accommodations for a former Iraqi stray. When the thermometer hit 120 degrees in the afternoon, we figured that Francine would go for a dip, but she wanted nothing to do with the water.

Pooty, a purebred German short hair, hung out in a cordoned-off area adjacent to the ops center. She had been found as a pup by SSG Michael Beardsley, and her origin remained a mystery. He figured she must have been someone's lost pet, but Iraq had no system for reuniting lost and found animals with their owners.

The one dog I couldn't locate was Patton. From his photo, I knew he was short haired and mostly white except for black and brown markings on his face and ears and the dark freckles that splattered across the legs and belly of many dogs' coats in Iraq. I ran into Doug on his way to breakfast and asked if he had seen the missing puppy.

"Oh, he's around here somewhere," he said with a snicker. "Patton knows he's got a good thing going. He already acts like he owns the place and does whatever he pleases. I can't tell you how many times we tried to confine him yesterday, and the little bugger kept finding a way to escape. He is one determined puppy."

When Harry had gone over the compound rules with us the night before, he had asked us to make sure we kept all the animals outside and not to bring them into the villas. "If it were up to me," he said, "they'd all be allowed indoors, but we have local people working for us who are terrified of dogs."

After searching high and low in all the discreet places an Iraqi-fearing puppy might hide, I returned to our villa worried that we'd lost Patton. Entering the large, air-conditioned foyer, where staff members constantly came and went, I stopped in my tracks, not quite believing my eyes. Smack dab in the middle of that cool marble floor lay Patton, sprawled out and sound asleep. Rules may be rules, but Patton didn't think they applied to him. Every time people crossed the room, they lowered their voices and stepped over the puppy, careful not to disturb him. Patton certainly lived up to his name.

"How's Tom doing?" I asked as Bev collapsed into the ops center chair. I had just returned from putting Patton back where he belonged and was scanning my morning e-mails, hoping for some word from Lynda or Dave about the French connection. They were desperately trying to convince French authorities to ease the regulations for this one special mission. So far nothing from them had come in.

"Tom seems better, but we have another problem. I can't find Baby Leesa. I've asked every English-speaking person if they've seen her, but no one has. I'm really worried."

We hurried outside to where Mama Leesa and her puppy had been sleeping the night before. Mama Leesa was lying in a scraggly patch of brown grass, but Baby Leesa was nowhere in sight.

"Let's split up and look for her. She couldn't have gotten far; the compound is completely fenced in. Don't worry, Bev, we'll find her."

For the next forty-five minutes we turned the SLG compound upside down, eliciting the help of anyone willing to join the search. I suspected that Baby Leesa had found a shady spot to hide in because the morning temperature was already unbearable. With no luck from our first search, Bev and I decided to walk in opposite ways down the street that ran in front of the villas.

"Terri!" Bev hollered a few minutes later. I ran to find her pointing at the base of the perimeter fence.

"Look. There's a hole. Do you think she might have squeezed through?"

"I sure hope not."

For the rest of the day we kept watching for the puppy, hoping she'd return to her mother after the hot sun went down and hunger took over, but she never did. Baby Leesa's disappearance remains a sad mystery.

Until that morning I had witnessed only the last stage of SLG's role in our rescue efforts. When I descended the Gryphon plane stairs, SLG men would appear from the dark like magic, escorting another dog or cat to the waiting aircraft. It wasn't until Bev and I came to their compound in Baghdad that I grasped what hazards these men faced each time they collected the animals.

"The team is just about ready to head out for the next pickup," Doug said at 8:00 a.m. He walked into the ops center with a steaming cup of coffee in one hand and an automatic weapon in the other, carrying his tool of the trade as naturally as a carpenter would a hammer.

"Great. I'll go and see them off," I said.

Looking ready to charge into battle, five parked vehicles faced the main gate of the compound. Men dressed in bullet-proof vests, Kevlar helmets, and goggles milled around the heavily armored trucks and SUVs. Their shouldered weapons were a stark reminder that, before the day was over, any one of these men might kill somebody—or be killed himself.

I had met the American team leader on several occasions at BIAP. Each time he had handed over another animal, he had said what an honor it was to play a part in sending the animals to their new homes. Now, as I witnessed preparations for the animal pickup that day, I realized that the honor was mine to work with such brave and kind-hearted men.

The first dogs on the day's collection schedule were Beatrice and her pups. I had been working with SSG Roberta Green to get the dog home on a mission planned for late March. At the beginning of March, I had received the following e-mail from her:

Terri,

You won't believe what has happened. About four days ago SSG Thornton was playing video games and heard a strange noise coming from behind the game console. She investigated and found Beatrice giving birth. None of us have ever been around a pregnant dog, so we had no idea—we just thought Beatrice was fat.

Does this mean Beatrice has to stay here? We're at our wits' end with worry. There are people here, including some officers, who would like to adopt the five pups once they are weaned. What do we do, and how does this work now? We need your guidance. Thank you.

—SSG Roberta Green

Rather than take Beatrice off the list, we merely pushed her rescue date back a few weeks. Now that the puppies, Abibi, Taji, Hause, Rocky, and Chewy, had reached three-months, they complied with airline regulations and could fly with their mother on this mission.

The next animal scheduled for collection that day was our second cat, named "Caramel." After the security team picked her up, they would make four more stops to collect the dogs: Roxy, Rosie, Stubbs, and Charlie.

All of the animals had a story, some more touching than others. Charlie's story involved one of the saddest tragedies a person can experience. Charlie had come into one civilian contractor's life at such a perfect time that one wonders if divine intervention was involved. When Kenny's wife, Jolene, contacted me, I was unprepared for her heart-wrenching story.

Kenny had been working in Iraq for an American company that repaired and serviced mine resistant ambush-protected (MRAP) vehicles. These had been brought in to replace the Humvees, which gave soldiers no chance of survival when they drove over an IED. A strong V-shaped framework was installed around the sides and body of large military trucks and tanks. This barrier deflected the explosive force of any IED out to the sides and away from the vehicle base, protecting occupants from the full effect of the blast. Kenny's job saved many American soldiers' lives.

After long months of steady, hard work, Kenny took R&R and flew back to visit his family. The day he arrived, his two-year old grandson suffered a tragic death. Kenny was devastated. The child had been his pride and joy, and his death had taken its toll. As soon as the funeral was over Kenny went back to Iraq, still reeling and was unable to recover from a deep depression. Soon after he returned to work, Kenny's workmates approached him and asked what to do about a stray female dog they'd found while he was away. Kenny took one look at the five- or six-week-old puppy and thought how his grandson would have loved her. "Leave her with me," he said and named her Charlie.

By adopting Charlie, Kenny suddenly felt closer to the boy's spirit. He poured his love into that little dog, keeping her constantly at his side. With such a faithful companion supporting him, the pain of grief seemed more bearable. Kenny's wife, Jolene, had written to me saying, "I didn't know if I'd ever see my husband again. He was so consumed by our grandson's loss, I feared it would take away the edge that kept him from getting killed before now. Having Charlie with him has been a great comfort for me because when he looks out for her, he's inadvertently looking out for himself."

A story like Kenny's made me ever more aware of just how important our mission was. As the SLG team drove out the gate to collect Charlie and ten other animals, I silently wished them all Godspeed.

Still anxious to hear from Lynda or Dave on the French issue, I kept myself busy with Bev, constructing our temporary kennel. We needed to house as many dogs as we could in one area. With the assistance of Dutch, SLG's fleet manager, we scrounged through the compound's junk pile looking for any suitable building materials we could find. The discovery of a dozen wooden pallets proved to be the shelter builders' bargain of the year. One by one, we hauled them to the ops center building, where a courtyard fence connected two villas, creating a three-sided enclosure. We made a fourth wall by binding the pallets together with zip-ties. Dutch then produced a large section of camouflage netting, which we strung over the shelter area, giving the dogs at least some relief from the unrelenting heat of the Baghdad sun.

During the construction Iraqi nationals walked by with bemused looks on their faces. Several stopped to watch the extraordinary women from America. By the time we finished our construction project, we wouldn't win a prize for beautifying the neighborhood, but we sure could have won something, hands down, for ingenuity.

It was time to gather the dogs and settle them into their temporary home. We decided to leave Francine in the pool area, where she was safe and comfortable, and Tippy, who had no intention of moving away from the kitchen, stayed put as well.

"The only thing we need now is dog food," I said to Bev. "Some of the owners provided dry food they had left over from stateside care packages, but it won't be enough for the number of stomachs we've got to fill."

"I'll go see what I can scrounge from the cook," Bev said.

A short time later I found Bev standing outside the kitchen next to a large metal tub of raw chicken, beef, fish, and other leftover scraps the cook had set aside for the dogs. Using a waist-high courtyard wall as her worktable, she began to chop the meat and divide it among a row of paper plates. Bev's hands, covered with blood and

Staying cool in the Baghdad shelter *Terri Crisp*

Tippy, Bev's kitchen assistant, waiting for a
meal in Baghdad *Bev Westerman*

grease, were useless for wiping the sweat that ran down her face. She gritted her teeth, wiped each cheek with a shrugged shoulder, and carried on chopping.

"Things here are so different," Bev said as the sweat dripped off her brow. "It makes you realize how much we take for granted at home. It's no wonder soldiers talk about always being on edge. I can see why now."

"Did something happen?" I asked.

"No. But did you see the signs on the sides and back of the SLG vehicles?" Bev continued chopping as she talked. "'They were bilingual notices in big, bold lettering."

"You mean the 'STAY BACK 100 METERS' warning?"

"Yep. One of the guys translated the Arabic words for me. I don't know if he was pulling my leg or not, but after the order to stay back one hundred meters, the Arabic version contains the addendum, 'OR YOU WILL BE SHOT.'"

"Do you think they really mean that?" I asked, stunned.

"Like I said," Bev wiped the sweat with her shoulder again, "it's not like home."

Chapter 16

FULL HOUSE

Bath time in Baghdad *Bev Westerman*

Barking dogs announced the SLG team's return in the late afternoon. I turned the corner of the ops center building just as the line of vehicles passed through the gate. The men had tucked the airline-crated animals into every space they could find, leaving them panting from the heat. The cat Caramel, however, remained cool and comfortable like a typical feline that always gets her way. Throughout the trip one of the men had perched her crate on his lap and left the air-conditioning vent aimed directly at her. The satisfied look on Caramel's face suggested she had always presumed that the best seat in the house was hers. Of course it was hers; there was no question about it.

Bev and I looked at each other as the men climbed out of the trucks. Although we were full of gratitude for the safe return of men and animals, our next thought, expressed by slightly raised eyebrows, was, "Boy, are we going to have our hands full." With eighteen dogs and two cats in our care, that left just ten more dogs and one cat to collect the following day.

Beatrice's five puppies were offloaded first. They were definitely hot, but I had to remind myself, these dogs were acclimated to the heat, unlike Bev and me.

The men carried the crates to our new shelter, and when they saw the hodgepodge enclosure we'd built with camouflage netting, pallets, and zip ties, the teasing began.

"Hey, if we knew what you could do with a heap of pallets, we'd have let you come sooner," said the team leader as he set down Rosie's crate.

"It's just like having our wives around," one guy complained with a smile. "We go to work, and when we get back, the whole place looks different."

"Don't let their teasing get to you," the American team leader laughed. "I can see the two of you fit right in. This is how a lot of things are built in this country."

While getting the dogs settled in, we gave them a once-over to make sure they were okay. We filled their water dishes but held off on the food at first. They were all too excited, checking out their new digs as well as eyeing their new shelter mates. Unless the dogs had already been living together, we kept them separate; an all-out dogfight was the last thing we needed.

"I think it's time for your baths," I announced after the latest arrivals were tucked into their temporary homes.

The puppies had not been out of their crate for the entire trip back to the compound, so they were covered in excrement. Using the bottom half of an airline crate, I dragged a nearby hose into the shelter area and proceeded to fill it, grateful that the water happened to be on for the moment. Baghdad's water services were no more reliable than its power supply. Bev ran back to our room for shampoo, and soon we went to work.

In the 120-degree heat, I expected Chewy, the first puppy, to enjoy the tepid water, but he wasn't having it. He tried to wriggle free the entire time. His struggling resulted in my getting more of a soaking than the pup, but I was not complaining. That water felt great. One after another, I scrubbed most of the filth off the puppies.

All during the sudsy exhibition, a row of Iraqi men stood outside our makeshift wall and stared in fascination. This was the first time any of them had seen a dog get washed. Each time a dog shook, spraying water all over me, the men laughed and chattered in Arabic. When I allowed the dogs to plant juicy kisses on my face, they nudged each other and grimaced.

Taking care of the animals wasn't an easy job. With only sporadic electricity and water, tasks such as feeding, cleaning, and cooling the animals became difficult and time-consuming. As soon as the water was on, we quickly took advantage, but many jobs were only half done when the water cut off again.

That evening, when the SLG team members returned from BIAP, they brought us the microchips that Linette had delivered to the Kuwait airport. It felt good to have one more thing go as planned. According to my latest e-mail from our FedEx coordinator, the French were still not budging from their impossible demands. It was out of my hands, so I just had to trust that Lynda and the FedEx team would eventually find a way to get us home.

At the end of an incredibly long day, Bev and I dragged ourselves back to the villa. The moment we crossed the courtyard, the dogs started barking. This was not going to win friends among SLG staff members who needed as much sleep as they could get to stay alert on their jobs. Bev and I tried to quiet the dogs, but every time we walked away, Rosie and Roxy barked; then the whole chorus joined in.

"What are we going to do?" Bev asked.

"Rosie and Roxy are the instigators," I said while rubbing my sunburned forehead. "Let's take them back to our room."

"What about the 'No dogs in the house' rule?"

"We could wake up early and bring them back before anyone gets up," I suggested.

"I guess if it means everyone gets their sleep tonight, they'll be glad we broke the rule."

Bev and I tiptoed to the villa, and Rosie and Roxy cooperated in silence. We were just about to enter the courtyard again when we heard a sound behind us. Our hearts stopped.

"What's that?" Bev whispered.

Once again that darned puppy, Patton, had managed to escape. Not only that, but he'd made up his mind to join our slumber party. We were so exhausted by then, it was easier just to give in.

I got about four hours of sleep that night with Patton hogging three-quarters of my bed. How could such a small puppy take up so much room? By the time I dozed off with him cuddled up to me, I realized that he could have taken the entire bed, and I wouldn't have minded. Life was not about sleep or comfort. It was all about these animals.

Patton's paws were poking me in the ribs as the first light of dawn filled the room. Minutes later, wearing pajamas and unlaced work boots, Bev and I tiptoed down the stairs with Rosie, Roxy, and Patton. We crept out of the villa, but as soon as the other dogs saw us, they began to bark. Anyone who wasn't awake before certainly was now.

We quickly returned to our rooms to change out of our PJs, then went back outside and took turns walking the dogs, while the other person cleaned crates. After we finished, we each squeezed in a shower. Then Bev went to prepare breakfast for eighteen dogs and two cats, and I checked my e-mails, hoping for good news regarding the French. When I saw Dave's name sitting in my inbox, I didn't know whether to celebrate or cringe. The time on the e-mail showed that Dave had sent it several hours before. Was it good news?

June 1, 2008

Good morning, Terri,

All of us at FedEx want to do everything we can to transport the dogs and cats back to the States, but we must first ensure all regulatory concerns of the French are addressed before we take possession of them in Dubai.

I cannot allow FedEx to accept responsibility until we are reasonably assured we will not have any compliance issues. This could impact FedEx's reputation with the French regulatory authorities.

Based on what I've seen from the French so far, maybe we need to delay the shipment a number of days. I would suggest we reschedule for the following week, on Tuesday, June 10. Let me know your thoughts, as we would need to reschedule with Gryphon as well.

—Dave

With the increasing heat, staying in Baghdad another week would put the animals more at risk, even if we moved them in the middle of the night. I was also afraid we'd wear out our welcome at SLG, especially if we had to keep sneaking dogs into our room. I would agree to Dave's suggestion if I absolutely had to, but I was not ready to concede just yet.

I e-mailed Dave back and told him I'd like to stick with our plan to get the animals to Dubai that night. I reiterated that I would have a better chance of complying with French requirements from there. A short time later Dave's next e-mail arrived, giving me some hope.

Hi Terri,

I may not have mentioned before, but I'm participating as a guest at the Army War College's security seminar and will be here all this week. When our animal move hit the bump in the road this morning, I reached out to a U.S. Navy Captain and his wife. They've taken a real interest in Operation Baghdad Pups and believe they know the right people to pull some strings. I'm hopeful this may lead to a much-needed solution. Go ahead and get the animals to Dubai. I'll keep working the problem from here.

—Dave

I ran outside to find Bev hanging out with the dogs. When she saw the look on my face she groaned and said, "Please don't tell me we're stuck here until Christmas."

I couldn't keep a straight face any longer. "Pack your bags, partner. We're going to Dubai!"

Bev whooped and gave me a high-five before asking, "By the way, have you seen Patton?"

"He was in the ops center with me, but a guy walked out eating a bag of potato chips, and Patton followed him, hoping for a handout."

"I'd better go find him," she said. "We don't want him missing his ride to the airport tonight. Losing Burt yesterday was bad enough."

SLG's scheduled pickup of Burt, the two-timing cat, had not gone as planned the day before. When the team members had showed up at the designated location, they learned that Burt had escaped minutes before they arrived. The men stayed as long as they could, searching for the fugitive feline, but with several more pickups to do, they couldn't delay any longer. Burt would have to wait at the American outpost until we came back for our first fall mission.

In spite of continued efforts to locate Baby Leesa, we never found her either. Without time to arrange a pickup for two replacement animals, we'd be flying with twenty-six dogs and two cats that night—not the thirty we had hoped for.

The SLG convoy had left earlier to pick up three remaining dogs: Iraqi, Siha, and Samantha. On the team leader's last update he reported that they had collected two of the three dogs already. So far the day was actually going as planned.

Much remained to be done before we'd be ready for the evening flight to Dubai. I had managed to locate Aymen Almarrani, who was recommended by local Iraqis on the SLG team as someone who could administer the microchips. When Aymen answered his phone, I was relieved to learn he spoke English. For $25 per animal, plus the cost of hiring a car, he was willing to come to the compound and microchip each animal.

Aymen and his mother arrived in the late morning, so Bev worked with them to get all of the animals micro-chipped. After they were finished, Bev came in to check on Tom, who was not showing any improvement. Leaving Tom in Iraq meant leaving him to die. After careful consideration, Bev and I decided to bring Tom with us on the flight in spite of his condition. It was his only chance. We agreed to continue using the safety precautions we'd previously followed, keeping Tom isolated from the rest of the animals, thoroughly washing hands after handling him, and limiting Tom's nursing care to one person.

In order to move all the animals from our compound to the airport that evening, SLG arranged for a local national to bring his open flatbed truck. There would be no air conditioning, but we would load the animals at the last minute and make sure all their bowls were filled with water. The vehicle had metal rails on three sides plus a tailgate and was large enough to accommodate all the crates. Bev and I would bring the cats in the vehicle with us. The targeted time for our departure to the U.S. airbase at BIAP was 7:00 p.m.

I had my fingers crossed that the four owners, whose dogs SLG didn't need to collect, would be waiting for us at BIAP. Once we had Ralphie, Jolly, Buddha, and Moody, all the animals would be present and accounted for. I was especially anxious to meet Bryan Spears, who owned Moody. Bryan's mom, Janet, had originally contacted me by phone. After hearing the depth of emotion in this mother's voice as she spoke of her son, his dog, and the soldiers who rescued him, I would have moved mountains to bring that animal home.

Bryan's platoon was stationed in one of the hotspots of Baghdad where ethnic cleansing was still a major problem between Sunni and Shia neighbors. The platoon had been split into two teams: the Blue Team, which was Bryan's, and the Red team.

When the men heard from locals about a tiny abandoned puppy in their district, they formed a friendly competition called "Operation Puppy Snatch" and agreed that the first team to locate the puppy would get to name him. The Red Team won and decided to call the dog "Moody." A few days later their Sergeant discovered evidence of the contraband pup and told his men to get rid of him. When the soldiers went to get the platoon mascot, he was already gone, almost as if he had heard the command to leave. For two weeks there was no sign of Moody.

At this point in her story, Janet told me that Bryan had been her "smile" since the day he was born. Struggling through hard years, whenever she was at her wits' end, that boy's smile gave her courage to carry on. During her son's second tour in Iraq, he lost his best buddy to a grenade. After Bryan redeployed from that tour, she watched her son's smile struggle to surface and, each time, fail. Now, she said, he was on his third tour.

Two weeks after Moody's disappearance, the Red Team was on a routine patrol. An Iraqi man approached the soldiers and asked them for help. As they gathered around him with their interpreter, the Iraqi blew himself up. Five American soldiers and their interpreter died that day. Having lost so many of their buddies in such a horrific way, Red Team members, who survived the blast, and Blue Team members left behind all fell into a crevasse of sorrow. Things couldn't get much blacker. Bryan called his mom on the day of the military memorial service.

"All the life was gone from his voice," she told me, choking back the tears, "and for the first time since he'd joined the Army, I really feared for him. He said the military might want to send him home for R&R, but he was determined to stay and take care of his men. He said, 'If it comes down to me staying and getting killed, or my guys going home alive, I just want you to know, Mom, I love you,' and then he hung up. Well, I dropped the phone and got down on my knees, and I prayed like I've never prayed before. I told God, 'You've got to do something for my boy—right now—or I'm going to lose him.'"

That night a mother's desperate plea was heard. Moody, the little mascot whose Red Team rescuers were now dead, walked back into camp and straight up to Bryan, as if he knew how badly the soldier was hurting. For the next few days Moody's body absorbed hugs of grief while his fur soaked up soldiers' tears. Moody didn't judge the men. He just loved them. When an officer discovered Moody's forgotten food dish and alerted his CO that the dog was back, he was told, "Let the men keep the dog. It's about the best thing we can do for them right now."

"I'll never forget when Bryan called to say that Moody had come back," his mom continued. "I could hear the smile in his voice again. That's when I knew my boy was going to be okay."

• • •

"The truck's here," Bev said, poking her head in the door of the ops center.

"Great. I'll be out in a minute."

As I packed away my computer, I took a second to say goodbye to Brent, the alternate ops manager who had taken over when Doug left for some well-deserved R&R the previous day. When I got outside I discovered that most of the men on the compound had come out to help us load up. I was really going to miss these guys.

"That's everyone but Roxy," Bev said, standing at the back of the truck.

"I'll go get her." I had left Roxy inside the shelter area, thinking a few extra minutes to stretch her legs would be nice. When I came around the corner past our wall of pallets, I stopped dead in my tracks. An Iraqi man, who had spent more time watching us care for the dogs than any of the other local staff had, was sitting on the steps. Our only communication up to then had been an occasional smile or nod. This man, who had feared and disliked stray animals before we came, was now sitting inside the shelter with Roxy by his side. Gently stroking the dog's ears, he spoke to her in soft Arabic, his mouth only inches from hers.

I waited a moment, not wanting to break the spell. At last I stepped forward, and the two friends parted.

When we finished loading Roxy, there were no shy handshakes. Instead, Bev and I were wrapped in burly-armed hugs. I looked down the line of men in their beige SLG shirts and cargo pants and saw a heart-warming blend of Americans, Europeans, Pacific Islanders, and Middle Easterners standing together like a lineup of heroes. In just three days we had become fast friends. Living in a war zone certainly sped up the bonds of fraternity and friendship. When the reality that each moment could be your last comes into play, you don't waste time.

"Hey, next time you come," said one of the men, "bring us all some earplugs, would you?" A couple of the guys woofed and howled like dogs, and soon we were all laughing. Car doors closed behind us while raised palms and a firm double slap on the roof of our vehicle sent us off on our journey with a soldier's blessing.

● ● ●

The ride back to BIAP took place while there was still light, giving us a chance to see our route through the city, but so many fifteen-foot concrete blast walls lined the road that we drove through a gray maze, unable to see anything except the turquoise and pink sky above. The incongruence of hard blast walls against the soft evening heavens made the sky appear small and pathetic, while the war remained giant and brutal. This was what Iraqis had to deal with everyday; monstrous reminders of the dangers jeopardizing and controlling their lives.

We cleared the last checkpoint and drove onto Sather, the U.S. air base section of BIAP. Despite being thousands of miles away, I felt like we were already home. The American flag on soldiers' sleeves greeted me with the confirmation, "We stand together; we are family." I felt so proud to be an American among them. At the same time, another feeling took me by surprise. Iraq had grabbed a hold of me and wasn't letting go. I knew then that one day I'd have to come back.

The location that Doug had chosen for staging the animals worked out perfectly. Out of the direct flow of vehicle and foot traffic, we blended into the perimeter of the dimly lit airfield. It was two hours before departure, so we unloaded the dogs' crates and lined them on one side of the truck and placed the cats on the other, out of the dogs' sight.

The fact that none of the dogs was barking was a big plus. We didn't know if they were too hot or just too tired. Whatever the reason, we hoped the quiet would continue since we didn't want to attract any attention. The only dog to grouse about the whole situation was Patton. His complaints were expressed by an occasional growl that ended in a self-pitying whimper.

We proceeded to check water dishes and make sure everyone was doing okay. We had just begun when an Air Force soldier ambled up. Although he appeared to move slowly, his stride was so long that he covered the ground in much less time than I expected.

"'Scuse me, ma'am . . . Are these here dogs part of an Operation Baghdad Pups transport?" The soldier's southern drawl was as gentle as his walking pace.

"They sure are," I replied. Word of our program had certainly spread.

"Do ya mind if I help give 'em some water?" As the soldier squatted down to greet one of our charges, I imagined him at home in jeans and a T-shirt, working on a Georgia farm maybe, with dogs trailing behind him. Even stroking one soft muzzle for a few minutes must have felt like a little piece of home in his fingers.

"Glad to have the help," I said. "Thank you."

We finished watering just before a Humvee pulled up.

Is this friend or foe?

It had crossed my mind more than once that someone high up in the military might show up if he or she got wind of what we were doing and order us not to proceed.

A tall blond soldier with a lean body, and a dimpled smile that made me feel good just for looking at it, stepped out of the Humvee.

He held the door open while his dog jumped out. I recognized Moody right away from his photo and Bryan from his mom's description. Moody sat on Bryan's boot giving me a worried look as he pressed his shoulder against Bryan's leg.

Thank goodness. One down, three to go.

"Hey, Bryan, it's so good to finally meet you." I extended my hand while Bryan approached half-dragging his frightened dog.

"I still can't believe this is really happening," he said. "How you pulled this off, I'll never know, but I'll be forever grateful to you and SPCA International. You've saved Moody's life, and, boy, this is one life *definitely* worth saving."

As Bev helped Bryan get Moody into an airline crate, another soldier with a dog on a leash appeared from around the corner. Again, I recognized Buddha from the pictures that Bob Mullen had sent me. This time I got a big hug in addition to a "thank you" from SFC Mullen.

Amber Daigle was next to show up with Ralphie, who did not enjoy being confined to his airline crate and was barking nonstop to let everyone know.

"Please forgive him," Amber said with a worried look on her face. "He's never been in a crate before, and I suspect he's figured out something's up."

"No need to apologize," Bev replied. "I'd be acting the same way if I were him."

The last person to show up was Sergeant Sean Alexander. Sean's dog, Jolly, had quite a fan club, and all the members had come along to see him off.

The uniformed men and women circled around their dogs in the semidarkness, exchanging names and stories of where they were posted, all of them relieved to be sending their buddies to safety, yet not ready to let them go.

Spending time with these American soldiers confirmed all over again why Operation Baghdad Pups was so important. Hearing them talk about the inseparable relationship they had with their animal made me grateful that SPCA International and collaborating team members had been prepared to risk doing what others deemed impossible.

All of the animals were present and accounted for, but we still had about an hour's wait for the Gryphon plane. The four owners took advantage of the time, opened the crates and walked their dogs along the perimeter fence in the dark.

"Do you think we should get the others out one more time for a potty break?" Bev asked.

"That's probably a good idea. Just be careful to leash each one before letting them out of the crate. The last thing we need is to lose them now."

Bev and one SLG man walked the dogs, while I stood guard over the rest. Just then a uniformed man approached with a businesslike walk and a serious expression. When he asked, "Are you Terri Crisp," I got the feeling that he was not paying us a friendly visit. I felt my muscles tense and tried not to hold my breath, but trying and doing are two very different things when the stakes are this high.

"Yes," I replied.

"Your plane just landed."

Feeling weak at the knees with relief, I released my breath again and called Bev over, saying it was time to board the passengers. One step closer to home, we could hardly contain our excitement.

The Gryphon plane stopped about sixty yards from where we stood. It was hard to believe that the plane was there just to pick up twenty-eight animals and two people. After all I had been through to get to this point, this was about as close to a miracle as I could get.

"Well, guys, this is it," I said to the four owners squatting by their dogs' crates.

Bryan was the first to stand up and release Moody to the SLG man who was helping to load. Knowing how much Moody had meant to Bryan after all they had gone through, I wouldn't have been surprised to see him break down. But when Bryan turned around and looked at me, he flashed that big smile. "I am so glad he's getting out of here," Bryan said. "I can't tell you how relieved I am to know what good hands he's in." Bryan shook my hand, then turned on his heel and walked away without looking back. Before he disappeared into the dark, I saw him raise his hand and wipe his face.

Each of the soldiers surrounding Jolly took a turn to squat down and wish him luck on his journey, while Sean stood there soaking up the last view of his dog. As soon as his friends finished saying their goodbyes, Sean put his hand under Jolly's muzzle and sat nose to nose while silent tears streamed down his face. "See you back home, boy," he choked and then closed the door of the crate. With the help of a friend, Sean lifted the crate onto the baggage truck.

Bob Mullen looked so upset when he said goodbye to Buddha that for a moment I had to turn away. This soldier who had given me such a warm hug was already missing that physical contact with his buddy. As Bob put his fingers through the crate door, Buddha licked them and his eyes locked on Bob's, pleading with all the soul he could muster, "Don't leave me. Don't send me away."

Amber Daigle was last. "I just wish I could take him out and hug him one more time," she said, tears filling her eyes. "But I don't want to get his hopes up that he's coming back to base with me." Ralphie stopped barking long enough to lick her hand, but the moment Amber stepped away from him, he set to barking again, throwing himself against the crate door. If Ralphie could have busted the walls of that crate to get back to Amber, he would have.

After the baggage truck was full, it headed for the plane, and then, one by one, the SLG men carried the crates up the stairs. Because the cargo hold was too small for our purposes, we had been allotted one row of seats per animal. The Gryphon flight crew helped us to secure each crate with bungee cords.

When we finished, I stood at the front of the plane and looked down the aisle in amazement. Where passengers' heads and shoulders would normally be visible, there were only airline crates concealing puzzled eyes, four legs, and fur. Who would ever have thought it possible?

Roxie's new Iraqi friend *Bev Westerman*

SSG Bryan Spears, Moody, and Terri Crisp at BIAP *Bev Westerman*

"So, who's giving them the safety briefing?" the team leader teased as he came up behind me.

Laughing, I realized how much I was going to miss everyone at SLG.

"The pilot says we're good to go," he said, putting emphasis on "good."

"Okay then," I responded as tears stung my eyes, "I reckon this is goodbye."

"We'll look forward to seeing you in the fall when you come back for more animals," the SLG man said, confirming that we had not worn out our welcome.

"Okay, that's a promise. See you then!"

With the help of the Gryphon flight attendant, we made one final check to ensure that the animals were safely strapped to their seats, while Bev kept a watchful eye on Tom, who was situated next to her. Finally we were ready to go. I collapsed into my seat and closed my eyes, amazed and relieved that we'd made it this far.

When we reached cruising altitude, one of the flight attendants came down the aisle carrying trays of food. Bev and I ate like street beggars who hadn't had a meal in days. Between bites we joked that the number of peanut butter sandwiches we'd consumed in the last three days must have set a world record. After we finished stuffing ourselves, we checked on the animals. They had to be so confused. If only there was a way to explain what lay ahead.

Returning to my seat, I thought of the long journey still before us and of the people waiting back home, all the while praying this wouldn't come to a tragic end in France.

Chapter 17

THE FRENCH CONNECTION

Gryphon passengers strapped in and ready to fly! *Bev Westerman*

It wasn't until turbulence woke me two hours into the flight that I gazed down the plane's aisle again, still amazed to see it filled with four-legged passengers. We were scheduled to land in Dubai in about an hour and a half. What news would be waiting for us was anyone's guess.

"We'll be starting our descent into Dubai shortly," the flight attendant said to Bev and me at the back of the plane, where we'd gone to sit with the lonely Patton.

As the Gryphon plane touched down on the Dubai tarmac, dawn rose against the tops of city skyscrapers that pierced through the smog, while the sun struggled to breach a misty gray horizon. The animals began to stir in their crates, undoubtedly more than ready for a potty break. I hoped they'd be getting one soon.

Parking alongside a FedEx aircraft, the Gryphon pilots finally cut the engines. A set of stairs was wheeled toward our plane, and the men locked them into place. When the flight attendant opened the door, our official greeting committee of FedEx employees boarded the plane.

The manager of operations for FedEx's Dubai ramp and hub stepped forward to introduce himself as Justin. We had been corresponding for days, working through many of the details required for our undetermined length of stay in Dubai. The moment he greeted us, Bev and I knew we were in good hands.

"I can't tell you how good it feels to be here," I said. "Bev and I are anxious to hear what the latest news is regarding the French."

Justin's smile faded a little, and lines of worry appeared around his eyes. "Dave's last e-mail from an hour ago reported that the French are still not budging," he said.

Although the news wasn't what I wanted to hear, Justin assured me that the FedEx team was on our side no matter what happened.

Optimism is much easier to muster when you know you're among friends.

"We still have five hours until the flight, don't we?" I responded. "Maybe we'll get a miracle before then."

"Yes, that would be wonderful. We'll try to arrange one for you," Justin laughed. "In the meantime, let's get you two processed through immigration."

"But the animals—they're our number 1 priority. Any chance we can get them out for a potty break?"

"They'll be fine, don't worry. Our crew will get them offloaded and transferred to the airport quarantine kennel, where they'll stay until we know what the plan is. They'll be able to relieve themselves there."

"Okay," I said. "We're just concerned they don't get left somewhere and forgotten, especially as the day gets hotter." It was a few minutes past six, and already the temperature was rising. Losing animals to heat exhaustion was a real possibility if we weren't extremely careful.

"Not to worry, Terri. They will be indoors where there is air conditioning," Justin said. "The man in charge of Dubai International

Airport's animal regulations said that the quarantine facility has people who will see to the animals. He promised they'll be in good hands."

All of the FedEx men who entered the plane with Justin were dressed in western style except for one, who wore the traditional Arab clothing of full-length robe and white cotton headscarf. He stepped forward and asked for our travel documents. While he shuffled through the pages of our passports, Justin asked if he could meet our traveling companions.

"These are good-looking animals," he exclaimed as we made our way down the aisle. "I can see why the soldiers took a liking to them."

"Where are your stamps from Iraq?" the man with our passports interrupted, a puzzled expression on his face.

"We never got any," Bev and I said in unison.

"No one stamped your passport when you arrived in Baghdad or departed?"

"No," I replied. All of a sudden I remembered Tom Hanks's movie, *Terminal,* in which his documentation problem left him stranded in the airport for months.

"How did you get in and out of the country?" he asked, even more puzzled now.

"Well, we were on a kind of long layover."

"Okay, come with me," he insisted and motioned for us to follow. I hesitated and looked at Justin.

"It's all right," Justin assured us. "I'll stay here and get the animals squared away."

Bev and I grabbed our carry-on luggage and followed the man, who, still clutching our passports, led us over to the FedEx building and into Justin's office.

"Wait here while I see what I can do," he said. He left the room and closed the door behind him.

"Well, this is interesting," I said to Bev. "Makes you feel like we just committed some crime or something, doesn't it?"

"Do you think he'll be able to get this straightened out?"

"Of course! So far, everyone at FedEx has proven they have a 'can do' attitude."

An hour later the door swept open without warning, making Bev and me jump. Were the immigration officials coming to take us away?

Our white-robed FedEx friend entered with a big smile on his face.

"Follow me. We've got this all ironed out."

Wondering what exactly they had done but afraid to ask, Bev and I followed the man to the car. He drove us to the Customs and Immigration building and led us inside. A uniformed man greeted us and spoke to our chaperone in Arabic. After much discussion, nodding of heads, and direct glances at us, followed by more discussion, the uniformed man stamped our passports. We weren't going to jail after all!

As soon as we returned, Justin caught up with us. Bev and I blurted out at the same time, "How are the animals?"

"They're on their way to the quarantine kennel now. They looked a little bewildered when we unloaded them, but other than that, they seemed to be doing okay."

"When can we see them?" I asked.

"First we need to get you temporary FedEx IDs so you can enter the quarantine kennel; that means we'll have to get passport photos taken. Come with me; I'll take you to the mall."

Visiting a mall was certainly not what Bev and I had expected to be doing in Dubai, and the city's traffic put Los Angeles rush hour to shame. As Justin's car crept along the busy streets, all Bev and I could think about were the animals. How were they doing—especially Tom?

Justin filled the time by pointing out all the construction going on in the city. Bev commented on the fact that everywhere we looked, Dubai citizens were dressed in high fashion, designer clothes and driving Mercedes or other expensive cars. I pulled out my Blackberry and checked my e-mails, but two hours after landing in Dubai, no news had come through about the French.

We wove our way through a throng of shoppers at the huge, impressive mall. Expecting Justin to bring us to a photography studio, I was surprised when he stopped beside a photo booth. It was one of those booths you'd see at a fair where you put your five bucks in, stare at a camera, smile, wait for the click, and three minutes later a strip of pictures shoots out. Bev stepped in first while Justin fed the machine—but it kept spitting the money back out.

"It must be broken. Don't worry; there's another one at the other end of the mall," he said, his voice cheerful and confident. Justin's high energy made just about anything seem possible.

Back through the crowd we went. Bev and I looked at each other. *How much longer is this going to take?*

When the second booth proved to be in working order, we grabbed our strips of photos and just about ran back to the car. By the time we reached the FedEx building, we had been separated from the animals for nearly three hours.

"Let me check to see if there is any news about the French," Justin said, heading to his office. "I'll be quick, I promise."

"I got an e-mail from Dave," Justin announced as he returned to the lobby where we were waiting.

"Please tell me the French have reconsidered," I said.

"No, but Dave has arranged a conference call with the French ambassador to the U.S. Army."

"That sounds hopeful," I replied.

"Since we can't get you out of here today, I'll get someone to drive you to the hotel where we'll book you in for the night, and you can drop off your bags because you can't take them into the quarantine kennel. After you're settled, our driver will take you to visit the animals."

Justin left us in the hands of another FedEx employee, who drove us through the relentless traffic once again. He was tall, slender, and wore an Australian outback hat, which looked a bit odd with his Arabic features. I felt bad that Bev and I seemed to be monopolizing everyone's time, and I apologized to our quiet driver.

"Please," he said, "we are the ones who should apologize. All this running around must be very stressful for you. But don't worry; no matter what happens, we will take care of you as if you were family." A few minutes later the gracious driver pulled up to our hotel entrance. "Ladies, feel free to take your time. I will be waiting here for you whenever you are ready."

Everything seemed to be working against us getting back to the airport and finding our animals. Check-in took forever. Even the elevator moved from one floor to the next as if some old man were pulling it by a rope, hand over hand. When we got to our room, Bev and I just tossed our suitcases inside the door and hurried back down the stairs.

Between the traffic and road repairs, we spent more time sitting in one place than we did moving. I wondered if it would have been faster to walk back to the airport. It wasn't until we reached the airport that we learned the quarantine section was another twenty minutes away.

"Here we are!" At long last the driver's words sang out and he flashed a white-toothed smile from under his outback hat. He stopped the car in front of a block-long warehouse.

I had been feeling somewhat impatient while we were running to the mall and back, but at the same time, felt grateful for what everyone at FedEx was doing. Now I was only concerned about the animals. Their owners were also anxiously waiting for word about their dog or cat.

What was I going to say? *I haven't seen your buddy now for almost five hours, so I haven't got a clue how they're doing.* Those e-mails would have to wait.

"The quarantine kennel is through those double doors," our driver pointed as we stood beside him in the huge warehouse. "Then you make an immediate right. You'll see it on the right."

Before we could follow his instructions, I happened to glance to our left, and sitting on a nearby loading dock were our twenty-six dogs and two cats, still in their crates, strapped onto the pallets and covered in netting. No one had let them out.

"Oh, no. Look!" Bev and I all but ran to the animals. Thankfully, on first inspection the entire group seemed fine, even Tom. Our FedEx driver was just as surprised as we were that the warehouse staff had not moved the animals into the quarantine kennel. When FedEx dropped them off, the cargo handlers had assured them that the animals would be seen to promptly.

Considering the extraordinary measures that FedEx employees had taken every step of the way to ensure the animals' safety, our driver must have been just as frustrated as Bev and I to discover they'd been overlooked.

We needed to get the animals out of the crates as quickly as possible. They all needed a potty break and a meal. Our faithful driver located a warehouse worker and explained the urgency of the situation. After the worker located several employees to help move the animals, we thanked the driver for his kindness, and he returned to the FedEx office.

The quarantine kennel turned out to be one room containing four dog runs, each about six feet by four feet. Four cat-sized cages sat at one end of the room above a larger cage where a dog was already situated. The open space in the center was maybe one hundred square feet at best, approximately ten by ten. Anyone with claustrophobia would have had one hell of an attack. Bev and I looked at each other and then at the animals, who had no one but us to rely on. We had to figure out a way to make this work; what choice did we have?

Our first decision was to put Beatrice and her pups into the largest run. Poor thing, when we put her into the run, the pups pounced all over her. All the puppies had messed in their crates, so their fur was matted and streaked with poop. We'd have to give them a baby-wipe bath as soon as we could.

Mama Leesa, Diwo, and Crusader went into the second run. They had become fast friends during the time they hung out in Dutch's office. Longtime friends Rosie and Roxy got the third run. We decided to use the last run as a dog-walk area and lined the floor with puppy training pads, which we had brought from the States. We fed the dogs and cats some dry food we had packed. Although Bev tried, she couldn't get Tom to eat. If we stayed in Dubai much longer, I'd have to figure out where to get more food.

We finally let the remaining fifteen dogs take turns to relieve themselves and stretch their legs in the small run. I wished I could have assured them that the worst was behind us, but I really had no clue as to what lay ahead. I had been monitoring my Blackberry all day, and still there was no news from France.

Bev and I were just getting Samantha back into her cleaned crate when a young man and woman in casual clothes entered the quarantine kennel carrying a large bag of dry dog food.

"We heard about you and all the animals from Iraq," the young man said as he put the food down. "We thought you might need some help. When animals are in transit, we take care of them until they leave."

"We sure could use some help," Bev replied. "Any chance you have a way to get a hold of a veterinarian? We have a cat that needs to be seen."

The woman pulled out her cell phone and called the vet. "He will be here in about an hour," she said after hanging up. "In the meantime, we brought some cleaning supplies, too. Can we help you clean the crates?"

"Yes, please! Any chance we could take the dogs outside for a proper walk?" I asked. "It's awfully cramped in here."

"Sorry," the guy said. "All animals in transit have to remain in the quarantine kennel."

With our new helpers, we got through the remaining dogs much faster. By the time we finished, the dogs and cats seemed fairly content, considering what they had been through so far.

The veterinarian finally arrived, and while he and Bev attended to Tom, I stepped outside to send an update to the owners. It was long overdue, and I needed to tell them we would not be leaving Dubai that day.

I also had to break the cost of our layover to JD without giving him a heart attack. Earlier I had received an e-mail with a cost breakdown from Jovitson Muthiah, the Middle East operations management specialist for FedEx.

> **From: Jovitson Muthiah, FedEx**
> **To: Terri Crisp, SPCA International**
> **June 3, 2008**
>
> Please note the breakdown of airport tariffs that have accrued for the twenty-eight animals:
>
> - AVI storage charges: $27 per day/animal
> - Kennel crew care: $950 per visit (it is recommended that kennel crew attend to the animals every eight hours)
> - Veterinarian charge: $410 for the visit already made
> - Delivery order charges: $25
> - Agent handling charges: 0.05 cents/kg
> - Agent storage charges: 0.05 cents/kg
>
> Animals may not stay in the quarantine kennel for more than twenty-four hours. We are presently working on alternative arrangements. As you can see from the above, if we do not find a quick resolution we will not only jeopardize the safety of these animals but run into high costs for maintenance.
>
> —Jovitson

Using my Blackberry, I calculated just the AVI storage and kennel crew charges for twenty-one days, the minimum time for getting rabies antibody blood test results. I was in absolute shock when I saw the amount—$75,726.

How can you soften that kind of news? Knowing it would be several hours before JD woke to read my e-mail, I prayed that Dave's string pullers were working overtime and that I would be able to write to JD, "Ignore my previous message; we're on our way home."

My next e-mail was to Justin. "Any word from Dave yet?"

"Nothing," was his reply. What he wrote next caught me off guard. "We've been tossing around some ideas to avoid going through France. There is another route. How does going through China sound?"

What would be worse, remaining in Dubai for nearly a month or traveling thousands of additional miles?

Justin ended the e-mail by saying, "We'll talk about it more in the morning."

It looked like a flight to the States was not happening anytime soon unless we went through China. If I was not mistaken, going through China was a whole lot farther—maybe twice as far. By this point I was so thoroughly drained that my ability to problem solve was completely maxed out.

I walked back to the quarantine kennel, and my head began to pound. Extreme heat, lack of sleep, and the relentless problems I'd been dealing with for weeks contributed to the pain. I really could have used a time-out, but that just wasn't an option.

If we were held over in Dubai for much longer than originally planned, I had another pressing problem. Bev couldn't stay more than a few days; she had to get back to work. Employers don't take kindly to people whose week of vacation suddenly stretches into three weeks or more; I had to figure out who could take her place. My daughter Jennifer was the logical choice. I decided not to call her until the next day. Maybe, just maybe, I wouldn't have to make that call.

"We found out what Tom's problem is," Bev said as I came through the door of the kennel. "He's got an abscess at the base of his tail that has become infected."

"I'm surprised we never saw it."

"He kept lying on it, so we couldn't. The vet cleaned it up, though, and he's going to bring back some antibiotics. I feel so bad that we couldn't do more for him." Bev's voice broke as tears welled up in her eyes.

"He'll pull through this, Bev. Don't worry." I mustered as much assurance as I could and gave her a hug. "Tom's a real survivor, just like all these animals are. It would take a lot to knock him down."

We'd been in Dubai for almost twelve hours. With all the animals tended to, we decided it was time to take care of us. Saying goodnight to each dog and cat, we promised we'd be back first thing in the morning. When we stepped outside, I couldn't believe how sweltering hot it still was. How people and animals survived this heat was beyond my understanding. I didn't want to stick around and find out either.

Back at the hotel, Bev staggered toward one bed, and I aimed for the other one. We collapsed onto the pure white duvets, fully clothed in what we'd worn for two hot, stinking days, boots included. Dirt, fur, and remnants of dog and cat excrement were forgotten. Thirty seconds later, Bev and I were sound asleep.

I woke to a pitch-black, air-conditioned room and, for a few seconds, had no idea where I was. I knew only that my body was freezing. Pulling the no-longer-white duvet over me, I was about to go back to sleep when Bev whispered, "Are you hungry?"

Bev turned on the table lamp and located the twenty-four-hour room service menu. Each item sounded better than the one before, so we ordered everything worth drooling over. Too tired to even consider which of us was going to shower first, we lay on our beds and stared at the ceiling, silent and motionless, until a knock on the door signaled food.

Our feast tasted sinfully good. My taste buds danced from a savory bit of macaroni and cheese to chocolate decadence cake, to Greek salad, to veggie burger, to ice cream, to pizza, and back around again. Between bites, our whole conversation consisted of one word: "Mmmmm." When we couldn't stuff another thing down, Bev and I looked at each other and let out two moans. Seconds after the bedside light turned off, we were back in dreamland.

At 1:00 a.m. my Blackberry rang. Startled awake, I managed to get the phone to my ear.

Dave Lusk's voice said, "Are you awake?"

"Sort of," I yawned.

"Well, you need to be awake to hear what I have to say."

I sat up just as Bev rolled over and turned on the light. She crawled out of bed and headed for the bathroom.

"Okay, I'm awake and alert. What's up?"

"The French have waived the requirements."

I dropped my phone and covered my eyes with both hands as tears spilled down my cheeks. My relief was indescribable.

"Terri, are you there?"

"Dave," I said and picked my phone off the floor. "Did I hear you right? Is it really over? Are we going home?"

"Yes, you'll all be on the plane tomorrow."

For the next half-hour Bev and I danced around the room, called home, took showers, and finally, when all our energy was spent, went back to bed.

It turns out that while Bev and I were asleep, an unbelievable series of events had been transpiring on both sides of the Atlantic. While Dave was a guest at the U.S. Army War College's final week of security training, he had spoken with his friend, an Army Captain, about the French situation. Determined to help get the animals home, the Army Captain talked to one of his classmates knowing that this person had a working relationship with the Deputy Commandant for International Affairs. When the Captain's classmate asked the Deputy Commandant for help, he in turn reached out to an Attaché at the U.S. Embassy in Paris. The Attaché then intervened with a key person in the French Ministry of Agriculture. Between these two individuals, a workable compromise was finally agreed upon.

The outcome, Dave told me, was that Operation Patriot Pets would be allowed to make a stopover in Paris. The veterinary officials would not interfere as long as we stuck to our flight schedule and kept the animals on the plane at all times. I wondered if this would jeopardize FedEx's relationship with French officials at the airport, but Dave assured me that FedEx's reputation would remain in good standing.

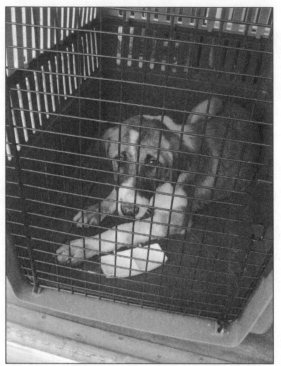

Buddha, one of twenty-eight animals stuck in Dubai
Bev Westerman

Tight quarters in Dubai airport quarantine kennel *Bev Westerman*

Considering the U.S. military's ban against befriending or assisting stray animals in the war zone, it was particularly gratifying to know that the people who got the ball rolling when we were stuck were members of the U.S. military. Their actions saved these animals' lives when they stepped up to do the right thing.

Chapter 18

AU REVOIR!

"We did it!"—Bev and Terri finally landed in Newark, New Jersey.
Bev Westerman

The saying, "What a difference a day makes," never rang as true as it did the next morning when Bev and I entered the quarantine kennel. Such a happy chorus greeted us; we swore the animals knew we were leaving that day. I don't know who was more excited—the animals or us.

The anticipation of heading home gave us the energy we needed to water and feed, clean crates, and walk dogs in the miniature run. Even Tom perked up; his antibiotics seemed to be doing the trick.

When Justin offered to let us hang out at the FedEx office until our flight, I said, "Thanks, but no thanks." I was not letting those animals out of my sight until I saw every one of them safely boarded on the FedEx plane for our 2:00 p.m. departure. I am not a pessimist by nature, but given how often we found another fly in the ointment, I could not believe we were home free yet.

208

The only downside of leaving in the mid afternoon was the heat. Just before we transferred the animals back to the FedEx location, we filled all their water bowls and soaked the absorbent puppy pads that lined the airline crates. Since we'd have access to the animals during the flight, we could switch the wet pads for dry ones when we reached cruising altitude.

"It's time to go," I said to Bev after the last animal was loaded for the ride across the airport. As our driver took us back to the FedEx office, all I could think about were our twenty-eight charges. These animals had been the focus of my life for twenty-two days, and they had become as much a part of my heart as my animals at home. There wasn't much that Bev or I wouldn't have done to protect them, and from the trusting looks in their eyes, we concluded they knew it.

Just before departure I grabbed my Blackberry to turn it off and found an e-mail message from Dave. All it said was, "Fly safe, and bring those animals home."

During the flight we made regular checks on our passengers, and the animals were always glad to hear us coming as we squeezed sideways down the tight maze between giant stacks of other palleted cargo. A chorus of barks, whines, yelps, and even meows heralded our arrival. The FedEx crew in Dubai had packed seven or eight crates per metal pallet and had carefully configured them to give us easy access to each animal. Feeding and cleaning up after twenty-six dogs and two cats at thirty-five thousand feet were new experiences for Bev and me, and we were having the time of our lives.

Paris is a destination that many people dream of reaching, but in our case, I wouldn't have objected to bypassing France altogether and heading straight for New Jersey. When the pilot announced we had started our descent into Charles de Gaulle Airport, the knot in my stomach tightened. Despite our having received clearance from the French Minister of Agriculture, something could still go wrong.

The only window available to Bev and me was about the size of a child's head, so it didn't provide much view of the world outside. When the plane came to a halt, I jumped up and peered out, looking for French officials. What I saw instead put a huge smile on my face. FedEx employees, ground crew, and equipment surrounded the plane. If I wasn't mistaken, the resolute expressions on their faces seemed set to warn any French officials who dared to approach: *Don't even think about messing with these animals.*

"Cross your fingers," I said to Bev as the door of the plane opened.

"Believe me if I can cross it, it's crossed."

"Other than our FedEx friends, let's hope the only people to come on board will be the airline caterers, delivering a huge box of French pastries."

"Mmmm, yes, pastries oozing with chocolate."

"*Bonjour, mademoiselles,*" said the FedEx employee after he opened the door. "Welcome to Paris."

Bev and I acknowledged the welcome with what little French we knew.

"Can you tell me if anyone with the look of an official is waiting to see us?" I asked.

"No, the coast is clear," the man replied with a grin.

Dare I believe that another miracle was in the works?

An Attaché from the U.S. Embassy in Paris and a handful of truly good-natured FedEx employees were our only visitors during the stopover. We had a great time at Charles de Gaulle Airport, introducing everyone to the animals. Our furry companions seemed to enjoy all the attention, especially Patton, who had been feeling out of sorts from not having the freedom which he usually demanded and got.

Two hours after our arrival in Paris, the cargo was loaded, the engines were warmed up, and we headed back to our oversized seats. A ground crewman reached through the open door, and just as he pulled it shut, his last words slipped through: "*Au revoir!*"

As we taxied down the runway, I relaxed for the first time in weeks. Other than a two-hour cargo exchange in England, we were on our way home.

· · ·

Twelve hours later, the plane began its descent into Newark Liberty International Airport. Bev and I could not stay in our seats. We checked on the animals one last time, making sure that all the doors to their crates were locked and that the netting over each metal pallet was secure. After twenty agonizing minutes of circling, our pilot said the magic words, "We've just been cleared to land."

War veterans have been known to get down onto their hands and knees and kiss American soil upon their return. For the first time in my life, I experienced that same urge.

We weren't allowed to exit the plane until a U.S. Customs officer came aboard to inspect the paperwork for all the animals and to check our passports. When everything met with his approval, he cleared us to reenter the United States. Before the officer turned to leave, he extended his hand for a shake and said, "Job well done."

We stepped out of the aircraft into a cool drizzle that felt magnificent. Every pore of my body wanted to absorb the moisture after one week of the dry desert climate. I wondered how the animals would handle the chilly late-night air since only two days before we had all been sweltering in 120-degree heat.

As the massive cargo door opened and the crew slid the first pallet of animals forward, the eyes of Ralphie, Taji, Samantha, and Charlie stared back at me. I got so choked up I couldn't even call out their names.

Bev and I walked down the steps onto American soil just six minutes short of midnight.

"Welcome home, my friend," she said, putting her arm around me.

Upon hearing those words, I lost it. A sound halfway between a sob and laughter escaped me while my tears joined with Bev's in the hug of a remarkable friendship.

"Let's go give these dogs a much-needed pee break," I laughed.

Waiting on the flight line were our friends and volunteers: Kathy Deem, Linda Pullen, Andy Showers, Sheri Thompson, and Dena DeSantis, as well as Stephanie Scroggs from SPCA International.

They were a welcome sight indeed. Dave Lusk, our FedEx friend, had arranged clearance for them to be there, knowing we would need to see some familiar faces when we exited the plane. He couldn't have thought of a better way to welcome us home.

The FedEx team at Newark moved the animals from the plane to a nearby warehouse with extreme care. Parked inside the building was the strangest collection of transport vehicles I'd ever seen. Dena DeSantis had enlisted a team of local plumbers who offered to haul all the crated animals to Building 95 on the airport property. Their motley collection of plumber's trucks and motorcycle trailers formed a caravan of vehicles, all lined up and ready to go.

As soon as all the dogs were unloaded at Building 95, each person grabbed a leash and released a dog from its crate. One could almost hear a communal sigh as the dogs relieved themselves on the nearby grass. Most of them had never laid a paw on green turf until that moment.

Dena followed Bev and me inside and showed us all the donations that local people and businesses had provided. Just about everything that a temporary shelter could possibly need was neatly stacked at one end of the large room. Volunteers, in the meantime, were scrubbing the travel crates, getting them ready for the dogs to sleep in when they came inside.

Linda Pullen brought Caramel the cat indoors and placed her in a small room off the main shelter area. Andy Showers, a devoted cat lover, brought Tom into the quiet room beside Caramel's. Andy promised to keep an eye on our sick friend, and we later learned that she sat up the whole night with him curled up in her lap while she kept vigil over him.

The next day, just after 6:00 a.m., a very concerned Andy called Bev at our hotel to report on Tom, who was even more lethargic than before and was now refusing all food and liquids.

"Andy doesn't think Tom can wait for the vet who is coming later, so Dena called her own vet and got her out of bed," Bev announced. "The vet said to bring Tom in, and she'll see him as soon as we arrive."

Bev and I quickly got dressed and drove to the shelter, where Dena was already waiting with Tom. Bev dropped me off while Dena climbed into the car with our poor sick friend.

Some while later, three mobile groomers arrived, donating their time, supplies, and equipment. Each dog went into the spa with a coat dulled by Iraqi sand and came out brand spanking clean with a patriotic bandanna tied around its neck. When I peeked in to see how Stubbs was doing, the groomer said, "Not one of these dogs has objected to having a bath. They all just stand in the tub and let you scrub them from nose to tail. I wish my regular clients were this easy."

Amber Daigle had arranged for Ralphie to be picked up at Building 95 by her brother. When two young men pulled up, saying they had come to collect Ralphie, Bev took them inside to meet Amber's dog. When one of them sat down, Ralphie collapsed onto his lap and, throwing his head against the young man's shoulder, gazed into his eyes with unfettered adoration.

"He certainly likes you," Bev said with a laugh. "I don't think he's going to have any problems adjusting to his American family."

"I can see now why Amber didn't want to leave you behind," her brother said to the dog. "Well, Ralphie, we'd better get you in the car and start heading home. There's a whole bunch of people just dying to meet you."

"We recommend that the dogs ride in their crates," Bev explained when they got up to leave. "But I have to warn you, Ralphie is a bit of a Jekyll and Hyde when it comes to being confined. His bark is a little frightening."

"Oh, he'll be okay," the young man said, ruffling the dog's head. Sure enough, as the car drove away, ferocious barking emanated from the windows for a long distance down the road. "Bye, Ralphie!" the volunteers shouted as they rode away. Although everyone was laughing, many were sad to see the sweet dog go.

I was just about to walk one of the dogs when my cell phone rang. Bev's voice revealed she was not calling with good news.

"I'm just leaving the vet's office now," she said. "They want to keep Tom under close observation. He's really struggling. They said that when cats fight and get scratched, some pretty nasty bacteria enter the wounds. The ensuing infection travels quickly throughout their body, deep under the skin, and it's almost impossible to check if it isn't treated within a day or so. Poor Tom, no one even knew he had a wound for God knows how many days. The vet says his condition is now quite serious." At this her voice broke.

I tried to comfort my friend, but no words could promise Tom's recovery, and that's what we both longed for. Tom had to pull through. I didn't know what it would do to Kevin if his beloved friend died.

After walking the dog, I went to the news conference with Tom on my mind. It was supposed to be a time to celebrate, but for me the event was overshadowed by sadness.

Stephanie had been busy while Bev and I were in the Middle East. Coordinating with the mayor's office, she had organized a major news conference for the morning after our arrival in the airport administration building. She told me she expected a big turnout. So many people had called to say they wanted to meet some of these Iraqi desert dogs and to hear more about their incredible rescue.

When I arrived, satellite trucks and news media cars filled the parking lot of the airport administration building. Putting on a happy face, I entered the large lobby, which had been turned into a makeshift press room where maybe one hundred people had gathered. Waiting were dozens of reporters and camera operators, along with staff from the airport and port authority, as well as many officials and residents of New Jersey.

Accompanying me were my close friend, Sheri Thompson, and Stephanie. Also with us, ready to make their first public appearance, trotted the freshly groomed Taji, Tippy, and Iraqi. While Stephanie and I worked our way through the crowd with Taji and Tippy, Sheri took Iraqi into another room. His entrance would be saved for the last.

Cheryl O'Brien from FedEx greeted us as we walked up to the end of the lobby where microphones had been set up. I proudly introduced her to Tippy and Taji and explained that I had chosen them to represent the animals from Iraq, since they were used to being among large numbers of people and had calm personalities. After the introductions, we all walked together to the podium.

"Thank you all for coming," Stephanie said into the microphone. Taji and Tippy sat beside me and were sweeping the room with curious gazes. Standing next to Stephanie, I introduced each of them, giving a little background on the owner and the circumstances in which they'd been rescued.

Stephanie then introduced Cheryl, grateful that FedEx had allowed us to publicly acknowledge its employees' extraordinary efforts provided we emphasize that this was a one-time-only mission.

Cheryl took over the microphone.

"FedEx, as you know, doesn't carry passengers; we transport cargo. So we wanted to make sure we did everything right for our four-footed friends. We strapped the animals' crates onto specially designed pallets and secured them amidst a sea of giant containers in an aircraft that was described by one person as a stadium on wings when they first saw the size of it.

"Traveling all those miles is a daunting prospect for people, let alone animals from Iraq. But I'm proud to report that the animals never registered a single complaint or caused any fuss at all. The only feedback we received from them was wagging tails and looks of gratitude."

At this a chorus of "Awh" filled the room, and both dogs pricked up their ears. "All of us at FedEx," Cheryl continued, "would like to honor our special friends with a little thank-you gift and a great big welcome to America."

Cheryl motioned for me to join her by the microphone. She reached into a box that had been placed beside her and pulled out a dark gray and red canvas tote.

"Knowing that most of these animals still have a way to travel before they reach their final destination with soldiers' families, we arranged for each one of them to carry their own personal flight bag, containing everything a four-footed traveler needs." Cheryl handed me the bag.

"Open it up, Terri! Show us what's in there," someone shouted from the audience.

The image of children crowding around the birthday girl as she opens her presents crossed my mind. People moved closer to the podium and stretched their necks, while television cameras zoomed in on the bag in my hands. My eyes began to fill with tears. I had to keep blinking just to see as I pulled each item out. Inside were a brush, treats, and two collapsible bowls for food and water.

"I can't believe this," I said. "After all FedEx has done . . ." I turned to the crowd. "These gifts are from extraordinary people who went above and beyond to get the animals home. I wish I could tell you everything they did, but I'd have to write a book to fit it all in. Cheryl, please tell everyone at FedEx that our Patriot Pets will be thrilled with these." As I turned to give her a hug, the room exploded with window-rattling applause.

The next speaker was a man from the office of New Jersey's assemblyman, and where staff members had put together welcome-home bags for the animals. These bright sacks contained collars and bandannas in patriotic colors, Frisbees, brushes, and more dog and cat treats. This speaker was followed by Newark's Mayor Corey Booker, who played a key role in acquiring Building 95 for our use as a shelter.

Finally, Stephanie returned to the microphone. "There's no doubt about it," she said. "The citizens and leaders of Newark certainly know how to give a warm welcome for our four-footed friends!" The atmosphere could not have been more jubilant as people responded with noisy applause and cheers.

At last it was time to let everyone witness the heartwarming introduction they'd all been waiting to see.

"SPC Alishia Leitheiser," said Stephanie, "is the owner of a dog named 'Iraqi,' who is waiting in another room at this moment. Alishia is still deployed in Iraq, but her mother, Melissa Moore, has driven up from Pennsylvania to meet her daughter's dog for the first time. Before we bring Iraqi in to join us, I'd like to read the original e-mail Alishia sent to Terri, which is how each Operation Baghdad Pups rescue begins."

Stephanie unfolded the e-mail. "It is dated April 13, 2008."

The room went dead silent as she cleared her throat and began to read:

Animals befriended by U.S. troops all need the same thing—love and food. I never expected to come to Iraq and find a dog. But it happened, and it was love at first sight.

Iraqi listens to me when no one else will. He has been there when I needed a good cry, and his slobbery kisses have always let me know everything will be okay. He's become a huge part of my life. From the day I found this puppy, I felt like it was my duty to take care of him. I'm an avid animal lover, and I couldn't turn my back on him. Iraqi is like my son. I would do anything in the world for this dog.

I am begging SPCA International to help me get my beloved dog out of this horrible place. I don't have much time before I leave Iraq. It would kill me if I had to leave my best friend behind, knowing he was wondering where I've gone and when I'll be back. Please help me save Iraqi.

—Alishia

The buildup to the next moment was riveting. Not a shuffle or cough was heard as I left the room to collect Iraqi from Sheri. After a few quiet words to Alishia's dog, I returned to the lobby with Iraqi at my side and walked him up to Melissa. Everyone waited in silence. Handing her Iraqi's leash, I backed up and stood to the side. Melissa bent down and wrapped her arms around the dog her daughter had saved. The onlookers finally got what they had been waiting for. Waves of emotion spilled out across the room; several people pulled out tissues and wiped their eyes.

After taking a moment to collect herself, Melissa stood by the microphone and addressed the crowd: "Iraqi brought joy to my daughter everyday in a place where there is little happiness. I don't know how Alishia would have endured if not for this animal's loving companionship." Melissa looked at Alishia's dog, placed her hand on Iraqi's head, and the dog looked back into Melissa's eyes as if she understood their connection. A tear rolled down Melissa's cheek and she turned back to the microphone. "Our family will always be grateful to Terri, to SPCA International, and to all the people who gave so much to make this possible. Thank you all so much." A bright smile flashed across Melissa's face and she straightened her shoulders. "Well, it's about time I get a move on and bring this puppy home!"

People stepped back and cleared a path as the mother of one American soldier turned to leave the room. Proudly trotting beside her was the dog that carried her daughter's heart.

When it came time for me to close the news conference with a few words, I stepped over to the microphone. I had not prepared a speech like the speakers before me had. My usual way is to talk from the heart.

At first I just stood there, scanning the room. But my attempt at forming words, with nothing coming out, confirmed I was in trouble. I found it impossible to talk. Each time I simply tried to say, "I want to thank all of you for coming," my voice cracked and stayed in my throat. I paused and took a deep breath, but it was no use. My emotions had finally caught up with me.

For the previous twenty-two days, I had remained strong and focused. Sure, there were those moments when the tears appeared, but they did not stay for long. There was always something more pressing to attend to, so I'd suck it up and get on with it.

Now, with tears in my eyes, all I could do was gaze at the crowd of assembled people and then at the two Operation Baghdad Pups dogs standing beside me. My gratitude enveloped every single person who had turned an impossible mission into an amazing rescue. Working together, we had pulled off a miracle for twenty-six dogs and two

Dr. Alan Pomerantz and his team from Franklin Lakes Animal Hospital
preparing to do vet checks on all the animals *Bev Westerman*

Bev and Pooty inside Building 95
in New Jersey *Terri Crisp*

Andy Showers with Caramel at the New
Jersey shelter *Bev Westerman*

cats. No wonder the words could not come easily. Finally, in a trembling voice I just said, "Thank you."

The crowd began to applaud. Catching a glimpse of my longtime friend, Sheri, with tears streaming down her face, I stepped away from the podium as the applause continued. It was time to find a Klcenex and start making the arrangements to send the animals to their homes.

As a result of that news conference, word of our mission spread farther than we could even keep track of. Publicity raised by the media event quickly began to bring in the necessary funds to pull off the next series of rescues when the travel embargo lifted in October. The lessons I'd learned in the four months since rescuing Charlie would prove their worth in the months to come.

Chapter 19

LETTING GO

Siha and Bev taking a break at the New Jersey Shelter
Terri Crisp

Appearing on the CBS *Early Show* the next morning with five rambunctious pups and their mother was not something I had ever imagined doing. After dodging New York traffic and a mob of pedestrians, Sheri, Stephanie, and I put up a small exercise pen for Beatrice's pups in the plaza outside the CBS studio.

Maggie Rodriguez, one of the show's hosts, held onto one puppy's leash throughout the interview, while I kneeled beside Beatrice, the proud mom. In seconds we were surrounded by a throng of tourists who had come to be seen on TV, but on June 7, the cameras were not scanning the crowd. The massive lenses stayed down at knee level instead, recording nonstop movement of tan and white fur, floppy ears, question-mark tails, and oversized paws. Maggie's pup became so intrigued with one camera that she walked up to the lens and gave America a close-up view of the inside of her nose.

Throughout the interview, the puppies did what animals in the spotlight always do—they stole the show and everyone's hearts as well. With every heart they won, another donation would surely come in, helping to bring home another soldier's beloved animal. Grateful that the media event had great potential for producing a fundraising success, we packed up the puppies and headed back to the shelter.

"I wonder how Tom is doing," I said as Sheri and I got into the car. "I haven't heard back from Bev yet."

"Did you manage to get hold of Tom's owner?" Sheri asked.

"Not yet." I had been in touch with Kevin while we were still in Baghdad but hadn't heard back from him since we left Dubai. I kept hoping that Tom hadn't used up his nine lives yet, but in Iraq, cats go through them pretty darned quick. That morning I had sent Kevin another e-mail to let him know Tom's condition was grave.

A few minutes into our drive, Bev's name appeared on my Blackberry screen. Something in my gut told me that this was not going to be good.

"Tom was just euthanized" she said.

"Oh, no," I said, too stunned to take the news in. Bev and I sat with the silence between us, thinking of Tom and all he'd been through. Finally I needed to comfort my heart-broken friend. "Bev, I will always remember how well you took care of Tom in the time we had with him. In the last days of his life, Tom knew he was loved, right to the end. No one could have loved or cared for him better."

After we returned to Building 95, I got out of the car, sat down on the curb, and sent an e-mail to Kevin. With the way things happen in a combat zone, I knew I might not hear back from him for days.

Dear Kevin,
I am truly sorry to have to tell you this, but we made the tough decision this morning to have Tom euthanized. He had a systemic infection that overwhelmed his body's immune system.

The vet and her staff did everything they could to fight it, but without any sign of improvement. Tom was suffering, and I knew you wouldn't want that.

It's just not fair that Tom didn't get to know the life he would have had here in the States. Thank you for wanting to give him that life. I know he appreciated everything you were able to do for him. He was indeed fortunate to have you as his friend! I just wish your time with Tom could have lasted much longer.

—Terri

The volunteers were starting to bring the dogs out for their noon walk. As I sat on the curb watching them, I couldn't help but smile through my tears. These were the lucky ones, the ones that would never again experience the kind of pain inflicted on animals in Iraq. I guess in a way Tom was lucky, too.

Our shelter residents were settling in nicely. They were thrilled with all the attention the volunteers were giving them, especially Patton. He still knew how to get his way, and he figured out that the volunteers were real pushovers. People constantly remarked how the puppy lived up to his famous namesake. At one point Patton grabbed someone's duffel bag and ran off with it. The fact that the bag was bigger than Patton never slowed him down for a second.

"Lead me, follow me, or get out of my way!" a visiting Port Authority worker quoted the famous general and laughed at the puppy. He respected strong character when he saw it.

Another dog soaking up the attention was Mama Leesa. When Bev and I first met Mama Leesa, she seemed to have lost her desire to live. During our time in Baghdad, whenever we took her for walks, she'd barely move, and her head hung low the entire time. She never once made eye contact with us or anyone else. Seeing a dog so emotionally beaten was heartbreaking, but now she was slowly coming to life and telling us what she needed.

When Linda Pullen, one of the volunteers at the airport shelter, took Mama Leesa out for her walks, the dog would refuse to come back inside, unlike the others that wouldn't leave the air-conditioned building for more than five minutes. They would walk to the edge of the grassy area, do their business, then turn around and drag whoever was walking them back inside. They loved American comforts!

Not Mama Leesa. She just wanted to lie in the sun. Even in the mid afternoon, when temperatures teetered around ninety-five degrees, Mama Leesa preferred the heat. She'd collapse on the grass, stretch out like a true sun worshipper, close her eyes, and refuse to move. We were all concerned that she might succumb to heat stroke, but she never did.

Linda tried to tolerate the heat as long as she could but would soon reach a point where she had to find shade. Out of necessity, she came up with a solution by tying two leashes together, end to end, so she could stay out of the sun while Mama Leesa basked in the blissful sleep of contentment. Linda marveled at this dog that had been through hell and survived. Many things were about to change for her, but one thing Mama Leesa was determined to keep was her love of scorching hot days.

Stubbs had also become a real attention getter. He moved into the volunteers' room on his second night and took over one of the girl's sleeping bags. A wise and gentle soul, he had suffered extensively at the hands of Iraqis. Believing that a dog grows tougher when his ears and tail are cut off, they hacked Stubbs several times in preparation for fighting other dogs. His torture became their pride and entertainment. Everyone at the shelter took one look at Stubbs's horrible scars and wanted to smother him in love. No dog deserved what he had endured.

Veterinarians also donated their services and equipment for our temporary shelter. A holistic veterinarian who ran a mobile service saw the animals first and issued domestic health certificates for those that had to fly within the United States. The next day Dr. Alan Pomerantz and eight of his team from Franklin Lakes Animal Hospital spent the entire afternoon giving the animals a thorough exam. Their comments during the examinations indicated how extraordinary these Iraqi animals were.

"These are some of the healthiest animals I've ever seen," Dr. Pomerantz said with clear admiration. "I really didn't expect this, considering where they came from."

One of the vet techs added, "And they just let you do whatever needs to be done, without objecting. They're a joy to work with."

. . .

It was time to start getting the animals onto the final stretch of their journeys. Instead of coming to New Jersey to help, volunteer Barb Hartman had stayed at home in Virginia in order to coordinate flights for the remaining dogs and our one cat, Caramel. Barb called me in New Jersey with regular updates. Her latest report was not good.

"The record-breaking heat wave that started yesterday along the east coast has brought airline travel for animals to a halt. I just can't get any flights; the airlines won't take them. That's not all," Barb continued, "I'm afraid the weather reports are predicting the heat wave won't be ending any time soon."

Checking airline schedules and reporting back to families were much more time consuming than people realized. So many questions came up, and the families all wanted to talk. This was a big deal for them. On top of her full-time teaching position, Barb was on the phone for hours every night. Since I had more time on my hands, I offered to help her with the flight arrangements. Over the next few days, many flights had to be rescheduled, some seven or eight times, due to the continuing heat wave.

"I can't believe how grateful these people are," Barb said. "Their stories prove how important the animals are to them. When I called Jolene about scheduling Charlie's flight, she mentioned making her preparations. I asked what she meant, thinking she was planning a welcome party or something. But it seems North Carolina has strict rules about imported animals from Iraq.

"Jolene said they have to put Charlie in quarantine for six months and there was no way she was going to part with that puppy for a single day. So guess what—right now she is having a quarantine kennel built on their property. It has to be made of chain link, one ten-foot-by-ten-foot enclosure inside another twelve-foot-by-twelve-foot enclosure, set on concrete, and padlocked. This is costing them nearly $7,000, but Jolene says that for Charlie they're glad to do whatever it takes."

"Wow, talk about commitment," I responded. "It sounds like Charlie is going to have a really good life with that family."

"Has anyone else had to quarantine their dog?" Barb asked, curious about the other owners.

"Not so far," I said. "Health regulations are set according to state law and sometimes county. In some places people are allowed to quarantine in their home, while others have no quarantine requirement at all. In those places our veterinary health certificates are considered enough."

"Changing the subject," Barb continued, "did I tell you about Wilma Lacey's reaction to the CBS *Early Show*?"

Wilma was the mother of a soldier named "Sandy" who had agreed to give a home to Taji, one of Beatrice's five puppies.

"No. I hope she wasn't upset about us bringing the puppies to New York."

"Not a bit! The minute the show finished airing, she called me right away, saying, 'Barb! My grand-puppy is a celebrity!' She was so excited, you should have heard her. Over the last few years Sandy has been on several deployments to Iraq, so she's missed years of birthdays, Christmases, and family holidays. That's been awfully hard for Wilma. Now she's thrilled. She is looking forward to hugging Taji, she told me, because she'll be hugging a little piece of Sandy."

The steady stream of e-mails and calls on my Blackberry was like a constant ringing of bells and whistles. While I enjoyed dealing with all of them, I missed receiving messages from the person whose hard work and friendly banter had filled my previous weeks. It was high time to send Dave Lusk another e-mail.

June 8, 2008

Hi Dave,

I have missed our daily discussions! Most of my conversations since I arrived in New Jersey have been with airline agents, trying to arrange flights so our four-footed passengers can finish the last lap of their long journeys. Booking flights has been a challenge due to the extreme heat. After this is over, I believe I could find work as a travel agent, claiming my on-the-job training.

A few of the animals have arrived home, so I've been reaping the rewards of hearing those peoples' happy voices after they meet the new addition to their family. It's difficult not having my soft buddies around, though. Our mutual attachment grew, and we bonded during this incredible journey. They will always feel like my own.

Please keep in touch. In the meantime, stay well, and, as you have said many times in the past few weeks, may there never be flies in your ointment again.

—Terri

I was delighted when, only a few minutes later, Dave's e-mail popped up on my screen.

Hi Terri,

It's good to hear from you. I'm still buried with work after being gone for that last week at the Army College, and as you know, we were both a little busy before that. But I'm not complaining; I had the time of my life.

I've seen and read all the media reports that Stephanie sent, and I've shared them with everyone here at FedEx. You and your team have done an amazing job. You are the real heroes in this story.

Your friend,
Dave

Dave was right. All the members of the Operation Baghdad Pups teams showed an unmatched level of commitment and compassion toward the twenty-six dogs and two cats.

One example of that commitment was shown by the volunteers who stayed overnight at the shelter. Their attempts at undisturbed slumber were constantly foiled. Sleep was next to impossible when sharing living accommodations with dogs that seem to bark all night and sleep all day. We joked that the dogs were still on Iraqi time. One afternoon I found Sheri asleep on the concrete floor with no pillow or blanket, doing the same thing a smart mother does when there's a baby in the house: She snoozes when the kid does.

As the weather finally began to cooperate, we rebooked flights, and, one by one, the animals headed home. Each time I accompanied another dog to the airport and handed it over to the animal-cargo handler, it was equally difficult to say goodbye. Every single animal had moved into my heart and staked a claim.

But it was time to let go. Families had waited a long time to meet the four-footed friends they had heard so much about, and some of the owners were due back from Iraq any day. What better homecoming than to see their wartime buddy waiting alongside everyone else in the family? These were the moments we'd all been working so hard to make possible.

By June 12 all the volunteers had gone home except for Sheri, who stayed behind to help clean and make sure that we left Building 95 in tiptop shape. On our final morning, I dropped Sheri off at the airport to catch her flight back to Oklahoma City, leaving her with heartfelt thanks and hugs of goodbye.

At long last I loaded up my car with Tippy, Stubbs, and Patton, and the four of us hit the road. Our destination was Bev and Barb's house in Virginia. In two day's time, Tippy was going on a flight from Washington, D.C. to Texas, and later in the week I would be driving Stubbs and Patton to their respective homes.

With Patton riding shotgun and Stubbs and Tippy crated in the back of the SUV, we cruised along the New Jersey Turnpike. My iPod started playing Lee Greenwood's song, "God Bless the USA." I turned the volume way up and listened to the words with new appreciation for how lucky we are. As the song played, it evoked images of countless stories that soldiers had told me—heart-breaking tales of young men and women they'd known and loved, the ones who died in Iraq and Afghanistan—the ones whose names were tattooed on their bodies and hearts.

I thought about Jennifer Mann, Patton's owner, and of all the soldiers her mental health team had struggled to help, some so emotionally shut down that it took a puppy named "Patton" to start them talking, yet they continued to serve and sacrifice for the sake of us at home.

I had been to Iraq. I had felt the undercurrent of constant tension throbbing through the air of that country of extremes. Despite the camaraderie of wonderful people, it was always there, that unspoken fear of soldiers, and animals whose thoughts still whispered in the parched, gray soil, *don't leave me here—don't forget to bring me home.*

"We won't forget them, will we, Patton?" I asked. I began to sing the chorus again, joining the iPod song with all the volume I could muster.

Patton suddenly raised his muzzle, stretched out his chin, and his voice resounded with the loudest, most exuberant chorus of howls I'd ever heard a puppy make.

My little friend had seemed to epitomize General Patton's maxim, "You're never beaten until you admit it." The strong-willed puppy's spirit never admitted defeat, and neither did Stubbs, the gentle dog who still trusted people after the horrible things human hands had done to his body. Tippy didn't know what beaten meant. He knew where he wanted to be, and he always found a way to get there. These three dogs had pulled me through some of the toughest times in Baghdad and during our long journey home.

Patton continued to howl, throwing his little chest from one side to the other, as if his heart was leading his body. "Are you singing along?" I asked. "Or are you just complaining about my singing?"

As I drove south, each passing mile seemed to fill with its own set of memories, some funny, others sad, and many full of frustration or jubilation. What an amazing journey it had been.

Although grateful for what we had accomplished, I was also aware of the tremendous number of rescues yet to be achieved and of the greater need for world attitudes to be changed with education and healthy exposure to these precious animals. The upcoming partings and goodbyes for my three canine companions would not be the end of Operation Baghdad Pups. If anything, I knew more than ever, it was only just the beginning.

Stubbs, a true survivor and gentle friend
Bev Westerman

Mama Leesa and me *SPCA International*

AFTERWORD

By Cynthia Hurn

Barb and Tippy in Virginia *Bev Westerman*

While it's difficult to say goodbye to an animal you've traveled thousands of miles to bring home, it is also hard to leave behind the ones who've captured your heart through their stories. When working with Terri on this book, I had the wonderful opportunity to interview many of the people included in these pages. I heard the emotion in their voices, felt the love they have for their country, and especially the incredible devotion between them and their buddies.

As Terri and I completed our final edits on the last chapter, it was hard for me to put the pen down and say goodbye to my new friends, both human and animal. I couldn't help but wonder, "How are they doing now?" If your heart was moved by their stories, you may be wondering the same.

Almost all of the dogs and cats in *No Buddy Left Behind* are alive and well today, living with the person who befriended them, with members of their family, or with close friends. Sadly, some of the animals have died. Before their death, however, they experienced freedom as we know it in this country. They felt safe and loved and were well cared for. If that's all their rescue earned them, I believe the incredible effort to bring them home was worth it.

For the readers who want to know a few more details about the animals' lives since coming to America, the following owners kindly agreed to share just a little bit more with us and with you. In the order that they appeared in the book:

• • •

Charlie (SGT Eddie Watson)—Charlie is living the good life these days, fine tuning his dog-agility skills while Eddie completes his training for a career in the nursing field. The first Iraqi desert dog brought to the United States by Operation Baghdad Pups still has a few behavior issues related to living in a combat zone. He barks non-stop when fireworks go off, and people who look like Iraqis frighten him to this day—sad reminders of the damage done by cruelty and war.

Eddie and Charlie have also become family men. A special young woman walked into Eddie's heart and life soon after he was reunited with his dog. They are now proud parents of a toddler daughter, and she keeps Charlie on his paws.

Charlie has proven himself to be an all-American dog right from Day 1. When Terri took him on his very first pet store shopping trip after arriving in the States, out of all the toys he could have chosen, the only one Charlie wanted was a football. Now he enjoys everything American, from baseball to hamburgers, and he is proud of his promotion to the new rank of OCP (official couch potato).

• • •

K-Pot—Although he no longer fits into a Kevlar helmet, K-Pot still loves to curl up on anything soft. He moved in with Matt's sister Danielle and her kids, where he could romp around acres of land and have another dog to play with. During Danielle's wait for Matt to redeploy, K-Pot gave her a few challenges. The high-energy, intelligent dog could not get over his nervousness about strange noises, people, and situations, and Danielle soon realized she needed the help of a trainer with specialized skills. But try as hard as she could to find the right trainer, K-Pot got kicked out of every class he attended.

Inspired by desperation, Danielle went back to school and became a certified dog trainer and behavior specialist. Now she works with other dogs that have special needs and is always happy to help any owners who need advice on how to deal with their Iraqi dog.

"K-Pot is still a work in progress," Danielle says, "but he's made a 100 percent improvement from the frightened animal that came out of Iraq."

Today Matt works in Charleston, South Carolina. He lives in an apartment, which is an unsuitable environment for a dog with as much energy as K-Pot, but Matt visits his old buddy at his sister's house as often as he can. Danielle said, "The whole time Matt is here, K-Pot won't leave Matt's side. The bond between my brother and that dog is incredible. It's really special to see."

In February 2011, Matt and Danielle flew to Iraq as part of Operation Baghdad Pups' Missions # 84 and 85, bringing between them five animals home to the States. After they returned from their long journey, Danielle wrote to me:

"All I can say is that my life has been forever changed by the Operation Baghdad Pups program. I cannot imagine my life, or those of my family, without K-Pot in it.

"I have experienced the adventures of a lifetime, forged incredible friendships, and renewed old ones. I have witnessed the healing power of animals in even the most horrific conditions and seen humane programs blossom in places where animals are considered garbage. I've learned how to become a true pack leader among incredibly challenging animals as well as humans!"

• • •

Hope—Today Hope's burned leg is fully recovered except for slight stiffness. She, along with two other Iraqi cats, lives with Bruce and Pam in Virginia. The other two cats were adopted by the couple when their pregnant Iraqi mother was brought to the States and her American-born kittens needed good homes. All of them were placed with Operation Baghdad Pups' families. The three Iraqi felines are full of energy, Bruce says, and there is never a dull moment when it comes to their antics.

Last year Bruce was diagnosed with cancer and has been unable to work during his last bout of treatments. "Hope has been an excellent companion throughout this ordeal," Bruce said. "She is such a great comfort while I recover from chemotherapy. She always knows when I need a little boost and refuses to let me get depressed. She brings me hope and confidence that I'll soon be well enough to go back to work."

• • •

Jasmine—Although the Operation Baghdad Pups program requires that all animals brought to the States have to be spayed or neutered, by the time Jasmine came into America, she'd already had a fling with an Iraqi tom. Weeks later Jasmine gave birth to a beautiful kitten that resembles his feral father, except this kitten is well fed and much cleaner! Jasmine and Simba, and a rescued American cat named Kilo, have been living with Thomas in southern California, where he is still on active duty in the Marines.

In the summer of 2010, Jasmine pushed open a window screen and escaped. Her Marine buddy searched for weeks, but this time he was unable to locate his beloved friend. Tom prays that Jasmine is alive and living with someone who loves her, and he hopes that one day they will be reunited. If any reader recognizes Jasmine from her photo and knows anything of her whereabouts, please contact Terri Crisp through the SPCAI.org website. In the meantime, Tom is grateful that he still has Kilo and Jasmine's beautiful Iraqi son, Simba. Unlike his mother, Simba loves to stay at home.

• • •

Tiger—Tiger has grown into a fluffy, 125-pound lovable dog that purrs like a cat when you rub his tummy. Standing on his back legs, he measures five feet eight inches. He lives on the east coast with Jessie, and their regular run along the beach is his favorite pastime. To this day, more than twenty-five people from the camp in Afghanistan where Tiger was found call regularly to ask how he is doing. Every Christmas, Tiger gets cards from Dena and the girls who raised the funds for his rescue.

"He's got rock star status as far as they are concerned," Jessie said.

While Jessie is away on deployment, she knows that Tiger is in good hands. "I prefer to be forward fighting the fight. I have a phenomenal job in the Army, and I'm proud to serve our country. When I'm out there, knowing Tiger is safe at home is an indescribable boost for me. Most people wouldn't understand what it truly means to a soldier to bring back the animal that was forward with them, staying alongside them while they served. It's a special way of bringing light into some of the darkness that is part of war. The people who helped to save Tiger will always be in my heart."

• • •

Burt—Erin is happy to report that the two-timing Burt, who 'missed the boat,' managed to catch the autumn flight and made it home to America in October, 2008. He is alive and well and has grown into a big, bed-hogging cat. "Burt is fit enough to make any Marine proud," she says. "There's not an ounce of fat on him. He's all muscle."

"Burt has a few postwar quirks, just like I do. Once when I was in a bookstore, somebody popped a balloon, and it took all I had not to fall apart. I hit the ground, and then I found a corner to stand in, where it took me fifteen minutes to calm myself down and stop shaking.

"Burt does the same kind of thing. When somebody was using a nail gun for home repairs, my other animals took the sound as normal, but Burt scrambled onto my lap, and he tensed and jumped with every pop. I knew exactly what he was feeling. It's something we share. He's one of the few people I know that understands what it is like for a soldier after they return home from war. Having Burt here is such a gift; I can't describe how much it means to me.

"As Marines, leaving one of us behind is against everything in our being, and if we'd had to do that to Burt, it would have been so hard on the people at our FOB and would have absolutely destroyed me. I hope Terri and SPCA International are able to continue their work for U.S. troops. There was absolutely no way we'd have got our buddy home without her."

• • •

Mama Leesa—When Linda, one of the Operation Baghdad Pups' volunteers at the New Jersey shelter, opened Mama Leesa's crate door, the animal was too frightened to move. No amount of coaxing would bring her out. Linda reached in, scooped the dog into her arms, carried her to the grass, and gently lowered her body to the ground.

"When I put my hand on her," said Linda, "she looked deep into my eyes, as if aching for a loving touch. And that's the first time the thought entered my head, I could love this girl."

Linda fostered Mama Leesa until her owner returned, but his renewed work contracts in Iraq meant he would spend little time in the States, so Linda became Mama Leesa's new owner.

"She looked at least eight years old when she arrived, even though she was only two," Linda said. "Today she looks younger than her age, and she's a glowing, healthy girl. It took her a long time before she learned to trust people. She usually likes men, especially if they're in uniform. Sunbathing is still a favorite pastime, and she enjoys long walks. Mama Leesa stays just ahead of me when we're out; she's very alert and constantly scouting our surroundings for danger. If anyone wearing headphones approaches, carries a backpack, or appears strange to her, she will stop in front of me and shield me from harm with her body.

"I live fairly close to Bev and Barb, so I often help out with the incoming Operation Baghdad Pups. Whenever Mama Leesa sees Barb, Bev, or Terri, she recognizes them instantly and goes into spasms of delight, nearly putting her hips out of joint wagging that beautiful tail. She adores those women and has never forgotten they were the ones who rescued her and brought her home.

"Mama Leesa has the most grateful eyes of any dog I've ever known. It's like she remembers how it was and doesn't take her new life for granted. I've learned a lot from her. She's a remarkable dog, worth all the effort it took to save her."

. . .

Charlie (Contractor Kenny)—As soon as Charlie arrived at her new home in South Carolina, she spotted the lake with a pontoon platform in the middle. Never had Charlie seen a body of water, and this one was as big as a football field. She couldn't take her eyes off it. Before securing her in the state-specified ten-foot-by-ten-foot quarantine kennel, which they'd specially built on their two-and-a-half-acre property, a member of Kenny's family rowed the dog across the water to the floating platform. From there Charlie dove in for her first swim ever and had a wonderful time paddling through the water and barking at splashes when she reached the shore.

During Charlie's six-month quarantine, Jolene sat outside the enclosure every day, while the dog amused herself watching the family's pot-bellied pig, goat, and chickens from behind the chain link.

In December 2008 Charlie was given her long-overdue freedom! Full of joy, she ran and ran on the fenced-in property for three days. It seemed as if she'd never get enough running out of her system. Finally, on the fourth day, Charlie rediscovered her animal companions. Never chasing them, she took it upon herself to be their protector instead and spent all her time herding the pot-bellied pig, the chickens, and the goat.

That spring, while Charlie played in the warming sun, she stood on a nest of emerging fire ants and was stung multiple times. Before Kenny and Jolene could get her to the vet, Charlie died of anaphylactic shock. To Kenny it seemed incredibly unfair: first losing his grandchild and then his beloved dog.

Over the next sad days, a realization slowly dawned upon Kenny. Charlie had come to him needing love and protection, and that's what he and Jolene gave her. Maybe that was all she ever needed. Now, perhaps in gratitude, Charlie had taken that gift to the other side of the rainbow where she would play with his grandson and bring to the child all the love, protection, and companionship that had been so freely given to her.

• • •

Kujo—Adela reports that Matt and Kujo remain inseparable. When the 30-pound puppy came to the States, they had no idea he'd grow into his current weight of 115 pounds. "He may be big," she laughed, "but he's afraid of the strangest things. Small dogs and laundry baskets are a big worry to him, but the worst thing of all is worms. Whenever he sees one wiggling, all four of his paws leave the ground at once, and he growls like crazy."

Warming to strangers on their own terms seems to be a common thread among the Iraqi dogs. "Kujo doesn't like strangers to approach him too quickly. If someone new comes to the house, they have to enter slowly and sit down. Kujo gives them a good once-over with his nose, and when he decides they've passed his inspection, he'll offer them his paw. Once he accepts a person, he considers them a friend for life."

"Kujo played such an important role in Matt's life in Iraq, having him here is like a miracle," Adela continued. "We are now in the process of getting a sister for Kujo. She'll be a rescue from a local shelter, and we're looking forward to giving her a good home."

• • •

Francine—Kevin knew he wouldn't see his beloved cat, Tom, when he got home, but he was looking forward to being reunited with his dog, Francine. Kevin's wife met him at the train station in Fredericksburg, Virginia. As the reunited couple walked out of the station, Kevin glimpsed, from the corner of his eye, a foot-wide rubber mat that had been placed across the road for counting the cars as they entered the station parking lot. It looked just like the sort of thing used by Iraqi insurgents to hide IEDs, initiating a bomb attack. A classic post-trauma reaction hit Kevin like a thunderbolt.

"I almost blacked out," he said later. "It was so strong—this feeling came over me like a kind of rage—and it overwhelmed all my senses.

"My wife realized something was wrong, and she got me to the car as quickly as she could. That's when I saw Francine. Maybe Tom was gone, but my canine buddy was there. The moment I touched her, all the feelings of disorientation dissipated, and I knew I was going to be okay." Today Francine lives with her family, who are all grateful to have her.

· · ·

Pooty—When her husband's normally upbeat voice sounded unusually down during their overseas call between Iraq and the States, Rhonda asked him what was wrong. She had also served our country in the military and was quite familiar with the stresses of deployment.

"It seems like everyone I care for is being taken away," Michael said. "And this year, it's been one too many."

Michael's father had died during his latest deployment, and long months of separation from Rhonda had been extremely difficult. But that wasn't the last straw. "It's this dog at our FOB," he explained. "We're moving out of here, and she'll get left behind. I've been taking care of her, and I've grown to love her. Now it looks like I'm losing her, too."

During Michael's tour he had been blown up by an "S vest" (suicide bomb) and spent ten days in a German hospital before returning to duty in Iraq. Throughout his absence the camp mascot stationed herself on the soldier's cot. Except for potty breaks, Pooty refused to move until Michael came back. Rhonda suddenly realized that this dog meant more to her husband than anything else at that moment, and she made a vow to bring the dog home, no matter what it took to do it.

Days later the desperate Rhonda contacted Terri. Pooty became one of the twenty-eight animals to join the FedEx rescue mission. When she finally reached her new home in Washington State, Pooty weighed twenty-nine pounds and was nothing but skin and bones. Immediately she fit in with the family's three rescue dogs from American shelters, and she seemed really happy to be a pack member again.

Today Pooty weighs fifty-four pounds and is as healthy as a German short hair from Iraq can be. The Army camp's retired mascot has recently been promoted to Nanny for Michael and Rhonda's toddler daughter. Pooty dotes on the child, forgiving her for pulled ears and tail, and protects her as if that's what she was born and bred to do. Pooty and the toddler visit Grampa's five-acre family spread several times a week. While Pooty enjoys the freedom to run, Grampa shares a plate of pancakes with his granddaughter.

Pooty regularly attends U.S. military and SPCA fundraisers, doing her best to support the troops, and she raises money for local SPCA shelters and the Operation Baghdad Pups program. She's now a hard-working American dog and proud of it.

• • •

Stubbs—The dog that won the hearts of volunteers in New Jersey has gone from hell in Iraq to heaven in Virginia. Perhaps the oldest dog rescued by Operation Baghdad Pups, Stubbs had lived a life of sheer misery. Every time Davey's unit returned from patrol, he found that Iraqi soldiers had brutalized this poor animal. During the writing of Terri's book, we decided that details of the trauma Stubbs suffered were too horrible to include in the stories.

Before Davey handed Stubbs over to the SLG team that delivered him to Terri, Davey told his dog all about the wonderful home he was going to in rural Virginia. Finally, with tears in his eyes, Davey said, "Give this to my mom," and hugged his buddy goodbye.

"All those days we waited for Stubbs to come home," Lorna said, "it seemed as if the dog was an extension of my son. I knew how important he was to Davey, and I couldn't wait to get my arms around him. When he finally arrived, I went up to his crate and opened the door. The first thing that dog did was lick me in the face. I felt like my son had sent me a great big kiss."

"Our family decided Stubbs would be happiest living at our daughter's house. They have a fenced-in yard with trees, grass, and a big dog house for shade on summer days. One of their two dogs had recently died, and the remaining dog, Carly, had been pining for her old friend. We didn't know if she and Stubbs would get along, but the moment they set eyes on each other, it was like they were instant friends. My daughter also has two kids, so Stubbs gained a whole family as well as a girlfriend.

"Everything was an adventure for Stubbs at first. Why, he thought grass was the nastiest-looking stuff he'd ever seen. We laughed when he wanted nothing to do with it and refused to walk on it. But pretty soon he learned from Carly and the kids not to be scared, and now he loves nothing more than lying down on all that green stuff and having a good roll.

"Despite the mutilation and torture he suffered from human hands, Stubbs never hardened his heart. He looks at us with the softest, most loving eyes you've ever seen, and he's the gentlest creature you could imagine with those kids.

"Before Stubbs came to America, Davey thought he wasn't going to survive his tour in Iraq. But the moment we sent the message, 'Stubbs made it—He's here!' my son kept talking about what he was going to do when he got home. I know in my heart that the saving of Stubbs was also the saving of my boy. When anyone wonders out loud at the fairness of bringing an Iraqi stray to America, I just tell them a soldier's dog is always worth saving because it's a part of him. And when my son comes home, I don't want any bit of him left behind."

• • •

Iraqi—Alishia's mother, Melissa, brought Iraqi home to Pennsylvania, where state regulations required her to quarantine the dog in her home for six months. By the time Alishia redeployed and was able to visit her buddy, her mom and the dog had totally bonded. Now called "Iraqi-Roo," the much loved dog has become attached to Bean, an American-born Dachshund.

"I didn't have the heart to break them apart," said Alishia, "but I visit him about twice a year. Each time I come, Iraqi and I go hiking in the woods. He loves chasing every bird he sees, and he jumps like a gazelle through the trees; it's beautiful to watch."

Alishia, now separated from the Army, plans to dedicate the rest of her life to animals. In the summer of 2011, she begins her first semester of veterinary school.

• • •

Dusty—The dog with intense gold eyes, rescued by Alan, has been both a comfort and a challenge to Jean, Alan's mother. When Dusty arrived in New York, Jean, a skilled dog trainer, described him as shut down, often frozen, and unable to respond. He was a highly stressed animal with classic symptoms of PTSD, shown by his sweaty pads, dilated pupils, and constant hair loss. He was reactive to fast-moving objects and people, and whenever anyone with a Middle Eastern appearance came to the house, Dusty had to be muzzled.

Dusty was used to taking care of his soldiers, and that behavior didn't change. When Jean's senior dog disappeared in a three-foot snowdrift and was unable to climb out, Dusty reacted by barking nonstop while running from window to window. Finally he sat down and gave a distress signal of three short howls, a sound he'd never made before. Dusty's behavior alerted the family to the other dog's predicament and saved its life.

Alan served as a Green Beret in the Special Forces in high-risk, top-security missions for six years. No one in the family ever knew where he was stationed, and when or even if he would come home for R&R or redeployment. One day Alan just appeared on the front porch unannounced and stood at the glass door looking in. Dusty froze with hackles up until he recognized Alan. He stood up and pawed the lever of the French door until it opened, and he jumped into Alan's arms, delirious with joy.

Jean's heart bled for this young man who now seemed like a stranger. Alan had come home about as emotionally cut off as a soldier can be. He was unwilling to talk to anyone, even his parents. For six years he had served in the most dangerous, high risk, ugly war situations that our country can ask of any soldier to endure. Due to the sensitive nature of his work while on deployment, he could never discuss the traumatic memories that would reveal where he had been and what he'd done. He had no way, therefore, to release them and to heal.

It was incredibly difficult for a mother to see her son in so much pain and be unable to help him. Her first hope finally came when she looked out the window one morning and saw Alan seated with his arm around Dusty's shoulders, and talking for all he was worth. From that day forward, Alan talked to Dusty for hours while the dog sat and listened.

"That was when I realized," said Jean, "that the war took my son away, but Dusty was bringing him back. The connection between those two was so intense; even today I can't explain it."

Three years later, Alan is working and living a productive life, while Dusty still lives with Jean and plays paper chase every chance he gets. "We have four bathrooms," said Jean. "When I'm out of the house, Dusty goes into each bathroom, grabs hold of the toilet paper and runs. By the time I come home from work, paper is strewn everywhere, and that dog sits there grinning at me like he's Goody Two Shoes. Considering what he's done for Alan, though," she laughs, "I forgive him."

• • •

Patton—For a puppy that provided so much comfort to soldiers and counselors on the mental health team in Iraq, it's not surprising to learn that Patton also suffered postwar symptoms. Now weighing sixty pounds, he still seeks the safety of someone's lap when frightened by a loud noise. Patton also needs assurance when strangers approach, and exposure to new situations has to be on his terms—typical behavior for dogs that have lived in a combat zone.

Patton is enjoying life in Ohio with the retired Air Force major and her family. Only a month into her retirement, Jenni discovered that she had cancer. Her dog became a great source of healing and humor while she underwent chemotherapy. Patton helped her through difficult months to stay positively focused on her goal of complete recovery. He now claims the title of Canine Coach and accompanies Jenni as she practices for her first marathon.

"Patton is still a character," Jenni laughs. "His favorite thing of all is puddles, the bigger and dirtier, the better. Try as we might, my daughters and I just cannot keep Patton out of them. He claims our laps on the couch, keeps me laughing, and we all love him. Thank God, he's here."

• • •

Moody—Bryan's mom, Janet, was taken aback when someone asked why she and her son wanted to bring home a foreign stray dog, while so many American dogs needed homes. With two sons serving multiple tours in Iraq and a daughter married to a soldier on deployment, Janet was quick to respond, "Not one of those American dogs saved my son."

After serving three tours of duty and losing several close friends to enemy action, Bryan did what many soldiers do in order to just survive. He shielded his heart behind a nearly impenetrable wall of reserve.

"I dated a little between tours," Bryan said, "but I never allowed myself to get close to anyone or have a long-term relationship. Yeah, I was lonely. But when you're overseas, and you get a letter with the news she's tired of waiting and found someone else, it can destroy you. Distractions like that will get you and your men killed."

When the Military cable TV channel showed Bryan and Moody's Operation Baghdad Pups rescue story, a nurse in New York couldn't get the beautiful dog or the soldier with the sad eyes and gorgeous smile out of her mind. After several days she broke down and e-mailed the soldier, who had just started his fourth tour in Iraq. The nurse said she'd be glad to send stuff to Bryan and the other soldiers of his unit, so he quickly responded, "Yes, please!" hoping for a big care package filled with homemade cookies. They corresponded regularly, and Bryan found it easy to open up to this person unlike any of the women he'd dated before.

Three years later Bryan is still serving in the military, and he's back in the States living with his dog and the special woman he loves.

"Every time my son looks at that girl, his beautiful smile lights up his face," said Janet happily. "If it weren't for Moody, they'd never have met. Moody has been like a miracle to our family. He saved Bryan, and he brought the most wonderful woman into his life.

"I can't thank Terri Crisp and SPCA International enough. The work they do is so important for U.S. soldiers and their families. I pray they will continue their missions for as long as we have people serving overseas and that Americans will continue to generously support this program."

• • •

Due to the scaling back of American troops in Iraq during 2010 and 2011, many of the working dogs, owned by private companies and contracted out to U.S. troops for bomb-sniffing and other security duties, are no longer needed. As of March 2011, Terri began another Iraq-based rescue mission that resulted in eight retired working dogs making it safely back to the States, where forever homes were waiting for them. No more sniffing for bombs or facing the dangers of war; these dogs will now get to live happy, carefree lives. Terri promised that her efforts to find permanent homes for these war service animals will not stop until every unwanted dog that risked its life for our troops is brought home.

As of May 31, 2011, Operation Baghdad Pups brought a total number of 340 animals—280 dogs and 58 cats from Iraq, plus two dogs from Afghanistan—to the United States, determined that there will be *no buddy left behind.*

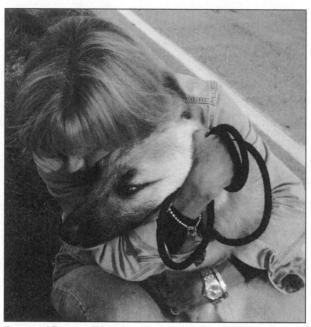

Jean and Dusty—"Hugging him was like holding a part of my son." *Jean Mathers*

LETTING GO